Towards a Rhetoric of Everyday Life

Towards a Rhetoric of Everyday Life

New Directions in Research on Writing, Text, and Discourse

Edited by

Martin Nystrand and John Duffy

THE UNIVERSITY OF WISCONSIN PRESS

The University of Wisconsin Press
1930 Monroe Street
Madison, Wisconsin 53711

www.wisc.edu/wisconsinpress/

3 Henrietta Street
London WC2E 8LU, England

1   3   5   4   2

Printed in the United States of America

Library of Congress Cataloging-in-Publication Data

Towards a rhetoric of everyday life: new directions in research on
writing, text, and discourse / edited by P. Martin Nystrand and John
Duffy.
p. cm.—(Rhetoric of the human sciences)
Includes index.
ISBN 0-299-18170-7 (cloth: alk. paper)
ISBN 0-299-18174-X (pbk.: alk. paper)
1. Rhetoric. I. Nystrand, P. Martin. II. Duffy, John, 1955– . III. Series.
P301.T64 2003
808—dc21
2002010218

Publication of this book has been made possible in part by the generous support of the
Anonymous Fund of the University of Wisconsin–Madison.

Contents

Part 4. Closing Remarks

Preface

Rhetoric, Writing, and the Everyday
Some Preliminary Remarks

Martin Nystrand and John Duffy

If composition studies became a field in the 1970s and 1980s when researchers asked the Big Question, *What is writing?* almost no one asks this question today. *What is writing?* strikes us today as a naïve question seeking an oversimplified response. Indeed, the field today displays little consensus among its members regarding its goals and principles, but might be thought of instead, as Andrea Lunsford (1990) has expressed it, as "a postmodern discipline, a postmodern profession" (p. 77), in which fragile boundaries are easily redrawn and hegemonies are regularly threatened. While the field has historically been consumed by the monistic requirements of the Freshman Composition (that is, Department of English) essay, cutting-edge issues now concern writing and something else in contexts that more often than not invoke the particulars of some *place* else: writing and technology in the workplace (e.g., Haas, 1996), writing and culture in communities and community centers (e.g., Cintron, 1997; Farr, 2000, forthcoming; Farr & Guerra, 1995; Flower, 1994, 1996; Freedman, 1994), writing and communication in industry (e.g., Barabas, 1990; Herndl, Fennell, and Miller, 1991), and investigations of writing in numerous other nonacademic settings (e.g., Bracewell and Breuleux, 1992; Duin & Hansen, 1996; McNamee, 1992; Palmer, 1992; Schriver, 1992; Geisler, 1992).

In short, the leading edge of research on writing, reading, and literacy these days is defined by its intersection with sociocultural, historical, political, disciplinary, institutional, and everyday contexts—each situated and domain-specific. Much current work in composition studies and rhetoric seeks to understand writing under the rubric of "cultural studies." One might well wonder if writing researchers have done such a terrific job expanding our understanding of writing *qua* writing that they may be in danger of putting themselves out of business. As interest in written discourse has matured, it has become transformed, connected, and increasingly subsumed into other, broader interests, especially in the world beyond the academy.

Perhaps the most recent published piece to ask *What is writing?* was Witte's important (1992) piece on context. But we must consider his argument: we need to broaden our conceptions of writing to include more than alphabetic texts (Witte, 1992). Indeed, efforts to broaden conceptions of writing have been relentless over the last decade, and they continue with no end in sight: relating writing to discourse and disciplinary communities, Bazerman (1991) has shown how text production is shaped by the writer's social, historical, cognitive, and rhetorical context. Myers' (1991) study following Miller's (1984) seminal work on genre as social action shows how the publication review process has shaped scientific discourse. Brandt's current historical work of literacy development (Brandt, 1994, 1995, 1998, in press) in over nine Wisconsin generations illustrates how conceptions of literacy are transformed by sociocultural change over time. Dyson's work (1989, 1993, 1997) documents the continual and intricate relationship of children's literacy development in school with their social worlds beyond. And Flower's (1996) recent cognitive rhetoric investigations are set in a community literacy center. All the big abstractions—"literacy," "cognition," "writing," "reading"—are increasingly linked to real-world and institutional contexts. Long gone are any lingering fantasies that texts can be 'autonomous' or that writers' agency completely shapes their texts.

This volume examines these recent trends by bringing together in a single volume contemporary studies focusing on what we call "the rhetoric of everyday life." By this, we mean the rhetorical character and dynamics of language in mundane contexts especially beyond school, and also the rhetorical interpenetration of school discourse and political and cultural forces transcending the academy. The contributors to this volume show how discourse both in and out of school is mediated by the material conditions and multiple circumstances of the everyday world. Their studies focus on individuals of all ages in a wide range of professional and cultural contexts, showing how their everyday, mundane interactions continuously shape and refract their understandings of themselves and the world, as well as their positions and identities within it. "Rhetoric" here refers not to the classical arts of persuasion, or the verbal ornamentation of elite discourse, but rather to the ways that individuals and groups use language to constitute their social realities, and as a medium for creating, managing, or resisting ideological meanings. The discourses of institutions and popular culture are rhetorical in the sense that they situate us in our worlds: they shape our ideas about "the way things are," who we are, where we belong, and guide what we talk about and what we say (and don't say).

Moreover, while traditional theories of rhetoric concern the role of persuasion in the affairs of government and men, the rhetoric at the heart of composition studies over the last 30 years has examined the language of other, nontraditional rhetors, including immigrants, women, and college freshmen, long on the margins of political forums. In short, composition studies has focused the rhetorical character of literacy development, helping us understand how the various contexts of literacy and literacy development profoundly shape the very location and meaning of "everyday life" as the learners know it, and sometimes resist (Duffy, 1997).

Towards a Rhetoric of Everyday Life

The purpose of *Towards a Rhetoric of Everyday Life* is to examine the leading edge of research on writing by elucidating the entanglements of writing and writers with their quotidian contexts. Collectively, this volume unveils the rhetorical character of popular culture and institutional discourse as they situate us in our worlds, shape what we learn, and fix our ideas not only about who we are and where we belong, but also what we choose to say and often, of course, what we resist saying (Duffy, 1997).

Towards a Rhetoric of Everyday Life is organized into three parts: Rhetorics of community life, Rhetorics of education and classrooms, and Rhetorics of modern institutions. In the introduction, "The Sociocultural Context for the New Discourse about Writing," Nystrand and Duffy set the tone for the volume by relating recent academic conceptions and uses of composition and rhetoric to social forces beyond the academy. They examine the role of demographic and cultural shifts in American society as these affected the establishment of composition studies as a new discipline in American universities characterized by empirical research programs and the professionalization of college instruction.

Perhaps the most fundamental dynamic of rhetoric in everyday life concerns struggles over power between those on the margins and those in control. For example, in his chapter about young urban Latino street-gang members that opens Part 1, Rhetorics of Community Life, Ralph Cintron probes the "rhetoric of violence" as the intersection of personal vulnerability and street ideology. Here, gang members' language about rivals is largely about establishing and sustaining "the way things are," as well as resisting their rivals' constructions of them. At the same time that such language "fixes" a view of the world and the identity of the Other, the concomitant reductiveness of that fixation inevitably does violence to the Other. Rhetoric here is a struggle for what gang members believe to be real and true.

Cintron's conception of rhetoric as "violence of fixation" captures several other chapters in this volume. In "Other Gods and Countries: The Rhetorics of Literacy," Duffy examines the rhetorical context for literacy development among Hmong-Americans, relating the forms, genres, and issues of their writing to the sociopolitical forces buffeting Hmong society in Laos and the United States.

In "Writing in a Culture of Simulation: Ethos Online," Carolyn Miller argues that the Turing test, proposed by Alan Turing in 1950 to assess whether computers can think, is not so much a test of cyberlogic as it is a test of ethos (Turing argued that computers would pass the test only if those judging the computers could not reliably distinguish their response from human response). Like Schwebke and Medway, Miller argues that the answer depends on what computer users ascribe to the machine; it depends on their active fixations.

Drawing on the work of Henri Lefebvre, John Ackerman, in "The Space for Rhetoric," examines the rhetorical force of architecture insofar as it consummates, reinterprets, and/or resists the scenes and contexts its constructions adjoin. As Ackerman puts it, architecture is rhetorical when it isolates actions and consequences in social space.

A key concept in all these investigations is what Cintron, following Henri Lefebvre and Susan Ruddick, calls the "social imaginary," which, argues Ruddick "signals an image that exists within the popular imagination or unconscious" and which, "far from reflecting the object to which it seems to refer (be it a social, political, or other imaginary), is, in fact, *produced* by the discourse that surrounds it" (Ruddick, 1996, p. 12; emphasis in original).

Focusing on the historical development of social imaginaries, Nystrand's "Janet Emig, Frank Smith, and the New Discourse about Writing and Reading" relates the development and influence of process pedagogy during the late 1960s and early '70s as a confluence of constructivist academic ideology (the formative context) that celebrates the power of mind, with social struggles, particularly related to the Civil Rights movement, that seek to affirm the legitimacy of minority voices (the receptive context). In the following chapter, "The Stolen Lipstick of Overheard Song: Composing Voices in Child Song, Verse, and Written Text," Anne Dyson examines how young school children appropriate learning from their identifications and cultural practices outside the official school world and, thus, the cultural, social, and semiotic negotiations that ensue inside the official world.

Modern institutions, including government, also play a key role in shaping (and resisting) individuals' identities. In her case study of a schizophrenic, "On the Rhetorics of Mental Disability," for example, Catherine Prendergast shows how diagnosis and treatment of the mentally ill can strip the stricken of their agency, and how total and devastating this loss of "rhetoricity" can be. In "Subjects of the Inner City: Writing the People of Cabrini-Green," David Fleming's study of the Cabrini-Green urban housing project in Chicago, we get a close look at the role of language by both urban and federal governments in "building the city, in making some people our neighbors and others, not."

Finally, in closing remarks on "The Future of Writing," Robert Gundlach reexamines the last 30 years of empirical research on writing from a linguistics perspective and urges a renewal of research on writing in terms of language.

Collectively, the contributors to this edited volume trace the ways in which literacy development intersects with rhetorical concerns, which are themselves circumscribed by the material contexts of the everyday world. The volume is addressed to researchers and teachers of writing, rhetoric, literacy, and education.

References

Althusser, L. (1969). *Lenin and philosophy, and other essays.* Trans. B. Brewster. New York: Monthly Review Press.

Bakhtin, M. (1986). *Speech genres & other late essays.* Trans. V. W. McGee. Ed. C. Emerson & M. Holquist. Austin: University of Texas Press.

xii   PREFACE

Barabas, C. (1990). *Technical writing in a corporate culture: A study of the nature of information.* Norwood, NJ: ABLEX Publishing Corp.
Bazerman, C. (1991). How natural philosophers can cooperate: The Investigation in Joseph Priesley's *History and Present State of Electricity.* In C. Bazerman & J. Paradis (Eds.), *Textual dynamics of the professions.* Madison: University of Wisconsin Press.
Bazerman, C. & Paradis, J. (Eds.). (1990). *Textual dynamics of the professions.* Madison: University of Wisconsin Press.
Berkenkotter, C. & Huckin, T. (1995). *Genre knowledge in disciplinary communication: Cognition, culture, and power.* Hillsdale, NJ: L. Erlbaum Associates.
Bishop, W. & Ostrom, H. (Eds.). (1997). *Genre and writing: Issues, arguments, alternatives.* Portsmouth, NH: Boynton/Cook.
Bracewell, R., & Breuleux, A. (1992, April). *Cognitive principles for the support of technical writing.* Paper presented at the 1992 Convention of the American Educational Research Association.
Brandt, D. (1994). Remembering reading, remembering writing. *College Composition and Communication, 45,* 459–479.
Brandt, D. (1995). Accumulating literacy: Writing and learning to write in the twentieth century. *College English, 57,* 649–668.
Brandt, D. (1998). The sponsors of literacy. *College Composition and Communication, 49,* 165–185.
Cintron, R. (1997). *Angel's town: Chero ways, gang life, and rhetorics of the everyday.* Boston: Beacon Press.
Clark, H. (1996). *Using language.* Cambridge, UK: Cambridge University Press.
Duffy, J. (1997, March). *Literacy, immigrants, and the struggle for "our town": competing rhetorics of community in a Wisconsin city.* Paper presented at the 1997 Convention of the American Educational Research Association, Chicago.
Duin, A. H., & Hansen, C. (1996). Nonacademic writing: Social theory and technology. Mahwah, NJ: Lawrence Erlbaum Associates.
Dyson, A. (1989). *Multiple worlds of child writers: Friends learning to write.* New York: Teachers College Press.
Dyson, A. (1993). *The social worlds of children learning to write in an urban primary school.* New York: Teachers College Press.
Dyson, A. (1997). *Writing superheroes: Contemporary childhood, popular culture, and classroom literacy.* New York: Teachers College Press.
Emig, J. (1971). *The composing processes of twelfth graders.* Urbana: The National Council of Teachers of English.
Fairclough, N. (1992) *Discourse and social change.* Cambridge, UK: Polity Press.
Farr, M. (forthcoming). *Rancheros in Chicagoacán: Culture and identity in a Mexican transnational community.*
Farr, M. (2000). Literacy and religion: Reading, writing, and gender among Mexican women in Chicago. In P. Griffin, J. K. Peyton, W. Wolfram, & R. Fasold (Eds.), *Language in action: New studies of language in society.* Cresskill, NJ: Hampton Press.
Farr, Marcia and Guerra, Juan. (1995). Literacy in the community: A study of *Mexicano* families in Chicago, *Discourse Processes* Special Issue, *Literacy Among Latinos, 19,* 7–19.
Flower, L. (1994). *The construction of negotiated meaning: A social cognitive theory of writing.* Carbondale, IL: University of Southern Illinois Press.
Flower, L. (1996). Literate action. In L. Z. Bloom, D. A. Daiker, & E. M. White (Eds.),

Composition in the twenty-first century: Crisis and change. (pp. 249–260) Carbondale: Southern Illinois University Press.

Freedman, A. & Medway, P. (Eds.). (1994). *Genre and the new rhetoric.* London: Taylor & Francis, 1994.

Freedman, S. (1994). *Exchanging writing, exchanging cultures: Lessons in school reform from the United States and Great Britain.* Cambridge, MA: Harvard University Press.

Garrod, A. and Larimore, C. (1997). *First person, first peoples: Native American college graduates tell their life stories.* Ithaca: Cornell University Press.

Herndl, C., Fennel, B., & C. R. Miller (1991). Understanding failures in organizational discourse. In C. Bazerman & J. Paradis (Eds.), *Textual dynamics of the professions: Historical and contemporary studies of writing in professional communities.* Madison: University of Wisconsin Press.

Lake, R. (1991). Between myth and history enacting time in Native American protest rhetoric. *Quarterly Journal of Speech, 77,* pp. 123–151.

Linell, P. (1998). Discourse across professional boundaries: On recontextualizations and the blending of voices in professional discourse. *Text, 18,* pp. 143–157.

Lunsford, A. (1990). "Composing Ourselves: Politics, Commitment, and the Teaching of Writing." *College Composition and Communication, 41*, pp. 77–86.

McNamee, G. D. (1992, April). *The voices of community change.* Paper presented at the 1992 Convention of the American Educational Research Association.

Miller, C. (1984). Genre as social action. *Quarterly Journal of Speech, 70,* pp. 151–167.

Myers, G. (1991). Stories and styles in two molecular biology review articles. In C. Bazerman & J. Paradis (Eds.), *Textual dynamics of the professions: Historical and contemporary studies of writing in professional communities* (pp. 45–75). Madison: University of Wisconsin Press.

Nelson, J., Megill, A., & McClosky, D. (Eds.). (1987). *Rhetoric of the human sciences: Language and argument in scholarship and public affairs.* Madison: University of Wisconsin Press.

Odell, L, & Goswami, D. (1985). *Writing in nonacademic settings.* New York: Guilford.

Palmer, J. (1992, April). *The rhetoric of negotiation: Professional writing at Apple Computer, Inc.* Paper presented at the 1992 Convention of the American Educational Research Association.

Ruddick, S. M. (1996). *Young and homeless in Hollywood: Mapping social identities.* New York: Routledge.

Schriver, K. (1992, April). *Collaboration in professional writing: The cognition of a social process.* Paper presented at the 1992 Convention of the American Educational Research Association.

Shaughnessy, M. (1977). *Errors and expectations.* New York: Oxford University Press.

Vološinov, V. N. (1973). *Marxism and the philosophy of language.* Trans. L. Matejka and I. R. Titunik. New York: Seminar Press.

Vygotsky, L. (1962). *Thought and language.* Cambridge, MA: MIT Press.

Wertsch, J. V. (Ed.). (1981). *The concept of activity in Soviet psychology.* Armonk, NY: M. E. Sharpe.

Witte, S. (1992). Context, text, and intertext: Toward a constructivist semiotic of writing. *Written Communication, 9,* 237–308.

Introduction

The Sociocultural Context for the New Discourse about Writing

Martin Nystrand and John Duffy

Much has been written about the "revolution" in ideas about writing as a composing process that took place in North America during the late 1960s and early 1970s. Until this time, discourse about writing in North America was largely an instructional affair focused simply on prescriptive text features of model prose written by exemplary writers. Thinking about composition in the mid-twentieth century (and earlier) focused at the college level on model texts of the sort collected in countless Freshman English readers; by far most ideas about writing concerned expository writing and reflected prescriptive-grammar, "current-traditional" views (Fogarty, 1959). Composition instruction typically occurred exclusively in English classes and culminated in mastery of the humanities essay genre or, for many students, the five-paragraph theme. At this time, discourse about writing was largely captured in formalist maxims and rules of the sort offered by Lucas (1955), Strunk (1959), and Warriner (1950).

Starting around 1970, however, a new perspective on writing developed that sought to refocus discourse on writing from a prescriptive concern for text features to a description of cognitive writing processes. It brought methods of empirical inquiry to a largely pedagogical concern that, until this time, had largely been unaffected by such methods. The resulting new discourse about writing inspired considerable research. Moreover, these developments led eventually to the institutionalization of this research in national and international professional organizations, as well as in department of English graduate programs. Today, not all of these are characterized by a focus on empirical research; nonetheless, these developments were not just a passing notion in discourse and thought about writing. Circa 1970, discourse about writing took a serious scientific turn.

The new investigations sought to understand the unique character of writing, focusing especially on processes of mind and communication. More recently, the field has looked more closely at the contexts of writing, and today writing is increasingly linked to sites and conditions extending far beyond the classroom ranging from studies examining the role of writing in the construction of mental illness (McCarthy & Gerring, 1994) to the socialization of Hmong refugees in a small American community (Duffy, 1997). While this recent research might seem to suggest that, appropriate to a new millennium, writing studies have started a new, post-process chapter, we believe these recent developments are in fact completely in character with the field as it has developed over the last 30 years. Indeed, the seeds of this transformation were planted in the late 1960s, a period usually remembered as heralding a shift of emphasis from "product" to "process." Yet the move to process-based models of writing in the late 1960s and 1970s was but part of a far more widespread and encompassing transformation of academic interests of the times, one that extended beyond departments of English as schools and scholars alike sought to respond to widespread demographic and cultural shifts in the larger society. The new discourse and debates about writing were an important forum for this transformation, especially as new research efforts came to seriously regard the writing of ordinary and so-called marginal students (cf. Emig, 1971; Shaughnessy, 1977), and served as the basis for subsequent research that was increasingly focused on written discourse in multiple and nonacademic contexts.

In this article, we examine the social and intellectual forces during the late 1960s that led to a new discourse about writing circa 1970, and show how these developments provided the foundation of much contemporary research in rhetoric and composition. We seek to outline how this new discourse about writing, which became institutionalized in the 1970s and 1980s, shifted over the last 30 years from formalist, prescriptive conceptions realized almost exclusively in pedagogical contexts, to empirical descriptions of writing in particular settings, including the world beyond school. This is not to say that there was no empirical research on writing prior to the 1970s. Braddock et al. (1963) succinctly review such studies. Yet these early empirical studies were almost entirely pedagogical in nature and notably not intended to be theoretical. In contrast, the 1970s and 1980s witnessed the start of a sustained, international effort on the part of many researchers at many sites to formulate, empirically examine, and flesh out theoretical conceptions of writing. Moreover, these efforts became institutionalized through the establishment of new doctoral programs, new journals and publication outlets, and the creation of new professional organizations. All of these developments supported an approach to writing—empirical, situated, and often focused on the practices of writers once considered "marginal," including "basic" writers, minorities, immigrants, women, and students.

Over the last several decades, many competing stories of composition have been told in many different guises: as a formal model for correct discourse and social success (Fogarty, 1959); as a rediscovery of the classical canons of rhetoric (Corbett, 1965); as an expressive revolt against institutional authority (Macrorie 1970); as the systematic study and application of individual cognitive processes (Flower and Hayes, 1981); as a move away from individual cognition toward social meanings of language (Bizzell, 1982); and as a struggle among competing ideologies instantiated in discourse (Berlin, 1987). We do not seek to discount these narratives; rather, we seek to construct a genealogy of current research in composition as it has evolved over the last 30 years with emphasis on the material contexts of the greater society. We take our cues from Burke's view of all forms of language as motivated and therefore rhetorical, and from Bakhtin's concept of language as dialogic—always enmeshed in history, ideology, and the languages of other speakers and institutions. We are interested in the relationships between intellectual (conceptions of writing) and sociocultural processes both inside and outside the academy, and how awareness and conception of these relations have shaped the discipline during this period. This emphasis is significant for two reasons. First, it offers a historical perspective that has been overlooked in previous histories that have focused more exclusively upon conceptions of writing. Moreover, we believe this account—what composition research is today and how it became that way—suggests directions for the future of the discipline.

The Contexts of the New Discourse about Writing

The new discourse about writing drew both from the social sciences, especially cognitive psychology, and from rhetoric, especially the ideas of

Richards, Burke, and, recently, Bakhtin. These ideas, of course, had particular uses within their own disciplinary contexts of use (psychology and rhetoric). In the 1970s and 1980s they came to have new uses within the interpretive contexts of composition, that is, established voices gained new resonance.

Yet while these intellectual sources seem clearly to have fueled new ideas about composition, their availability alone is not sufficient to explain why and how they became salient and influential in the 1970s and 1980s, or just how they came to inform composition studies. To do this, we focus on the sociocultural contexts of the times—the social upheavals and demographic changes of the 1960s and 1970s that involved racial unrest, student protests against the Vietnam War, public perception of a literacy crisis in American schools, and the increase of non-English-speaking immigrants in the United States. These were the events that provided the critical catalyst. We do not argue that all the changes in our field were indelible or irreversible, only that the sociocultural contexts of the times helped set agendas of change and define issues in the particular forms they took.

The interaction of academic contexts with the world beyond academe is important for historians to consider if their histories are to be more than chronologies of great people and important events. Our effort is not so much to depict the way things were (a synchronic conception of history) as it is to examine (diachronically) *why and how events unfolded as, when, and where they did*. Why were ideas about writing process and marginal writers taken seriously in North America in the 1970s, but not before? Why did empirical research on writing take hold at about the same time, but not before? Ideas take hold because some receptive context valorizes them. The efforts of principal actors (in this case, authors and researchers) provide but one small, though critical, part of the story. Actors only have influence to the extent that their voices are heard by and resonate with others. For example, even though many articles appeared about writing as a process as early as 1912 (in *English Journal*, for example), the idea didn't really take root, especially as a focus of research, until Emig published her study *The Composing Processes of Twelfth Graders* in 1971. Similarly, although Professor of English Henry Sams of the University of Chicago promoted interest in invention in the 1940s, his visionary efforts went nowhere amidst the formalist literary currents in his department. For invention to be considered a topic with currency in the field, it had to wait 35 years after Sams to be discovered once again at the Conference on College Composition and Communication, and especially in Richard Young's department of English at Carnegie Mellon in the 1970s and 1980s, when the climate in the cognitive sciences there was receptive to ideas about invention as it affected cognitive plans and goals. The influence of the Carnegie Mellon school of cognitive rhetoric, exemplified by the research of Flower and Hayes, ultimately derives from the currency it achieved during the 1970s and 1980s within the professional and research contexts of the Conference on College Composition and Communication, the National Council of Teachers of English, the new doctoral programs in departments of English (and the departments where Carnegie Mellon subsequently placed its graduates), and federal research support, especially in the Center for the Study of Writing funded in 1985.

The Expansion of Higher Education and the Material Contexts for the New Discourse About Writing: The Social Context

Rarely have the problems of the world influenced school and university instructional programs as strongly as during the late 1960s, when riots ignited in cities and Vietnam War protests ripped through university campuses. The Johnson administration vigorously sought to increase educational opportunities as a key weapon in its War on Poverty, and by the late 1960s, a new community college opened every week.[1] This dramatic expansion of post-secondary education seems almost unimaginable to us today.[2] In the 1960s and 70s, these changes were nowhere more profound than at urban universities like Brooklyn College, City College of the City University of New York (CUNY) and the University of Illinois at Chicago Circle (UICC, now UIC, the University of Illinois at Chicago): on all these campuses ethnic diversity among students increased sharply. Freshman Composition courses were especially affected. Most notable of the responses to these challenges were the efforts of Kenneth Bruffee at Brooklyn College and Mina Shaughnessy at City College, both of CUNY, as the university implemented its open admissions policy guaranteeing admission to any student with a high school diploma. The development of their thinking in this context provides a unique view of the effects of material contexts such as changing student demographics and radical campus politics on the development of ideas, such as social constructionism.

A recent oral history by Peter Hawkes (1996)[3] documents how Bruffee's use of collaborative learning and response groups in freshman composition at Brooklyn College was a direct response to the daily foment of social and political change both on and off campus during this time. Student demonstrations, strikes, takeovers of campus buildings, smoke bombs, vandalism, and fires were persistent: police brutality against demonstrators was common. The demonstrations were largely about student draft deferments: Of Brooklyn College's 10,008 students in 1968, only 119 were black and only 42 were Puerto Rican (Khiss, p. 48 cited in Hawkes, 1996, p. 2). Because few African Americans and Puerto Ricans qualified for student deferments, they were drafted in disproportionate numbers and shipped to Vietnam to fight, and in many cases to die.

According to Hawkes, in the fall of 1970, six months after four Kent State students were shot dead by National Guard troops, CUNY expedited its policy of open admissions five years ahead of its planned start in 1975. In the next three years, Brooklyn's enrollments jumped from 14,000 to 34,000 students.[4] There, Kenneth Bruffee, a young assistant professor hired to teach British Romantic literature, was assigned to design and direct the new Freshman Composition Program. As he planned his new program, he noted that such traditional methods as lecture, Socratic questioning, and seminars were all ineffective in the climate of the times because, he said, they all belonged to an "authoritarian-individualistic mode of education" ("The Way Out," p. 458). By contrast, he noted that certain innovative alternatives, such as an undergraduate drop-in counseling service staffed by peers, had more positive results. Bruffee augmented his new writing program by establishing a storefront tutoring facility near the campus subway exit, and staffing it entirely with students to help other students with their writing. He also experimented with peer groups in his own composition classes, often leaving the classroom in order to encourage student talk. The key to all these changes was radically altering, even inverting, the traditional teacher-student authority relationship. To understand the dynamics of collaborative learning, Bruffee did additional graduate work. During 1972 and 1973, he attended Columbia University's School of Social Work to study small groups practices, and then in 1980, the New School to study philosophy. There he read the social constructionist work of Richard Rorty, Thomas Kuhn, and Stanley Fish. Bruffee's political education at Brooklyn College provides a succinct vignette of how the culture in the 1970s outside academe shaped the intellectual ecology within it, including ideas about composition, language, meaning, and instruction.

Meanwhile, as CUNY implemented open admissions and as community colleges opened at a record pace, educators and pundits alike condemned an apparent decline in writing skills, and hysteria about a "literacy crisis" and calls for "Bonehead English" could be heard throughout the nation. Some instructors responded by developing new materials relevant to the contemporary world. At Queens College, for example, Van Laan and Lyons introduced a freshman anthology called *Language and the Newsstand* (Van Laan and Lyons, 1968, 1972), and McQuade and Atwan published *Popular Writing in America* (McQuade and Atwan, 1974).[5] Mina Shaughnessy, Director of the Instructional Resource Center of City College of CUNY, undertook a research-oriented approach. She set about empirically to uncover what she called the "logic and history" of student errors in the writing of four thousand "basic" (remedial) writers. Influenced by Labov's (1969) research on the logic of nonstandard English, Shaughnessy sought to show patterns and unconventional patterns in what the critics of the schools saw as so much sloppiness and ignorance. She was among the first to conceptualize writing as a social act (1977, p. 83) and viewed writing instruction as an essential tool in the empowerment and socialization of minorities and basic writers into the middle and professional classes. This view, echoed later by Bartholomae (1985) and Bizzell (1982), was profoundly rhetorical. Shaughnessy drew upon the Aristotelian concept of topoi (1977, pp. 257–272), or lines or argument, to stress that what students most needed to learn was not how to think, but rather how to write in the particular social and cultural milieu of the academy. At a time when many critics equated academic discourse with "logic" and "higher" cognitive abilities, Shaughnessy understood academic discourse as a culturally learned and socially validated form of reasoning. She argued that basic writers were not cognitively deficient, but rather simply unfamiliar with the social and cultural conventions of academic prose. Moreover, she understood writing skill itself rhetorically, as a validating element of persuasion helping those on the margins of society enter the mainstream. Basic writing instruction came to be about helping outsiders get in. The new discourse about writing challenged educators to define the discursive communities that students were attempting to enter, and to understand the rhetorical situations in which students were asked to write. Emig's (1971) work, for example, decried the sterile rhetorical environment of the typical English class and its withering effects upon students writing.

Shaughnessy and Emig believed that the writing of students in everyday classrooms raised issues requiring careful study and research. In this sense, their work laid the groundwork for much contemporary research in writing. Although many innovative ideas about writing had been proposed prior to Shaughnessy and Emig's work, it was the particular nature of social and cultural change in the 1960s and 1970s that allowed their particular innovations to resonate within the discipline and help shape a research agenda focused on ordinary student writing. Prior to this time, research on student writing, where it existed, was nontheoretical and noticeably disconnected from social and material processes.

The new discourse about writing was also shaped by the material circumstances of researchers and practitioners who had, in varying degrees, committed themselves to the study and teaching of writing. For many at the university level, a focus on composition was the equivalent to a professional backwater. The problems of composition were seen as intellectually inferior to the normal concerns of the academy, and professionally unrewarding. English departments "belonged" to specialists in literature, the result of developments that began in Britain in the eighteenth century (Miller, 1997) and a century later in America at Harvard (Berlin, 1987). Faculty members whose main occupations and interests were in writing were often hired on a part-time basis, or had difficulty getting tenure. In late–twentieth-century American academe, the increasing influence of these academics in establishing their professional credentials, in conjunction with the changing demographics of many American colleges, provided a key material site for the growth of composition studies and developments in writing research and pedagogy.

For example, urban campuses beset by new challenges in writing instruction became key sites for the new discourse about writing, and the interaction of individual practitioners and researchers promoted the institutionalization of the discipline. By 1980, many departments of English in American universities had begun to organize Ph.D. programs in composition and rhetoric. These programs sought to train graduate students in methods of basic research, and to prepare a management class of administrators who could direct Freshman English, writing-across-the-curriculum (WAC) programs, and tutorial writing centers. Urban universities like the University of Illinois at Chicago (UIC) were among the first to offer Department of English doctoral programs in composition studies. The more established campuses, like the University of Illinois at Urbana, came on board later.[6] As often as not, state boards of higher education tended to regard both writing and urban campuses as second-tier institutions: The Illinois State Board of Education was not willing to approve a literature Ph.D. at a second state campus, especially during the recession of the late 1970s when few tenure-track positions were open to new Ph.D.s in English. Hence, UIC saw a doctoral program in composition as its ticket for Ph.D. program approval. Not coincidentally, these new program initiatives also breathed life into department of English graduate studies programs at a time when tenure-track positions in literature were on the wane. Between 1980 and 1995, these programs grew from only a few to currently dozens generating hundreds of Ph.D.s each year. The story of composition studies is very much about the dynamics of a marginalized academic concern involving marginalized students on marginalized campuses, and what happened when they each, in their own way, strove for legitimacy.

The Intellectual Context

Where did the new ideas about composition come from? Among its themes, we can discern clear traces concerning the structure of everyday life that is characteristic of twentieth-century modes of inquiry, themes clearly present in the discourse of such fields as rhetoric, anthropology, and psychology.[7] In the twentieth century, many developments interjected elements of the everyday into rhetorical analyses. The work of Kenneth Burke and I. A. Richards, for example, were particularly influential in expanding the scope of rhetorical analysis to apply potentially to all forms of discourse. Both Burke and Richards were shaped by the social and political events of their own times, particularly the outbreak of World War I. The use of language as propaganda in this period, as well as the shift in literary meanings developed in modernist poetry, contributed to a "collapse of conventional understandings in the use of language."[8] This in turn led to radical departures in the work of Burke, Richards, and other rhetoricians and philosophers of language. Within rhetoric itself, for example, Burke and Richards were particularly influential. More recently, Bakhtin's work has been used similarly (though Bakhtin himself took a dim view of the formalist rhetoric of his time, which he viewed as ossified).

Burke and Bakhtin sought to counter both the New Critics and the Russian Formalists, who treated literary language as superior to ordinary language. With Medvedev, Bakhtin argued, "the [formal] linguistic analysis of a poetic work has no criteria for separating what is poetically significant from what is not" (Bakhtin/Medvedev, 1985, p. 85). Burke sought to refute literature scholars' valorization of literary language by showing that literature is as rhetorical as other modes of discourse insofar as authors and poets seek to move their readers. Bakhtin and Burke sought to elevate the status of ordinary discourse by analyzing the dynamics and structure of speech genres including advertising, propaganda, and everyday gossip. Today we can see how radically each of them expanded the scope of rhetorical analysis by normalizing literary language while at the same time universalizing rhetoric and extending its powers of analysis to all forms of discourse.

I. A. Richards, who came to rhetoric by way of the philosophy of language, articulated a theory of meaning based on then-recent work of linguists, anthropologists, psychologists, and philosophers of language. With C. K. Ogden in *The Meaning of Meaning* (1923), Richards contended that words have meaning not in terms of inherent qualities and the structure of argument, but rather in their use in particular contexts. In *The Philosophy of Rhetoric*, Richards defined rhetoric in terms of "how words work." The term "work" is critical here, for it suggests a transactional or pragmatic conception of text meaning having to do with effects on readers and listeners. As for both Burke and Bakhtin, meaning for Richards was an interpretive act of speakers and writers, listeners and readers.

At the time, these were radical contentions. Burke and Richard's universalization of rhetoric and meaning legitimated the marginal and conferred scholarly respectability to serious interest in difference. All of this, of course, strikes us today as quite modern, and in hindsight, we can readily appreciate the extent to which Burke's and Richards' ideas were part of early twentieth-century efforts to understand the structure and character of everyday life. For example, at about this time, by introducing intensive fieldwork to the empirical study of specific groups and cultures in their native contexts, anthropologists like Franz Boas debunked the formalist, grand generalizations of Victorian armchair anthropologists, who, like McGee (1899), promulgated a priori stage models of cultural evolution (for example, "Savage," "Barbarian," "Civilized"). The linguists Ferdinand de Saussure, Leonard Bloomfield, and Edward Sapir struggled against a philology concerned with the preservation and interpretation of classical Greek texts to make everyday, colloquial speech the central focus of research on language rather than canonical written texts. And in psychology, John Dewey and William James conceptualized experience as a dynamic construct of mind in everyday life—what James called "stream of consciousness." Writing about "The New Psychology" in 1885, Dewey argued,

> Experience is realistic, not abstract. Psychical life is the fullest, deepest, and richest manifestation of this experience. The New Psychology is content to get its logic from this experience, and not do violence to the sanctity and integrity of the latter by forcing it to conform to certain preconceived abstract ideas. (pp. 59–60)

In what can now be understood as an essential tenet of modern constructivism, James claimed that individuals cope with the incessant flux and temporality of experience through the power of mind. Like these early twentieth-century avenues of inquiry, the expanded conceptions of rhetoric promoted by Burke and Richards were but steps in the modernist intellectual odyssey situating language and meaning in the panoply of everyday contexts.

In the 1970s, the new discourse about writing followed these lines of thought, and it is in the new discourse about writing that some of the most fundamental postulates, themes, and emphases of both the New Rhetoric and the New Psychology have been developed. For example, Janet Emig, who was a Harvard doctoral student in the 1960s, is significant for breaking this new ground, for she was the first researcher to systematically study ordinary student writing as a cognitive process. This work was eventually published as *The Composing Processes of Twelfth Graders* (1971). In it, Emig reported results on case studies of several twelfth graders whom she asked to compose aloud, and the results, she claimed, showed that composing is recursive rather than linear; it is more learned than taught. Emig's work, like Shaughnessy's, helped shift the focus of writing instruction from prescriptions based on model texts by only the best writers to descriptions of ordinary, indeed even marginal, student writing. No move was more fundamental than this empirical orientation to the emergence of the new field of composition studies in the 1970s.

The intellectual legacy of both Shaughnessy and Emig can be said to be the legitimation of empirical descriptions of ordinary student writing as a focus of both instruction and research. Shaughnessy's effort to describe and understand marginal student writing, and Emig's pioneering efforts to investigate twelfth-graders' composition processes compelled an entire generation of teachers to emulate researchers by examining their students' writing as data. Their work inspired countless critiques of the formalist prescriptiveness of traditional grammarians, and of the then current traditional rhetoricians for their formalist obsession with ideal texts, and for their trivialization of the writing process through empirically empty maxims. The new compositionists sought to *describe* how ordinary people write, not *prescribe* how they should. Instruction was to be not based on arbitrary and traditional wisdom, but rather informed by empirical findings and basic research. The weakest writers were newly categorized in clinical fashion as Basic Writers, whose errors were approached not with worksheets and drills, but rather with research agendas designed to uncover the "history and logic" of their writing strategies. Such research became the mission of the National Institute of Education's new writing research program when it was launched in the late 1970s, and subsequently of the Center for the Study of Writing, founded in 1985. Like Richards and Dewey and the New Psychologists, a new breed of writing researchers, including especially Flower and Hayes and many others, posited the individual mind as the seminal organizing principle of behavior and experience. They sought to explicate the cognitive structure of writing processes that transformed thought and agency into text. In the new discourse on writing, meaning was as common and ubiquitous as consciousness and cognition itself, which were said to give rise to meaning in the first place. In other words, meaning was not a stable textual construct at all—to be found just in great texts—but rather a dynamic act of ordinary consciousness unfolding in "real time" through the composing processes of beginning, even remedial, basic writers. In North America, by the early 1980s, writing was nothing less than an act of mind in the world, an epistemic action shaping the flux of everyday life and ordinary experience.

Why the 1970s? On the Role of the Sociocultural Context

The central themes of both contemporary rhetoric and the New Psychology were already in place soon after World War I. Why, then, did the new discourse about writing emerge in the 1970s and not before? While the theoretical components for this new view of writing were available in the 1960s and earlier, many of the cultural components and necessary material elements of the receptive context became available only in the 1970s. In other words, the cultural context of the times played a key role in fostering a potential that existed previously almost exclusively in academe.

The Cognitive Revolution was well underway in the 1960s at the Harvard Center for Cognitive Studies and the emerging cognitive sciences that Gardner (1985) chronicles in *The Mind's New Science*. While political antecedents to the culture of difference in America may generally be traced to the Vietnam War protest movement, the Civil Rights Movement, the Women's Movement, and the counterculture of the late 1960s, the impact of those movements on academic accounts of language, as well as university programs and freshman English courses, began to be felt nationally, as we have seen, only with the implementation of open admissions and the attendant literacy crisis of the 1970s. In academic circles, Chomsky's (1957) definition of *grammatical* as whatever is "acceptable to a native speaker" (p. 13), unproblematic enough in the early 1960s, began to be challenged by sociolinguists asking, *Which* native speaker? (for example, see Labov [1969] and also Hymes [1974]). Among anthropologists, Rosaldo (1993) recalls from this time "the urgency of a social analysis that made central the aspirations and demands of groups usually deemed marginal by the dominant national ideology came from the counterculture, environmentalism, feminism, gay and lesbian movements, the Native American movement, and the struggles of blacks, Chicanos, and Puerto Ricans" (p. 35). In literature, scholars began to debate the validity of a canon composed overwhelmingly of white male European authors. In composition, we have seen, Shaughnessy (1977) awakened the composition community to the social and cultural complexity of writing as she systematically examined the errors in the writing of four thousand basic writers. Each of these debates transformed univocal conceptions of language and meaning into a pluralist semiotic, complicating easy generalizations about "cognitive processes," "the composing process," "the reading process," rhetoric, and text meaning. Composition was on the front lines of most of these transformations, and was a key forum mediating the changes.

The new discourse on writing focused radical, egalitarian contentions encompassing a far broader range of language (and language users) than the few elite, canonized texts (and authors) that had interested previous generations including Brooks and the New Critics, and in contexts far more particular than the conventional norms Bloomfield used to define meanings, which for him were always dictionary definitions.[9]

Related to this, the move towards empirical descriptions of how ordinary students write had political ramifications, celebrating social diversity and focusing political capital and constructive attention especially on the challenges of minorities. As such, the new discourse about writing advanced the egalitarian political impulses of 1960s America that motivated, for example, the Civil Rights and Feminist movements, and lent status to those previously excluded or marginalized. Basic, underclass writing was no longer simply "wrong" and "substandard"; rather it was presumed to express "nonstandard" "systems" of language, valid dialects of English, each with its own consistent rules and norms. Webster's Third Unabridged Dictionary, first published in 1961, which as a matter of policy eschewed usage labels, describing rather than prescribing the language, had foreshadowed such linguistic pluralism.[10] This pluralism also resonated in contemporaneous documents like *Students' Right to Their Own Language,* the 1974 white paper adopted by the Conference on College Composition and Communication, which made the case for nonstandard languages and styles in student writing. (As the 1990s flap over Ebonics clearly demonstrates, such egalitarian views of languages and dialects were scarcely the final word!) Nonetheless, these many initiatives of the 1970s can be understood as then-liberal efforts to valorize difference and legitimate the marginal and the peripheral-hallmarks of contemporary rhetoric and composition studies.

It is worth noting that the 1970s were not the first time that composition had mediated the forces of social change in colleges and universities. Miller (1997) shows that during the eighteenth century, English as an academic subject first gained currency in British provincial universities, not initially to teach literature—that came later—but rather to offer instruction in composition and rhetoric in response to demand stimulated by a rising middleclass and a radical expansion of literacy as a result of cheap newspapers. During the nineteenth century in America, the growing industrialization and the concomitant rise of a professional management class created a need for regularity and clarity in written discourse. Writing skill became a social grace—a power button, as it were—a way of exhibiting one's education, class affiliations, and upscale ambitions in an industrial economy. In this way, clarity, grammatical skill, and preferred style—virtues praised in Aristotelian rhetoric—were valorized in a modern capitalist economy. In his incisive "Rhetoric for the Meritocracy" (1976), Wallace Douglas documents the nineteenth-century American "devolution" of classical rhetoric into the modern school subject of composition as Harvard sought to transform itself from a college for sons of the landed gentry into a modern university dedicated to the education of middle as well as upper class managers in an industrial society. In short, Harvard shifted its focus from providing an education serving an agrarian aristocracy to one that provided specialized professional preparation for an industrial meritocracy, or an "aristocracy of achievement," to quote Charles William Eliot, president of Harvard in 1869. Eliot opened Harvard to "students in all conditions of life," including poor students of "capacity and character" (Eliot, quoted in Douglas, 1976, p. 127).

By the time Eliot assumed the presidency, Edward Tyrell Channing, Boylston Professor from 1819 to 1851, had already divined a new rhetorical curriculum well suited to the new mission. He first "purge[d] 'rhetoric' of its ancient connotations of public controversy carried on by members or clients of a ruling class before an uneducated, uninformed, and untrained audience" (Douglas, 1976, p. 124). The new rhetoric was to be clearly attuned to "the actualities of a society where opinion was more and more coming to be formed by the report and article, rather than by the debate" (Douglas, 1976, p. 124). Accordingly, Channing "first changed the locus of the oratorical situation from the public assembly to a generally private room, the medium from the spoken to the printed word, and the agent from the orator to the writer" (Douglas, 1976, p. 124). In this way, the new professional classes of the industrial world were to be given "a quite direct preparation of the work habits and thought patterns that are needed to function in any of the 'varied calls of life'" (Channing, quoted in Douglas, 1976, p. 125). This was the task of the new rhetoric of everyday life circa 1869.

Conclusion

As it departs from formalist and prescriptive models of written composition, those involved in contemporary research in composition have systematically moved toward carefully observed, meticulously reported studies examining the relationships between written language and the material contexts of culture, politics, and economics. Because much as this shift may seem to be a new chapter in composition studies, we believe its foundations are located in the currents of the social upheavals of the 1960s and 1970s, the intellectual climate of the day, and the efforts of early composition researchers such as Bruffee, Shaughnessy, and Emig to respond to their times. And while these early researchers have been associated with a shift from "product" to "process," or assigned to particular "social" or "cognitive" camps in the formation of the discipline of composition, the broader significance of their work lies in their examinations of the practices of writers in everyday life and the ways in which the material world shapes the writing in the classroom.

What do these conclusions suggest for the future of the discipline? We have argued that those involved in current research in composition increasingly look beyond classroom-based investigations of written language toward the roles and meanings of writing in diverse social, historical, and political settings outside of academia. From an activity once defined by pedagogical precepts—as ancient rhetoric was once defined by preceptive handbooks, composition and rhetorical studies had, by the 1980s, become a relentlessly empirical and theoretical discipline. Its boundaries, though often unclear, paralleled rhetoric, linguistics, the social sciences, and education. This suggests that composition is moving "further afield," in Deborah Brandt's phrase, away from a strict emphasis on classroom-based studies of writing and toward more expansive studies of the meanings and functions of written discourse in social life. The history presented here suggests that composition's beginnings, which are generally understood as a discovery of better and more efficient methods to teach school writing—as a product-to-process story—have in fact laid the foundation for a discipline which, as it investigates writing in all areas of social life, clearly seems to be moving towards a rhetoric of everyday life.

Notes

1. Hugh Davis Graham. (1984). *The Uncertain Triumph: Federal Education Policy in the Kennedy and Johnson Years.* Chapel Hill: The University of North Carolina Press. p. 223

2. When the Federal Government awarded the University of Wisconsin with an education research and development center in 1963, they not only funded the research but also built a new facility to house the projects.

3. Material used with Prof. Hawkes's permission.

4. Bruffee, *Collaborative Learning*, p. 15, in Hawkes, p. 3.

5. We are indebted to Charles Bazerman for this information.

6. Miller (1997) notes a similar process in the development of writing programs in Great Britain in the eighteenth century, which first happened in provincial colleges and universities, especially in Scotland, rather than elite institutions such as Cambridge and Oxford.

7. Twentieth-century modes of inquiry concerned with understanding the structure of everyday life are many and varied. In the arts, Baudelaire anticipated much we call modern by celebrating "the momentary, temporal, contingent, and the ephemeral (vs. stability, classic, eternal, universal); see "The Salon of 1846," esp. "The Heroism of Modern Life" (Pippin, 1991, p. 33). According to Baudelaire, the poet/artist's imagination redeems modern life by finding heroism and beauty which is not obvious to ordinary consciousness. Sub-

sequently, the French impressionists perfected the art of capturing fleeting moments of everyday life.

The structuralist programs of Saussure and Durkheim, as well as early efforts by Freud and Marx, were cutting edge in their time because they claimed to penetrate the surface of everyday life to reveal the underlying structures of, respectively, language, society, personality, and history. Statistics played an important methodological role in the nascent social sciences, and was used by Durkheim to great effect to show that suicide rates differed from one European society to another; such analysis enabled him to posit "social facts" as unseen but nonetheless real parts of daily life.

Recently, so-called postmodernist movements in the arts, literature, and the social sciences, have attacked the consistency, coherence, and harmony of modernist artifacts and ideologies, articulating conceptions of "blurred genres" (Geertz) and valorizing the place, function, history, and variety of local taste (Jencks). In the last 30 years, for example, anthropology has shifted its research focus from the identification of coherent, underlying structures to theories of practice that "explore the interplay of both structure *and* agency" (emphasis in original): "Rather than stressing timeless universals and the sameness of human nature, this perspective emphasized human diversity, historical change, and political struggle" (Rosaldo, p. xviii). In architecture, the International Style of Mies van der Rohe and others has come under sharp attack as an ideology seeking to impose the abstract coherence of a single will on local communities (Jencks, p. 26); consider Venturi, Brown, & Isenour's (1972) celebration of Las Vegas as art. Postmodernists' emphasis on eclecticism, pluralism, and difference highlights the heterogeneity of everyday life.

8. Conley, p. 261.

9. See discussion of meaning as reference (p. 139ff.) and of "the ordinary tie-up of phonetic form with dictionary meaning" (Bloomfield, 1933, p. 148).

10. This editorial policy set off a lively brouhaha among newspaper columnists, pundits, and outraged citizens. See Sledd & Ebbitt, *Dictionaries and That Dictionary: A Casebook on the Aims of Lexicographers and the Targets of Reviewers* (1962).

References

Bakhtin, M. M. (1981). *The dialogic imagination*. Austin: University of Texas Press.

Bakhtin, M., & Medvedev, P. N. (1985). *The formal method in literary scholarship: A critical introduction to sociological poetics.* Cambridge, MA: Harvard University Press.

Barabas, C. (1990). *Technical writing in a corporate culture: A study of the nature of information*. Norwood, NJ: ABLEX Publishing Corp.

Bartholomae, D. (1985). Inventing the university. In M. Rose (Ed.), *When a writer can't write* (pp. 134–165). New York: Guilford Press.

Baudelaire, P. C. (1964). The salon of 1846. In *Baudelaire as a literary critic: Selected essays*, Intro. & Trans., L. B. Hyslop and F. E. Hyslop. Jr. University Park, PA: Penn State Press.

Bazerman, C., & Paradis, J. (1991). *Textual dynamics of the professions: historical and contemporary studies of writing in professional communities.* Madison, WI: University of Wisconsin Press.

Berlin, J. A. (1987). *Rhetoric and reality: Writing instruction in American colleges, 1900–1985*. Carbondale: Southern Illinois University Press.

Bizzell, P. (1982). Cognition, context, and certainty. *PRE/TEXT, 3*, 213–24.

Bloomfield, L. (1933). *Language*. New York: H. Holt and Company

Bracewell, R., & Breuleux, A. (1992, April). *Cognitive principles for the support of technical writing*. Paper presented at the 1992 Convention of the American Educational Research Association.

Braddock, R., Lloyd-Jones, R., and Schoer, L. (1963). *Research in written composition*. Champaign: National Council of Teachers of English.

Brandt, D. (1995). Remembering writing, remembering reading. *College Composition and Communication*.

Chomsky, N. (1957). *Syntactic structures*. The Hague: Mouton.

Conley, T. (1990). *Rhetoric in the European tradition*. New York and London: Longman.

Corbett, Edward P. J. (1965). *Classical rhetoric for the modern student*. New York: Oxford University Press.

Douglas, W. (1976). Rhetoric for the meritocracy. In R. Ohmann, *English in America: A radical view of the profession*. New York: Oxford University Press.

Duffy, J. (1997, March). Literacy, immigrants, and the struggle for 'our town': Competing rhetorics of community in a Wisconsin city. Paper presented to the 1997 American Educational Researchers Association Conference, Chicago.

Duin, A. H., & Hansen, C. J. (Eds.). (1996). *Nonacademic writing: Social theory and technology*. Mahwah, N.J.: Lawrence Erlbaum Associates.

Dyson, A. (1993). *The social worlds of children learning to write in an urban primary school*. New York: Teachers College Press.

Dyson, A. (1997). *Writing superheroes: Contemporary childhood, popular culture, and classroom literacy*. New York: Teachers College Press.

Emig, J. (1971). *The composing processes of twelfth graders*. Urbana: The National Council of Teachers of English.

Farr, Marcia. (1993). Essayist literacy and other verbal performances. *Written Communication, 10*, 4–38.

Flower, L., & Hayes, J. R. (1981). A cognitive process theory of writing. *College Composition and Communication, 32*, 365–387.

Flower, L. (1994). *The construction of negotiated meaning: A social cognitive theory of writing*. Carbondale: Southern Illinois University Press.

Fogarty, D. (1959). *Roots for a new rhetoric*. New York: Russell and Russell.

Gardner, H. (1985). *The mind's new science.* New York: Basic Books.

Geertz, C. (1983). *Local knowledge: Further essays in interpretive anthropology*. New York: Basic Books.

Geisler, C. (1991). Toward a sociocognitive perspective on literacy: A study of an academic "conversation." In C. Bazerman & J. Paradis (Eds.), *Textual dynamics of the professions* (pp. 171–190). Madison: University of Wisconsin Press.

Greene, S. (1992). Mining texts in reading to write. *Journal of Advanced Composition, 12.1.*

Greene, S. (1993). The role of task in the development of academic thinking through reading and writing in a college history course. *Research in the Teaching of English, 27*, 47–76.

Haas, C. (1996). *Writing technology: Studies on the materiality of literacy*. Mahwah, NJ: L. Erlbaum Associates.

Hawkes, P. (1996). Open admissions and Vietnam protests: Tracing the politics of Kenneth Bruffee's collaborative learning. Paper presented at Thomas R. Watson Conference, University of Louisville, 11 October 1996.

Herndl, C., Fennel, B., & C. R. Miller (1991). Understanding failures in organizational discourse. In C. Bazerman & J. Paradis (Eds.), *Textual dynamics of the professions: Historical and contemporary studies of writing in professional communities*. Madison: University of Wisconsin Press.

Graham, H. D. (1984). *The Uncertain Triumph: Federal Education Policy in the Kennedy and Johnson Years*. Chapel Hill: University of North Carolina Press.

Hymes, D. (1974). *Foundations in sociolinguistics*. Philadelphia: University of Philadelphia Press.

Jencks, C. (1992). *The post-modern reader*. New York: St. Philadelphia: Martin's Press.

Kihss, P. (1968). Brooklyn College expands. *New York Times,* cited in Hawkes, 1996.

Labov, W. (1969). *The logic of nonstandard English. Georgetown monographs on language and linguistics. Vol. 22*. Washington: Georgetown University Press.

McCarthy, L. P. & Gerring, J. P. (1994). Revising psychiatry's charter document DSM–IV. *Written Communication, 11,* 147–192.

Macrorie, K. (1970). *Uptaught*. New York: Hayden Book Co.

McQuade, D. & Atwan, R. (Eds.) (1974). *Popular writing in America: The interaction of style and audience*. New York: Oxford University Press.

McNamee, G. D. (1992, April). *The voices of community change*. Paper presented at the 1992 Convention of the American Educational Research Association.

Miller, C. (1984). Genre as social action. *Quarterly Journal of Speech, 70,* 151–167.

Miller, T. (1997). *The formation of college English*. Pittsburgh: University of Pittsburgh Press. Myers, G. (1991). Stories and styles in two molecular biology review articles. In C. Bazerman & J. Paradis (Eds.), *Textual dynamics of the professions: Historical and contemporary studies of writing in professional communities*. Madison: University of Wisconsin Press.

Nystrand, M. (1982). The structure of textual space. In M. Nystrand (Ed.), *What writers know: The language, process, and structure of written discourse*. New York: Academic Press.

Ogden, C. K., & I. A. Richards. (1923). *The meaning of meaning; a study of the influence of language upon thought and of the science of symbolism*. London: K. Paul, Trench, Trubner & Co., Ltd.

Palmer, J. (1992, April). *The rhetoric of negotiation: Professional writing at Apple Computer, Inc*. Paper presented at the 1992 Convention of the American Educational Research Association.

Miller, T. (1997). *The formation of college English*. Pittsburgh: University of Pittsburgh Press.

Rosaldo, Renato. (1993). *Culture & truth: The remaking of social analysis*. Boston: Beacon Press.

Schriver, K. (1992, April). *Collaboration in professional writing: The cognition of a social process*. Paper presented at the 1992 Convention of the American Educational Research Association.

Shaughnessy, M. (1977). *Errors and expectations*. London: Oxford University Press.

Sledd, J. H., & Ebbitt, W. R. (1962). *Dictionaries and that dictionary: A casebook on the aims of lexicographers and the targets of reviewers*. Chicago: Scott, Foresman.

Strunk, W. (1959). *The elements of style*. With revisions, an introduction and a new chapter on writing by E. B. White. NY: Macmillan.

Students' right to their own language. (1974). *College Composition and Communication*

Van Laan, T. F. & Lyons, R. B. (Eds.). (1968, 1972). *Language and the newsstand: A critical reader*. New York: Scribner.

Venturi, R, Brown, D. S., & Izenour, S. (1972). *Learning from Las Vegas*. Cambridge, Mass.: MIT Press.

Warriner, J. E. (1950). *English grammar and composition: Complete course*. New York: Harcourt, Brace & World.

Webster's third new international dictionary of the English language, unabridged. (1961).

Ed. by Philip Babcock Gove and the Merriam-Webster editorial staff. Springfield, MA: Merriam-Webster.

Wertsch, J. (1985). The semiotic mediation of mental life: L. S. Vygotsky and M. M. Bakhtin. In E. Mertz & R. Parmentier (Eds.), *Semiotic mediation: Sociocultural and psychological perspectives* (pp. 49–71). Orlando: Academic Press.

Witte, S. P. (1992) Context, text, and intertext: Toward a constructivist semiotic of Writing. *Written Communication, 9*, 237–308.

Towards a Rhetoric of Everyday Life

1
Rhetorics of Community Life

1

"Gates Locked" and the Violence of Fixation

Ralph Cintron

Introduction

I begin with an ethnographic scene that serves both as a leitmotif as well as an object of analysis:

Rural Illinois . . . Friday afternoon . . . October 1996 . . . The waiting room of a medium-security prison. Less than a mile away are next year's cornfields and soybeans. I am waiting with a group of women. Many come from Chicago. Most are African American or Latina (Mexican or Puerto Rican for the most part). Typically, these mothers, girlfriends, wives come every other week. I come from a large public university, always on a Friday, not more than once a month. I am here to visit El Duque, a street gang leader who is about my age. Typically, the waiting, which usually lasts an hour or more, seems part of some vast system of punishment that imprisons us along with the convicted. Because this is one of my fieldwork days, I take notes on almost everything.

Suddenly, I feel an electric surge of confirmation: one of the women whom I have seen on a number of occasions has moved toward the front of the room and briefly turned so that I can read the words on her tee-shirt: Fear Is an Emotion/Bad Is an Attitude. After years of fieldwork in mostly Mexican/Puerto Rican neighborhoods in northern Illinois, those words embody what I have come to understand about street life, its passion and special ideology. Those eight words on a tee-shirt might neatly substitute for pages of data, analysis, speculation, and theory that I have been pulling together for years now.

I scribble hurriedly into my field-book. One of the perverse thrills of the kind of research I do is that sometimes the theory that one has been crafting for a long time swoops down and becomes embodied in the events of everyday life. What I might otherwise look at with indifference acquires a certain import, a flash of familiarity, as if yesterday's omen had materialized.

Although the above scene would seem not to have much to do with rhetorical studies, I will argue that, indeed, it has much to do with the study of rhetoric. The major concern of this essay is to show that rhetorical analysis can help make sense of everyday language use. I argue that rhetorical analysis need not be about famous speeches and/or the written word. Indeed, it need not be about the discursive at all, and should also include the non-discursive and performative. For instance, while doing ethnographic fieldwork in Chicagoland, I occasionally encountered a particular pose (arms crossed so that hands hook beneath the armpits, thumbs exposed, the body tilted slightly back) among some young males. The pose was meant to signal toughness or defiance, and I later found out that it was sometimes called "gates locked," a term that I now use to title this paper. The term is a wondrous metaphor, at least in my interpretive scheme, signaling the "locking out" of a potential challenger even as it "locks in" fear and vulnerability, making both invisible behind the performance of the pose. I take it, then, that a structure of meaning—I am tempted to say also a "structure of feeling" so as to acknowledge and honor the work of Raymond Williams (1965)—stitches this physical performance to a discourse so that the one cannot be understood without the other. Later in this essay, I will examine in more detail how the tee-shirt, Fear Is an Emotion/ Bad Is an Attitude echoes other "street" performances as well as the meanings of "gates locked."

My title, "Gates Locked," then, makes the very important point that through its gestures and adornment the body can "speak" rhetorically, thereby displaying the thought systems that a person identifies with and (implicitly or explicitly) "argues" for. In this sense, rhetoric would seem to be concerned with both discursive and non-discursive practices. The second part of the title, "Violence of Fixation," refers more broadly to that human tendency to fix or reify one's beliefs. Whenever we locate a belief, our own or someone else's, as natural, commonsensical, true, real, or correct, we have begun to manufacture a bit of artifice, one that reduces variability and complexity. These operations are, of course, utterly necessary, rational, and practical for the conduct of everyday life. Nevertheless, they entail at least a minuscule amount of violence, for it is hard to shape something without simultaneously losing something else—and this loss is the price that must be paid. In most cases, the price is negligible or at least worth it. In other cases, however, the price can be extraordinarily high. For instance, among the sorts of marginalized young males that I have come to know, some of the operations that reduce complex conditions to simpler ones so as to reify patented ideologies lead to real, physical violence. Even more pernicious and potentially more violent, however, are examples of policy making in which the policy makers can no longer critique their own positions because they too have reduced or "fixed" the complexities of real world conditions and reified frozen ideologies by labeling them "natural," "commonsensical," "real," and so on. This essay, then, also explores specific contexts in which the fixing or fixation of everyday language occurs.

So much for clarifying the title of my essay. Let me move on to explaining its structure.

The first part of the essay argues against disciplinary histories and expectations that, for the most part, have cleaved two areas of inquiry, rhetorical studies from anthropology. This problem is a personal one. The issues of everyday language and practice have become deeply engaging for me; they have also become relatively accessible through the tools of ethnography. However, these are not issues typically studied by rhetoricians. Indeed, most academics have a hard time at first believing that my research and teaching belong to rhetorical studies. Sometimes I quickly dodge their puzzled faces and reach for the shorthand explanation, "Well, you see, I do urban anthropology." To date, anthropologists have understood and accepted what I do. If anything, they wonder what I am doing in a rhetoric department. In short, I want to do something about this split. Interestingly, Kenneth Burke (1969) in a provocative passage both reinforced the cleavage and ushered in its possible dissolution: "We are not so much proposing to import anthropology into rhetoric as proposing that anthropologists recognize the factor of rhetoric in their own field" (p. 43). Thirty years or so after Burke's statement, anthropologists significantly rethought their discipline through the lens of rhetoric. It has now become impossible to list the number of anthropological texts that have either deconstructed the writings of anthropologists and ethnographers (and spilt much anthropological blood in the process) or, following Burke, taken seriously the ways in which field sites reveal the rhetoric of everyday practices. Certainly, Clifford and Marcus's *Writing Culture* (1986) is a watershed text for the first type, and James Fernandez's work, is one of the watersheds for the second; some of this work has been collected in his *Persuasions and Performances* (1986). But there is a third watershed that we might consider: the work of Dwight Conquergood (1991, 1992) is an example. In the work of Conquergood especially, one sees a clearer synthesis of rhetorical studies and anthropology. For instance, both fields for some time have been employing such shared terms as "performance" and "critical," but in Conquergood's work one sees how these terms can come to together to create a more compelling, shared terrain. This essay begins, then, by following Conquergood's lead and extending it. I will explore how the term "critical," as in "critical rhetoric" and "critical ethnography," has become one way to imagine the convergence of rhetorical studies and anthropology. Indeed, an examination of critical rhetoricians and critical ethnographers reveals that they are essentially both doing the very same work. The first part of my essay suggests a brief history of how and why this has come about. More importantly, it will suggest a terrain from which rhetorical studies can further imagine an ethnographic analysis of everyday life and language.

The second part of this essay arises from my motivation to unpack what seem to be polar forces operating in language. I describe these forces as "partiality versus presence." My use of the term "partiality" mobilizes a pun: that is, language *imperfectly* represents what it represents; hence it remains always *biased* or ideologically saturated. Imperfect representation suggests that a signified is, in a sense, run over by signifiers, which means that a signified cannot be satisfactorily grasped by any one signifier. This inexactness of reference suggests that words can, at best, approximate. People may use signifiers (words) in an attempt to couple them with signifieds (things), but, in the end, words and things are always of different species. This inexactness of words and language, this sense of words always missing their mark suggests to me that language is perpetually metaphorical, meaning that likeness is named, but exactness is not possible.[1] In short, language is a generalized poetics, a field of near misses and approximations. If language is always metaphorical, a kind of generalized poetics, it means further that language is ideologically saturated. In other words, if I do not name exactly, I must be naming subjectively. The pun "partiality," then, summarizes and connects two conditions, poetics and ideology. That is, a generalized poetics is the ground of ideology. I recognize, of course, that an ideology is much more than a set of subjective words grounded in a medium of poetics; indeed, an ideology is a thought system. However, I am trying here to unpack a different way to think about ideology and subjectivity, and so I have, for my purposes, limited what I mean by ideology.

Partiality has a companion I call "presence." Presence is that force in language that counters the forces of partiality. To explain briefly: what I find most peculiar about language use is the invisibility of partiality. How is it that at a moment of language use, most audiences, including myself, remain fairly blind and deaf to language's incompleteness and bias, in other words, to its partiality? How is it that words perform that magic of washing over us so that we believe that they are referencing, more or less accurately, something true, real, commonsensical, or correct. I suspect that this is a fantastically complicated process entailing much more than words. My tentative answer is that presence, by which I mean a kind of appearance of factuality or "beingness" that all words have, conceals partiality. Obviously, this mask sometimes is not complete, and an audience member sees, as if a through a window, into the incompleteness and bias of some discourse—this is the moment of critique. There are two examples that I will use to explore the details of partiality and presence and their relationship. The first example concerns a particular speech by Senator Tom Harkin of Iowa presented during the impeachment proceedings of President Clinton. The second example is taken from my fieldwork and concerns the talk of young, marginalized males.

My third motivation, which suffuses the entire essay, is to defend a particular preference of mine, which is to root all possible inquiries in the methods of ethnography. Academics tend not to talk very much about love (Dominguez, 1998), but ethnography is a method of inquiry that relies on forming bonds of trust and on listening to the hearts and minds of people and their ways of making meaning. The method also requires the ethnographer to have a subtle grasp of the social as a complex system. These are some of the opportunities, indeed, gifts that ethnography offers; I think that they require degrees of love and genuineness. Obviously, such statements seem embarrassingly naive and sentimental in the light of the postcolonial rebellion against sociocultural anthropology. In the eyes of its critics, ethnography represents colonialism's power imbalances so that its methods appear coldly inquisitorial, and in some instances mimic rape when they recasts human subjects as scientific objects (Tyler, 1986; Fabian, 1983). Moreover, given the sort of hermeneutics of suspicion that is practiced often with sterile brilliance in the academy these days, my comments may seem like antiquated essentialism. But why reduce ethnography to only one of its historical uses? What if agape were necessary to complete the mission of ethnographic inquiry? That is, what if ethnographic knowledge could only be understood if it awakened agape in the ethnographer? What I like about ethnography is the possibility of mobilizing a complex formula that utilizes empirical data, reveals sociopolitical constraints, delivers a tentative analysis of social structure, recognizes the limits of research, and is attuned to love (or at least to empathy and companionship), and purposefully awakens these inside the ethnographer and the readers of ethnographies.

Rhetoric and Sociocultural Anthropology

Before moving on to the sort of empirical work that ethnographic fieldwork represents, I wish to discuss two speculative issues. The first issue concerns certain intellectual movements in different disciplines that have been in place within the academy for quite some time. My purpose in this section, then, is to suggest that there is no inherent incompatibility between rhetorical studies and sociocultural anthropology, if we are allowed to follow certain trends that are already well in place in both fields.

Here is my broad definition of rhetoric that may help form the basis of my discussion: Rhetoric is that disciplinary art that imprecisely tracks the making of social imaginaries, including their histories, possible futures, and connections to material conditions; it assumes that individual thoughts and feelings, no matter how idiosyncratic, precipitate out of a social imaginary linked to specific material conditions. It would seem, then, that rhetoric is concerned with collective consciousness, its constituent parts and how they change over time. I am rather certain that my readers right now are asking for a definition of the term "social imaginary." My understanding of the term is influenced by Maffesoli et al. (1993), Stewart (1996), and Ruddick (1996):

"Social imaginary," a term used by [Henri] Lefebvre, signals an image that exists within the popular imagination or unconscious: social because the process which produces it is societal rather than individualized, and imaginary, rather than symbolic, because it indicates not a state of signification but a condition of possession. (Ruddick, p. 12)

I believe such a definition is consistent with Burke's (1969) vision of rhetoric and that it de-emphasizes another long-standing interpretation of rhetoric as a set of codifiable techniques for writing and speaking effec-

tively. Ruddick's definition would seem to be concerned with the production of culture, its discourses, webs of ideas, and even its artifacts. It is
true, of course, that I have manipulated such a definition in order to pluck
out a compatibility with sociocultural anthropology. Therefore, my bit of
artifice might not work for everyone, but it reflects the fact that I do not
recognize vast incompatibilities between these two disciplines. A small
comparison might suffice: Many anthropologists search for "key terms"
around which a community organizes behaviors and meanings. For example, in the ethnographic scene that began this essay, an ethnographer
might want to consider the terms "bad" and "attitude" and how they cir-
culate through a variety of communities in the United States, and what
sorts of actions, behaviors, thoughts, and feelings they describe. In contrast, someone following a definition of rhetoric that emphasizes the study
of social imaginaries might comb a community or a specific text for its
"cultural topoi" and encounter the terms "bad" and "attitude" and arrive
at the very same conclusions. In short, at an abstract level, to search for
key terms is to uncover "cultural topoi." However, the differing details and
audiences of these projects could result in one project being distinctly
rhetorical and the other distinctly anthropological. My point is, however,
that these two disciplines currently have models of cultural production
that are compatible: both disciplines are based upon a broad assertion that
cultures (including communities and groups) generate ideas, discourses,
and artifacts through processes of improvisation; hence, their analytic
techniques (key terms, topoi, and so on) are similar.

However, similarities between the two fields may be even deeper than
their common techniques. Let me examine a current branch of both rhetoric and anthropology: critical rhetoric and critical ethnography. These
two smaller fields differ in their origins, audience expectations, and their
objects of analysis, but do not differ in their overall goals and conclusions.
In the following definitions (the first by a rhetorician, the second by a
sociocultural anthropologist), the term "critical" becomes a unifying ad-
jective that dissolves disciplinary boundaries. A "critical rhetoric serves a
demystifying function . . . by demonstrating the silent and often non-
deliberate ways in which rhetoric conceals as much as it reveals through
its relationship with power/knowledge" (McKerrow, 1989, p. 92).

The critical-interpretive approach that I advance here, and that is advanced in different forms by Rabinow, Abu-Lughod, Rosaldo and me . . . calls into question

the epistemological and the political/moral status of the 'facts' and 'realities' under study. What matters to us is the means through which research data are acquired, the various meanings the findings have, and the relations between the
knowledge generated and the maintenance of dominant ideologies and power relations. (Scheper-Hughes, 1995, p. 436)

I don't know if McKerrow, the rhetorician, and Scheper-Hughes, the
anthropologist, are aware of each other's work. I doubt that they do because the histories of their disciplines are quite distinct. Nevertheless,
both disciplines employ the term "critical," to say the similar things. It is
almost this simple: without the word "critical" the disciplinary boundaries remain distinct. However, the addition of "critical" and the methods
it implies creates at the least overlapping disciplines and perhaps a single
discipline.

The term "critical," then, seems to unify. Our curiosity is piqued—
what does the term mean and how does it unify? Here is the briefest of
answers: "Critical" in these contexts is always associated with unmask-
ing. Critical work, a perspective that I generally subscribe to, requires a
trained and disciplined mind that is able to disregard the ideological satu-
ration that enshrouds any claim to truth. I think the underground terrain
of this thought system lies somewhere in Marx's notion of false consciousness and the need to crack through its falsities. For instance, says Marx, if
exchange values hide the misery of labor relationships, it is necessary for
the laborer to become aware of and dispel these mystifications. Today's
critical intellectuals may owe a debt to Marx, but, inevitably they have had
to move beyond his formulations.

And toward what have they moved? What has occurred in academe is
the steady dilution of Marxism as an analysis of the base (economic structure), but an expansion of its ghost-like presence in all sorts of analyses of
the superstructure (language and ideology, symbolic meanings, mediated
images, the social imaginary—in short, cultural stuff). This move can also
be described in the following way: from analyses of production to analyses
of consumption. Because consumption was not Marx's major preoccupation, Marxism's position in this newer scene, its reduction to formidable
ghost, causes consternation among those who want to retain an analysis of
production because in their view production continues to be the genera-
tor of the reality that matters—and in many ways they are correct. Nevertheless, the shift is now confidently in place so that today's critical analyses

of the superstructure (consumption, spectacle, desire, the visual, expressive culture, and the ideological formation of nation/states) operate within an interpretive framework that straddles numerous disciplines and never even needs to use the word Marxism. In other words, the unification of McKerrow, Scheper-Hughes, and many, many others under the heading "critical" has much to do with the diffusion and attenuation of Marxist thought across all matters of the superstructure. More importantly, it has to do with seizing the Marxist ethical thrust, a kind of battering ram ideology aimed at the forces of mystification, particularly at those daily oppressions and limitations and their attendant masking agents that are embedded in the superstructure and prevent the realization of justice.

All this drops us squarely into the garden of language and rhetoric. Take Scheper-Hughes, for instance. She does not wish to contemplate objects of knowledge shorn of their ideological functions. She wants her "'facts' and 'realities' under study" to reveal also their "political/moral status." McKerrow would agree. To do critical work in this view, then, means that any inquiry into an object of knowledge will become simultaneously an inquiry into how, why, and when the knowledge became knowledge and who made it so. Any inquiry into the namers of knowledge and the power that accrues and is maintained by such naming is an inquiry into partiality. "Partiality" is an interesting word. It has two senses, a sense of bias and a sense of incompleteness. When McKerrow, Scheper-Hughes, and others do the sort of critical work that is being described here, they assume that knowledge and knowledge-making are always biased, and always incomplete. The history of knowledge-making, they would say, reveals that even the most factual "discoveries"—for instance, the circulation of blood inside the body—occurred within a context of ideological interest, not disinterest, and continued to have an ideological dimension whenever and wherever modernity encountered tradition. Knowledge and knowledge-making, then, are inevitably partial, they would say. Indeed, we can probably go even further: to be immersed in the human condition is to be immersed in both senses of partiality, that of bias and that of incompleteness. At any rate, what is so intriguing about knowledge and knowledge-making is their tendency to hide their origins in partiality and to create the sense that they are somehow independent of the problem of partiality, that is, somehow real, true, or correct rather than partial. An investigation into partiality and the dense fabric of how it gets hidden behind a semblance of the real, true, or correct is, for me, "critical" work.

Moreover, because these sorts of investigations entail an analysis of how language itself does so much of the obscuring, one indeed might call this work critical rhetoric or, more easily, an investigation into how language supports ideology. No matter what we call it, it should be clear that Mc-Kerrow and Scheper-Hughes, as I stated earlier, are doing essentially the same thing, and their debt to the decay of one kind of Marxist thought and the expansion of another should also be clear.

So far I have described critical work as mostly a political project aligned to the progressive left. Does this mean that the left is the only thought system that can demystify? If so, I worry about the potential arrogance that McKerrow, Scheper-Hughes, and their coworkers might unconsciously subscribe to. My own sense is that responsible ideological readings can occur from within a wide variety of political positions and that, further, if we paid close attention to cynicism in the general public, we might uncover a kind of populist version of demystification. In short, I seriously wonder if the McKerrows and Scheper-Hugheses would be willing to release the term "critical" from a strictly left agenda.

However, it is clear that critical work is all around us and that one need not be an academic, or a leftist, to perform it. The availability of critical inquiry to everyone is a position that is important to take. Quite simply, rhetorical analysis is not just an endeavor of specialists but also an everyday affair. Let me consider the impeachment of President Clinton that occupied so much public time from 1998 to 1999. Such an example is particularly interesting because it steps out of the confinements of academic or formal knowledge and knowledge-making and puts us squarely into everyday knowledge and knowledge-making, a system far more vast, perplexing, and consequential than the academic. The example also broadens the prior discussion of "critical" as a project indebted solely to Marxist thought. Indeed, as will be seen, it places ideological demystification in the hands of everyone; it arises from every political persuasion.

During the impeachment proceedings, many members of Congress and the Senate from many political persuasions were busy examining people's motives, intentions, physical gestures, and, most importantly, words. Early in the proceedings, Senator Tom Harkin from Iowa abruptly stood up and interrupted one of the "prosecutors." Harkin, who is somewhat left-leaning, launched into a surprising speech that lasted under 10 minutes and called into question some of the basic terms that had become quite acceptable during the days leading up to the proceedings. He questioned the use of the term "juror" as a characterization of the senators and the word "trial" as a characterization of the proceedings. Both terms, he suggested, were reductive. He argued that the function of the senators was far broader than what the usual interpretations of juror and trial permitted. He argued that the senators were not just determining whether Clinton was guilty of the charges, but that they were also looking out for the welfare of the nation and that, therefore, their powers were larger than those of any juror at any trial. The senators, then, ought not to be compared to jurors at a criminal trial weighing evidence, he urged. Jurors, for instance, do not ask questions, but senators would be doing exactly that. Moreover, the senators had to understand the constitutional provisions for impeachment, to know something about American presidential history, and accept that even a guilty finding might be irrelevant given the extraordinary, weighty responsibilities facing them.

Prior to that peculiar moment, the words "juror" and "trial" had peppered the proceedings. They had become natural descriptors, limiting the public's imagination to those familiar denotations and connotations and no others. In short, they had circumscribed or narrowed the possibilities for imagining a set of proceedings that did not itself have more exact terms because the proceedings have been rare. Instead, these terms were merely the conventional ones, known to all. Harkin's speech, then, exposed this gap between a comfortable known and a less comfortable unknown. His speech released the terms "juror" and "trial" from their identification with the proceedings themselves and exposed their function in that context as approximate metaphors. For Harkin, the terms could not be more than metaphors or similes. That is, the proceedings were *like* a trial and the senators were *like* jurors, but we should not mistake "trial" and "jurors" as descriptions of actual reality. Not only did Senator Harkin expose the terms as inadequate, but he also revealed them as ideological and dangerous. In short, Harkin exposed what the Republican managers, knowingly or not, had hidden, namely, the partiality of their terms. He wanted to remind the senators and the American public of at least two things: that the matters under discussion were far more grave and finally of a different nature than what could be named by the word "trial," and that there was a certain violence that would be performed against the country if the senators continued to limit and fix these proceedings to those terms. In sum, in what at first seemed to be a puzzling questioning of "mere" words, Harkin pointed to an essential difference between "trial" as a term in the social imaginary and the portentousness of any impeachment. This difference was one that the public, according to polls, seemed to have realized all along, even though no one had publicly stated it in the manner that Harkin did.

Let me summarize: I have argued in this section that a certain kind of language analysis that focuses on the ideological character of language and that is broadly called "critical" is being examined from within a number of specialized disciplines in the academy. Such work can be mapped as a flowering of post-Marxism. The result of this confluence is that a certain kind of rhetorical work can be folded into a certain kind of anthropological work and vice versa until it all looks pretty much the same. More significantly, however, is that very similar work occurs among non-academics. The result of this second realization is that rhetorical analysis as an analysis of linguistic ideologies, these props of a social imaginary, is very much a part of everyday discourse. Perhaps this everyday analysis functions as a kind of generalized skepticism, even cynicism, aimed at power and authority. In the next section of the essay, I explore at greater depth the partiality of language and how it gets occulted. I wish to remind my readers that this next section is but another prelude leading, finally, to a discussion of empirical work.

Language, Ideology, and Poetics

How do we know that language is always, already partial? We can think this thought via a variety of linguistic theories, for instance, those of Jean-Jacques Lecercle (1990), or the linguistic anthropology of Stephen Tyler (1978), or Stuart Hall's analyses of ideology (1996). These theories are merely representative of what has become the generally accepted understanding of how language operates, an understanding that is derived for many from Derrida or Bakhtin:

Every act of saying is a momentary intersection of the "said" and the "unsaid." Because it is surrounded by an aureola of the unsaid, an utterance speaks of more than it says, mediates between past and future, transcends the speaker's conscious thought, passes beyond his manipulative control, and creates in the mind of the hearer worlds unanticipated. From within the infinity of the "unsaid," the speaker and the hearer, by a joint act of will, bring into being what was "said." (Tyler, 1978, p. 459)

Language is the medium *par excellence* through which things are "represented" in thought, and thus the medium in which ideology is generated and

transformed. But in language, the same social relation can be *differently* represented and construed. . . . Because language by its nature is *not fixed* in a one-to-
one relation to its referent but is "multi-referential": it can construct different
meanings around what is apparently the same social relation or phenomenon.
(Hall, 1996, p. 36)

If we take these arguments about the unpredictability of meaning seriously, about words having multiple trajectories, and about statements
and propositions not having stable reference because they are under the
aegis of the "unsaid," then we have grounds for saying that partiality is at
the heart of language use. In short, incompleteness and bias move through
the whole system and cannot be removed.

Here is a simple thought experiment that reveals the problem: Imagine a chair in the middle of a room and imagine also a group of speakers
trying to describe the chair to a blindfolded person whose back is turned
to the chair. The goal of the group is to create an "exact" picture of the
chair inside the mind of the blindfolded person. If the standard of what
counts as an exact picture is high, the project might very well fail. Words
will fall short of their intended targets. In order to even create an adequate
semblance, the speakers would have to speak at great length and carefully
choose the descriptors most essential to the listener's recognition of a
chair. How would they specify the limits of a specific color, the grain of
wood, the taper of the legs? Finally, imagine the removal of the blindfold
and the person actually seeing the chair. Might her reply be, "Oh that's
what you meant, now I see," and in that reply, do we not sense the material chair asserting dominance over the verbal "chair?" The group's description compared to the sight of the chair when the blindfold is removed
seems inexact, cumbersome, and lengthy. Once the material chair has
been disclosed (not completely, of course, because the physicist has yet to
plot for us its atomic and subatomic characteristics), do not the team's descriptions fall into the waste can? Clearly (and yes, I use the word ironically) isomorphism between discourse and its referents is an idealization.
Present in even the most exact verbal thought is its incompleteness and
bias, that is, its partiality. However, one might pragmatically reply (and just
as clearly) that few of us demand or even expect linguistic exactness to be
very exact, that all that should be asked is that it be "good enough."

Partiality reminds us of the elusiveness of language, how discourse
slips and slides beyond its referents and beyond the intentions of speakers. Because of these conditions we might think of poetics as organic to

language. By "poetics" here I mean that discourse in its descriptive and argumentative modes posits, at most, likeness but never exactness. For instance, we might be tempted to describe the blindfolded person as confused during the ordeal. But the word "confused," although probably "good enough," is at most an approximation, a semblance of how she felt over a stretch of time that undoubtedly contained a variety of reactions. Similarly, the descriptions of the chair may be good likenesses of the chair but not equivalences. But these examples and their inherent problems pale when compared to social science descriptions, for how does one speak about something as complicated as society? Take sociocultural anthropology, for instance. A statement like "the Boro Boro believe in X, Y, Z" would have to be revised in order to underscore the concept of partiality: "the statement 'the Boro Boro believe in X Y Z' is *like* but not equivalent to what the Boro Boro believe." The first statement seems naive because it assumes that its words are transparent windows revealing the actual beliefs of the Boro Boro. The second statement underscores the mediating role of language and says distinctly that the statement cannot be more than an approximation. In other words, the statement, at most, is a likeness, but not an equivalence. Moreover, it makes very good sense not to claim more than likeness, for surely all the beliefs of the Boro Boro cannot be subsumed under X, Y, Z, and, surely, the Boro Boro themselves are not stationary in time but are continually forming new beliefs. In short, likeness and approximation would seem to be organic to language, indeed, so organic that we could describe language as a kind of generalized poetics, that is, poetics stretches across its entirety. Lecercle (1990) has said, "The metaphor has turned organic rather than architectural, but it has mainly turned anarchic" (51).

Thus far, I have been stressing the poetics and partiality of language. One of the problems with my position, however, is that these are not conditions that most people think about in their daily use of language. For instance, when people argue or refer to this or that, they believe somewhat sturdily that their words are marking a real, true, or correct thing or situation. Senator Harkin certainly did, as did the Republican managers that he criticized. Indeed, even those theorists who professionally argue for linguistic partiality most often write in ways that seem to mask the conditions of partiality; that is, they labor at making their words mark a real, true, or correct position regarding the very conditions of inescapable partiality. Take this essay as an example. In a sense, it argues coherently that language use significantly thwarts our attempts to create coherence. How is this essay able to accomplish two seemingly contradictory actions at the same time? Speaking more personally, why do I enjoy arranging meanings that I believe embody clarity, exactness, and logical progression when the underlying argument itself undermines the possibility of its achievement? Speaking more broadly, why don't theorists who talk about the elusiveness of language and the multiple trajectories of a single word also reflect on how their own texts depend on (and perhaps even struggle for) degrees of exactness, clarity, and efficiency? The strangeness of this irony, I think, deserves some attention.

Let me try to work through this irony by first stating that partiality and poetics are always in relationship to another aspect of language. This other aspect of language might be humorously described as the vast "is-ness" of language. More seriously, language might be described as having an "is function," or, more precisely, each word has an "is function." Or, running with a friendlier descriptor, one might say that language has "presence." What do these terms, "isness," "is function," and "presence," refer to? These terms attempt to capture what I did not fully elaborate in the example of the Tom Harkin speech, the example of the Boro Boro, and the thought experiment of the chair. In other words, "isness," "is function," and "presence" attempt to explain how words and propositions appear to be identical with the things in the world they name. In order to better grasp what I am saying here, we might examine more closely the English verb "to be." "To be" grants a state of existence, of beingness, of objective reality, of actuality when in the affirmative and denies the same when in the negative. In short, it grants or denies "isness." The simple power of "is" is that it points to existence, beingness, reality, and so on and never points to itself as a naming of existence, beingness, and reality.

My point here is an important one, though I fear that, at first, it may seem bizarre or merely clever; therefore, let me push my analysis further: "Is," along with other words, does not point back to its wordness. Words do not constantly remind us of their wordness. Theirs is a simpler function: to help us get what we want or avoid what we don't want and so on. Words, then, do not emphasize their own wordness. Example: If I say, "The tablecloth is on the table" or "This essay is good," there is nothing in these words to remind us that words are being used to flash particular meanings inside the head, meanings that also exist inside the heads of others and have some relationship to the world.[2] Of course, discourse can point to discursivity (or what I am calling here "wordness")—and this very paragraph is an example of such. Discourse, then, can reflect back upon itself and thereby become metadiscursive, but words themselves do not have a phoneme or morpheme to signal the fact of their wordness. So what is the significance of this lack? It contributes to words having a very strong "presence"—not a presence of themselves as words but the presence of whatever they are referring to. Metaphorically speaking, the world shines brightly in words, particularly during moments of conviction. During such moments, we lose sight of wordness because there is nothing to tell us that words themselves are conjuring the presence of the world. Stated more simply, typically upon hearing words, we think of the world first and not the fact that words are mediating that world—except when someone like Senator Harkin points it out. In sum, words themselves do not tell us that they are words. Rather, it is our interpretive suspicion that senses partiality, that "reads" it in a speaker's tone, motivation, and situation. But even as we announce our suspicion, we articulate another round of partiality that our words by themselves do not disclose. No wonder that the realm of discourse seems so difficult, for it depends at all turns on its powers of transparency and its powers of partiality and we, as its users, are snagged in its operations.

So far, I have argued that linguistic partiality is probably the last thing that most people think about as they move through their daily routines. I have argued that one reason for this is that the world, as presence, pushes through words until we lose sight of them. This is in part because words do not signal their wordness. But the concept of presence is created through a variety of other means that are worth briefly exploring. For most people, language serves a functional purpose—and that's about all. The functional uses of language are probably heightened when people struggle against the pressures of life's events. For instance, the world constantly compels us to make decisions, to choose directions, and so on. In that moment of decision, the need to find the real, true, or correct—or at least a better real, true, or correct—comes to the foreground and a sense of partiality moves to the background. Do we make this life decision or this other one? Do we purchase this commodity or another one? Sometimes the time that we are given to make that choice is short indeed, but choices, whether one may deliberate over a long period of time or not, must be made. When we have the time to deliberate, we use words to make sense of evidence, and eventually to choose one possibility over another.

Throughout these deliberations, words will serve a functional purpose—
that is, to get the decision-making job done—and the major assumption
behind their use will be their transparent connection to whatever they refer. Under these conditions, what occupies our full attention is not wordness but all that our words are pointing to. In this sense, words become invisible, and once again the presence of the world shines through. The
illusion of transparency might shatter if others disagree with us, but even
the one who disagrees in good faith assumes that his or her words are
somehow transparent.

We need to acknowledge bluntly, then, that partiality is not the first
consideration of those caught in the push and pull of life. Indeed, from the
perspective of this approach, a philosophy of partiality is effete because it
prefers metalinguistic labyrinths to the practical world of action. What the
concept of presence tells us is that people must deal with the world, and
because language names its myriad parts, language helps people in that
fundamental struggle. However, in doing so, language as an active agent
for imagining that world becomes hidden. In sum, a functionalist approach to language always pushes linguistic partiality to the background.

What is the end point of this analysis of presence? Presence tells us
that words are constantly disappearing from the scene only to be replaced,
front and center, by the world. I suppose someone might reply that I have
not considered artistic uses of language that call attention to themselves
and their wordness. That may be a serious reply, but it does not affect the
major concern of this essay, which, as I stated at the beginning, is to make
sense of everyday language use. At any rate, the concept of presence begins to explain how speakers and writers so easily forget the screen of language. We tend to spy the world beyond the screen without realizing that
the screen is there. Presence tells us, in particular, that when speakers and
hearers share the same world view, the world seems to "shine through"
their words and thereby create conviction. At such moments, they lack the
resources to see language as a screen. That is, they fail to see how words
miss their marks. Presence, then, is always coupled with partiality. Presence explains how we tumble headlong into ideologies without ever knowing it, into the imaginative horizons that are persistently reinforced by particular conventions of language use.[3] These ideologies and imaginative
horizons—which *seem* to be verities because of their habitual correlation
to material realities—are constrictions of the world, not equivalences
of the world. Words and the ideologies that they build are partial, not

equivalent; approximate, not exact. Words cannot become equivalent to the unpredictable abundance of the world, and, therefore, they leave a remainder. However, what words can do is to constrict or reduce the world in order to manage it—and quite often they do a good enough job. In reducing the abundance, language seems to strategically shape the world even as it simultaneously occults the fact that it just did so. A point that will be considered in more detail soon is the extent to which this constriction or reduction is a kind of violence.

Finally, the relationship between presence and social power must be briefly mentioned. As I have been arguing, the naming of the real, true, or correct is not equal to the actual real, true, or correct. At most, it is the naming of a semblance. However, because of presence, this semblance or ideology might as well be real, true, or correct. When semblances become particularly convincing, we do not hear or see the mediations of language; rather, we hear the world outside of language speaking. We do not think of speakers and writers choosing a set of words from among a wide array of possible words. We do not think of how they have interpreted the world and inserted their partiality, borrowed, perhaps, from the social imaginary that they inhabit. As Senator Harkin pointed out to us, what we hear instead are identities between signifier and signified, identities that occult the most important aspects of any naming, namely, the partiality of the namer and the partiality of the names themselves. In that masking, the real, true, and correct emerge as seemingly independent of being named. They emerge as names not chosen from a range of potential names, as names not chosen by a specific speaker speaking from specific motives, predispositions, and speaking conditions. They emerge as if they had named themselves without human mediation—an impossible condition. One of the results of the discourse of power is that as it names the world, a semblance of reality appears to be more than a semblance. The extent to which this transformation occurs, that is, the extent to which the real, true, or correct seem to speak for themselves in contrast to being named, is one measure of the power an audience awards to a speaker. Thus, the acquisition of power would seem to have much to do with the masking of partiality by presence. But presence, as I have been arguing throughout these pages, is a form of make-believe, a semblance pretending to equivalence. In the end, presence is a form of mischief because an "is" statement is language functioning at its most ironic: Although a rhetorical commonplace, it props up power. (Of course, the acquisition of social power may take different routes. It need not depend on occultation, but, indeed, may occur via a full and open admission of partiality. If this sort of public confession can be delivered with convincing sincerity and other conditions are just right, such discourse can be awarded considerable credibility and social power.)

The Violence of Fixation: An Ethnographic Example

It is time to provide some grounding for the claims I have made I will rely on ethnographic fieldwork conducted during the early to mid-1990s, discussed at greater length in Cintron (1997); I have revised that original discussion for this chapter. Given my argument that poetics is organic to language, one might consider revision itself as a manifestation of poetics. That is, words never fully frame their referents, a problem that leads to revision.

Throughout fieldwork, I heard and tape recorded a number of stories from school-aged boys and girls as well as young men. Over time, vengeance stories, although not an original focus of fieldwork, became a pocket of interest. I began to wonder if they might have a particular pattern. For instance, most of the storytellers claimed that offensive words or actions had been aimed at them. In response, they felt compelled to "put things right" or "set things straight." The stories, typically, delineated the wrong and then justified their subsequent action as "righting the wrong." There was a cause and effect relationship, a logic that seemed to follow a fairly predictable sequence. In the following lightly edited transcript, Martín, the speaker, tells a story of vengeance. Martín had just recently finished high school and with two friends, Fidel and Gonzalo, had been arrested for selling narcotics. According to Martín, Fidel and Gonzalo turned against him after the arrest. His two former buddies began to spread rumors (aided by a go-between, Andres) concerning how Martín had "set them up" with the help of the police in order to collect money from Crimestoppers. What interests me in the transcript is how Martín "fixes" his interpretation and how that interpretation rationalizes violent action. (All names are pseudonyms. Martín is the speaker throughout, even though on occasion he drops into the voices of his rivals.)

Fidel never confronted me saying, "Hey Martín, I think you got money out of this shit, out of setting us up." That's all he kept saying to Andres. Andres would come and tell me . . .

Fuck this shit, I [Martín] got fed up with it. So I told Andres, "Hey, can you get me Fidel's plate number? You know what car he drives, I know what car it is, but there can always be more than one. . . . I need you to get the license plate of that car for me, act stupid, drive around the parking lot." . . . So I got it set up, fine, and he [Fidel] was driving around in his girlfriend's Mustang, and I asked him, "What the hell happened to your car?"

"Oh it's in the shop," he says, "getting work done, I'm dropping the car lower."
"Where the hell do you have your car?"
"Well, I got it at this and this place"
"When's your car going to be out?"
"Well, my car will be out about this time because they got to go through the suspension, they got to make sure that the weight of the car can handle the spindles."
"Well cool, are they going to do a good job?"
"Oh well, they are only charging me so much and so much."

Fine. . . . This was Fidel's Too Low Flow car,[4] a Caddie, a red Caddie. So in the car, he had a Alpine pull out, two Alpine amplifiers, one for each speaker with two 12-inch pyramid faze three pro series speakers and a kicker box and I had some guys take care of that, steal his shit out of the car, steal his alarm, and fuck up his car, in other words, key it up. They scratched his rims, they slashed his tires, they broke his windows, they fucked up the interior. . . . Because he kept insisting that hey, number one, that I had set them up because I wanted money [$1,000 from Crimestoppers for turning others in] and two, in other words, he was calling me a pussy, hey, you know, "Why you turning us in," this and that, "Why be a stool pigeon," you know, 'cause that is the kind of interpretation I took, and I was think-ing the only pussy here is Fidel because he does not want to come forward and tell me, you know, face to face: "Martín, I think you got money out of this shit." . . . I can call him a pussy because he doesn't come up to me forward and say, blah, blah, blah . . .

I did do something wrong [sell dope] and I got busted for it. And at this pres-ent in time, not proudly to say, I am facing up to a . . . maximum of 5 years in the state with 30 months of probation and $2,000 fine to follow, and he thinks that I set him up and that's why I'm going to jail, that's why I'm facing a jail sentence while those motherfuckers are out like a free bird. Shit, we'll see who's a pussy, you know, we'll see who's a man when he come out of jail or whatever. . . . But for one thing I know for a fact, if Fidel and Gonzalo were to go to jail, they'd be fucking jailbait, they'd be what you call the inmates' bitches, they'd be the ones getting [laughs] popped, because they're all pretty boys. . . . That seriously wouldn't scare me. . . . hey, I'd fucking just kick ass any dumb fucker who'd try to do that shit with me. That's the kind of attitude you'd have to take in jail. For the fact of gaining re-spect . . .

I still got a score to settle with them when once I come out of jail. Right now

I'm just hanging low profile, but his car got fucked up real good. It got fucked up nice, I mean, just to replace all the things he lost, the paint on the car, the tires, the rims. It was enough money to spend getting a new car. . . . And he asked me later, "Have you seen any of my shit?"

"Naw, what happened?"
He go, "Man, right where I had my car stored in the garage . . . it got fucked up, got keyed and everything."
"No, bullshit, are you talking about your Too Low Flow?"
"Yeah, man, the paint job, the interior, the speakers, the fucking tires and shit."
I said, "Damn, who the fuck would do that shit?"
"I don't know, dudes . . . I'm not really going to worry about it 'cause I'm going
  to report it to my insurance."

And that was it. I mean I didn't literally, literally, literally take any action, any physical action on the car, but you could say I was the one calling the shots about the car getting fucked up like that.

This story and others like it mobilized a certain ritualized language of the neighborhood, a language that functioned as a kind of street ideology. This language, brittle and predictable, was shared by both genders, and its key phrases often went like this: "So and so ain't showing me respect, no consideration"; "So and so's telling lies, talking trash—they ought to come talk to my face and I'll set them straight"; "You gotta show 'em they can't fuck with you"; "I got my rights"; "No way so and so's going to take advantage of me." These phrases were the triggers for decision making. They assumed a clear, unambiguous offense (for instance, "telling lies, talking trash") and an equally clear offender. If the conditions were this clear, then the response was obvious, even commonsensical. The humiliation of the offended party called, automatically, without hesitation, for an equivalent humiliation of the offender. There was not much space here for ambiguity and tolerance. Its ethos was "an eye for an eye, a tooth for a tooth."

I puzzled over these stories. Why was there so much clarity regarding the nature of the offense and the intentions of the offender? The story tellers seemed not to doubt the "facts" of the situation. Even when the "facts" were relayed to them by third parties or go-betweens (Andres, for instance), the information was typically accepted as factual. Furthermore, the storytellers believed that by not taking action quickly, the rumor or humiliation would spread further and, worse yet, confirm their weakness in the eyes of others. These were authentic social pressures that might "squeeze" clarity into situations that might otherwise have lacked any. But

were there other things coursing through the community that might encourage this sort of clarity and urgency? As I looked at these stories and
other instances of talk, I began to map a certain network of assumptions
that ran through their talk and actions:

- Life is tough
- Most people are not to be trusted
- Always be wary
- Defend yourself or get beaten up
- When a go-between reports the offensive remarks or actions of someone else,
  that someone reports faithfully without distortion
- Your enemies have simple motives: to hurt you
- Your enemies are basically "low life" and not much else
- When done wrong by your enemies, you occupy the moral high ground, a
  place of righteousness
- The wrongness of your enemies deserves punishment
- You always have the right to inflict such punishment
- You show more "heart" (honor, courage) when you take care of your own
  "business"

    As I tried to unpack these assumptions, it occurred to me that the core
world view was one of distrust. The world is not a place that is abundant
and gives of itself; rather, it is suspect and always ready to take from someone. Order is not a given, not something built into the fabric of human relationships. Rather, scarcity and the disorder that ensues are the givens. If
one desires order, one has to manufacture it and forcefully maintain it because it will always be threatened. How can we rely on something as slow
moving, unpredictable, and abstract as a legal-based society to deliver a
regime of order? How can such an unpredictable system right an injury
committed by someone against oneself? The answer, given the world view
outlined above, is that it can't. The result is the emergence of the last assumption: one shows "heart" when taking care of one's own "business."
What this last assumption means is that the only reliable entity is the individual operating independently outside the structures of a legal-based society. Honor and dignity are awarded to such an individual by like people
who vie for it, sometimes as direct rivals. In short, the act of vengeance becomes the tool of the "righteous" self putting order back into the world, a
world polluted by disorder. We might call all this the ideology of vengeance. The problem for a legal-based society in which this ideology of
vengeance arises is how to reinforce its own ideology in the face of it. That

is, a legal-based society must find ways to "reproduce" itself across the entire range of its fragmented population, fragmented through wide variations in ethnic culture and economic class. Counter ideologies seem to flourish in those sites where class and ethnic cultures remain undiluted by integration with other groups. (A case, of course, can be made that the ideology of a legal-based society is not itself whole, but also contested and evolving from within.)

Let me put it this way: Vengeance stories contained a language that seemed repetitious, a kind of ritualized thought and speech. Vengeance seemed embedded so deeply that one might call it unconscious and ideological. As an ideology, it explained real events, feelings, and social conditions. Embedded in its talk was a very tight knot of emotion, world view, and lived experience. Lived experienced, in particular, served as evidence proving the correctness of the world view. Lived experience represented a kind of reality that made the ideals and values preached by the educational institutions seem abstract, irrelevant, or, worse yet, hypocritical (because the practices of the educational system were themselves seen as unjust). In other words, this ideology made sense of "the way things are" and are expected to be. Moreover, it abstracted one's pain and dissatisfaction and placed it inside the nature of things. Thus, it functioned as a commonsense interpretation of street life. Creating another interpretation, cutting that knot, was no easy matter. It would have entailed making a different commonsense, and, more profoundly, making a new psyche: a new gut response to life itself. My experiences suggested that those who wagered certain life decisions on "the way things are" did not want to be proven wrong, indeed, would stubbornly resist the loss of that investment.

Like most ideologies, the ideology of vengeance hid its character behind claims of being a real, a true, or a correct view. As I have been arguing throughout this essay, ideologies, in general, mask themselves so thoroughly that strenuous reflexive thought is required to unpack how ideology insinuates itself into individual psyches and communities. As I argued earlier, the phenomenon of presence is central to this sort of occultation. Speakers believe that they have the ability to say what they mean and, furthermore, that what they say is true. These beliefs maintain that there is identity between the speaker, the words of a speaker, and what the words point to. For the most part, we *really* believe that what we say is *really* about *reality*. When we *really* believe, we have an instance of authority. Authority and conviction, then, have much to do with a fixing of the partiality of language. The process of fixation condenses ambiguity into a certainty, and from this minor act of violence emerges the potential for obsession as well as for forceful action. In one sense, all of us display this sort of authority and conviction when we gloss our propositions with very common expressions: "Here's the bottom line," "I'll stake my life on it," "You can bet your money on it," "I don't take no for an answer," and "See, I told you so." Even in these innocuous commonplaces, the identities described earlier are so packed together that as hearers, we too often forget that speakers speak from their perspectives, which are partial, and we forget that their specific words materialize out of a whole array of choices often at the moment of utterance. (Indeed, it is possible that idiomatic expressions may represent one of the best sites to consider the forces of ideology insofar as they embody those moments when speaking leans most heavily on the ideology of one's culture or community.) My central point is that when the identities mentioned earlier seem convincingly packed together, it is as if we are hearing the very words that reality would speak if it had a voice. The partiality of the speaker is masked as does the fact of word choice; instead, reality seems to shine through. We forget that the stated real, true, or correct is a semblance. (Such a position, by the way, does not mean that some semblances are not better than others.) At any rate, it is from the presumption of linguistic presence that conviction, decision, and action emerge—for better or worse. Moreover, it is through presence that ideologies hide their character and, thus, endure. Finally, presence tells us that we are at a scene of violence—even if only slight when compared to physical violence—in which the ambiguity of language became "fixed" and the world as that language presented it became our "fixation."

But the maintenance of an ideology depends on more than linguistic presence. As I suggested earlier, there is an emotional orientation as well as specific life events that act as evidence of a world view that must be synchronized with the ideological interpretation. When all three are synchronized, confirmation and conviction become more possible. Regarding the emotional orientation, what was salient to me about the lives of those who told me stories of vengeance was a history of pain, fear, and anger. I never scaled and compared the examples of pain and fear that many of my interviewees, but not all, experienced when very young. But some sort of early injury to psyche was common enough. Indeed, one might examine some of these psyches as accumulating violences, small and large, violences that had metamorphosed from wounds to faint scars, and metamorphosed further into a conviction that life was unstable or unjust. We might explain the emotional cycle in this way: The experience of pain generates the fear of some future pain and uses anger to protect oneself from pain, but anger, in turn, may destabilize the conditions around one and open the door again to a new round of pain. In other words, anxiety has captured such a life by the throat. Let me provide another example in the actual words of El Duque, a most formidable individual, a man very well respected in gang circles throughout Illinois. The following passage was written by him and represents a tiny fraction of the total amount of interview time and exchanges of letters that have passed between us over the years.

When I was about six or seven years old, it was at that time I came to the states. My father was young and had taken on a new wife and a stepmother for me. We lived in this old building that had so many doors to it, they were apartments but I did not know any better then. The apartments were small and had no toilets in them, the toilets were all at the end of the hall, as young as I was I had this bad habit of picking my nose all the time. It got so bad that my nose would bleed a lot and I would get blood on everything from towels, sheets, table cloth anything I could get a hold on to stop the bleeding. Since I was afraid to go out the door and down the hallway, I would grab the first thing in sight. One day my nose started bleeding after I had picked at it, there was blood all over the place and I got scared because my stepmother had told me that next time she would tell my father about it. . . . My father came home in a bad mood. He saw the blood on the sheets and everywhere else. Talk about someone being pissed. He grabbed me and took me over to the bedpost, tied my hands and feets to it, he also put a towel in my mouth and gagged me so that I would not be heard from anyone around. As much as I cried and screamed it was hopeless, he took a needle and stuck it under my finger nails. He did this to all my finger nails and then with a razor blade he began to cut an X on the tips of all my fingers. He left me tied there for awhile, until I stopped crying I suppose. I think, I cried myself to sleep though, because I don't remember anything else until the next day that I tried to pick my nose. One thing is for sure came out of that, I never picked my nose again and when I do now I remember that day so well.

This story, as far as I have been able to determine, is true. When compared to similar stories I have collected, it is atypical in its level of violence, but not atypical in this man's life. The story runs the danger of only appearing to be sensational (and, frankly, I worry about the use of such stories in furthering very negative portraits about working-class communities. The social sciences and popular press have been recording similar stories for over a century—and what are their motives? Such stories are examples of a "fixing" of social conditions through professional writing and a "fixation" on the part of audiences. They are examples of linguistic and social violence ascending to rather serious levels.) Although I cannot control how such a story will be used by my readers, my intent is to raise questions about anxiety, about how the feelings of pain, fear, and anger may become part of the structure of the sorts of ideologies that I have been describing. It is important to note that I am not granting a cause and effect relationship between anxiety and an ideology of vengeance. Indeed, this same man, by his own account, has passed beyond anxiety, and rather than reacting against others with vengeance, distributes punishment in calculated fashion in order to send strong messages to enemies that his organization cannot be pushed around, and to enforce discipline within the organization. Where in all his claims might we spy his own partiality, his own masking of partiality through "presence"?

Sifting through El Duque's account and those of others, what I have found is a world view that assumes that the possibility of serious, even life-threatening disorder and its escalation are always nearby. Controlling that is paramount. One way to do that is to "squeeze clarity" out of otherwise ambiguous events and to respond decisively. "Squeezing clarity" is another term, in addition to "presence," that describes linguistic violence that has preoccupied this essay. Both terms describe a reduction of the generalized poetics of language and a masking of partiality in the discovery of a real, true, or correct. But, of course, violent action requires more than just language operations. One has to be primed to discover threat. For such a person, even the rumor of a threat may be sufficient to make it real. The dense makeup of this ideology spanned a terrain that included one's emotional life, concrete life experiences, and a communally shared interpretation about the "way things are," as well as a deductive/inductive method for arriving at such interpretations. More specifically, this ideology rested on someone's specific history of anxiety, a set of assumptions about the "nature of reality," actual life experiences that served as evidence proving those assumptions, and the ability to wield a conventionalized "street" rhetoric. This ideology inhabited individual psyches as well as street life's social imaginary as a guiding ethos: a sensible way (in some cases, a sure way) to handle particular problems. In the end, vengeance could not stop its endless repetition, but it certainly answered deep-seated needs that were themselves forged within the furnaces of this ideology.

An (Anti)Ciceronian Replies

I have before me a remarkable *New York Times* article dated April 27, 1999 (Belluck). The town president of Cicero, Illinois, a working-class city of 70,000 southwest of Chicago, complains mightily of the city's gang problem. During the prior year, 64 shootings and 15 homicides scarred the city, and since the beginning of 1999 to the middle of April, another 24 shootings and 2 homicides have occurred.[5] (I presume that these offenses are gang related, but, actually, the article does not explicitly say that.) Interestingly, the article reports that in the last two decades the town has become half Latino. Many of the gangs mentioned are the very same ones that I have worked with in other parts of northern Illinois. All this resembles what I've seen before: fast-growing Latino populations, a bewildered city leadership, and an ideology of vengeance all revved up in overdrive. Even more interesting, however, is the fact that decades ago Cicero was the home of Al Capone; organized crime has had a strong presence in the city since his time. Indeed, the husband of the current town president pleaded guilty in 1991 "to Federal conspiracy charges and acknowledged being a bookmaker for the mob."

The ironies become thicker, sharper: The town president has drafted "an ordinance that would evict all gang members—and punish them if they returned, even to visit their families." In short, this is the "first gang-eviction law in the country," and its goal is to create a "gang-free city. 'I can't worry if they go to Berwyn or Oak Park or Chicago. . . . My concern is to protect the people of Cicero,' says the town president." The article goes on to say that despite the severity of this particular ordinance, it is related to a number of similar laws that have been passed in various communities around the United States. Needless to say, some of these laws and ordinances have been scrutinized closely by the courts and constitutional experts.

In discussing this story about desperate moves made in the name of self-preservation, I hope not to sound like a social critic decrying the provinciality, or worse, the false-consciousness of small town politicians. Provinciality and false-consciousness are not the issues here. The issues are more profound, for they go to the problem of communal fear and anxiety as a substratum in the vast difficulty of maintaining a secure public sphere that has been fractured by ethnic difference reinforced by economic inequalities. The town president, an (anti)Ciceronian, may be replying, metaphorically at least, to the excesses of El Duque and Martín, but she would be most surprised, I suspect, to know that on some issues regarding gangs, both El Duque and Martín might agree with her. El Duque, for instance, as he has often told me, is fed up with the waste of killings that has marked gang life since the late 1980s. He too would like to put a stop to useless murders, but how could such a man ever acquire the credibility to discuss such a thing with Cicero's town president? How can such a man escape the fixing of his identity in the eyes of a distraught community? I remember in the early 1990s discussing with the mayor of the city where my field-site was located an idea involving the solicitation of El Duque's support in order to stop the gang wars. The mayor knew of El Duque and also knew that his constituency would eat him alive if it ever found out that the city was collaborating with gang leadership to solve gang war. Such a policy awarded recognition and authority to gangs themselves. A populace that feels besieged begins to work within a narrower and narrower range of possible interpretations and solutions. Again, here is a form of fixing and fixation, of violence performed in the hermeneutic act, and that in time may lead to the larger violence of policy making.

But let me examine this quagmire that underlies the difficulty of making a community. Social imaginaries, it seems to me, are gargantuan containers of contradiction. For instance, surrounding the topos of street gangs in our social imaginary are all sorts of positions including those of gang members (who disagree among themselves), police officers (who have some of the most varied interpretations, as I have discovered to my surprise), social service representatives, gang experts, school officials, city officials, judges, legislators, the media, and the public. Winding one's way through this labyrinth is not easy, but it reminds one that positionality, even within supposedly polarized discourses, is not always predictable and tends to shift about considerably. There is room here for alliances, sometimes rather unpredictable ones that leap across economic and other material barriers. If we define rhetoric as an art that tracks social imaginaries always imprecisely, and if one does the tracking ethnographically, one certainly sees the divisions that split the social imaginary. However, one may also see the possible ways to reduce division. Perhaps I sound overly utopian and idealistic, but I want to recall a point I made earlier about the production of culture being distinctly improvisatory. Improvisation as a model of culture says that there is an underlying structure determining production, but structure does not replicate itself. There is space for change and chance—for improvisation. There is affinity between this space where the new has a breathing chance and a generalized poetics. All this is hopeful, I think, because it says that division is not inevitable, *if we can just see our way clear and improvise a new thought*. But it is also realistic, for it acknowledges that division in the social imaginary is rooted in anxieties anxieties and material conditions that are not easily alleviated. Anxiety tells us that we must fix, *now*, and it delivers to us our fixation.

Let me make my point as clear as possible: It occurs to me that the ideology and discourse of vengeance resembles the discourse of our (anti)Ciceronian. These discourses presume a fundamental collapse of community, a collapse of that ideal of getting along with those who offend us. In the midst of that debris, these discourses struggle towards what is imagined as a higher good. If the ideology of vengeance frames the higher good as a righteous individual righting a wrong and reprimanding a clear offender, our (anti) Ciceronian, also exasperated, splits her community between the infidels and the law-abiding: "The ACLU says gang members have rights. . . . How about our civil rights?" Both discourses are at their wits' end. They can no longer think beyond their categories. Anxiety has them both by the throat. What do we do, both as individuals and as communities, when the fixation of the world has become so complete that we resemble our own fixations? What gentle shift can we encourage in ourselves that might start to melt the frozen impasse between ourselves and our mirror images? I don't think our (anti)Ciceronian offers such a shift: "Asked how a 10-square-mile town with roughly 135 police officers would enforce [the gang eviction law], [our (anti) Ciceronian] said she might consider gating neighborhoods and establishing police checkpoints."[6]

Conclusion

I want to reintroduce here another woman from the Chicago area, the one who began this essay. She was wearing the tee-shirt "Fear Is an Emotion / Bad Is an Attitude." Ultimately, I cannot know the intentions of the manufacturer or the wearer. Nevertheless, I think the tee-shirt was consistent with a larger set of neighborhood meanings, and it is this consistency that I have been trying to outline in this essay. One day I asked El

Duque what the tee-shirt words might mean. He described the meaning of it this way: fear is something that you must hide; attitude is something that you act out and that hides fear; you don't dare show fear because fear is a sign of weakness. His words translated into my own suggest the following: In an unreliable, aggressive world, showing weakness encourages others to take advantage. In contrast, "badness" as attitude hides fear, masks it behind a public persona of toughness that protects one from the challenges of others. The tee-shirt, then, exposed an important dialectic in which the hiding of fear and emotion was paired against the display of badness and attitude. One way to cultivate badness and attitude was to acquire a "rep" for violence and vengeance. Remember Martín, who faced down the challenge of being thought a "pussy" by destroying his rival's car.

But if we examine this dialectic closely, we can conclude that one side of the dialectic, say, badness and attitude, could not exist without its other, that is, fear and pain. The public pose of "badness" and "attitude" was fragile at best, for the hidden world of emotion, fear, and pain that the public persona was paired to was dangerously close to the surface. In these spaces darkened by the sometimes hyperbolic performances of toughness, one might find the sorts of emotional experiences and anxiety that I have collected over time from El Duque and others. Indeed, this same dialectic was very much in evidence within the street corner poses of some gang members. With arms crossed over one's chest and the torso tilted slightly back (the street term for this pose is "gates locked"), the pose was a threat, a putdown, a sign of superiority, toughness, and attitude. In short, the pose signaled disrespect of one's foes. As a communicative system, it "spoke" most forcefully to those whose own histories of pain and humiliation were close to the surface. The putdown of "gates locked," then, worked when it tapped someone else's anxiety. The fact that this second person might be seen at some later date signaling his own gates locked suggested that the dialectic was more than just part of the code of the streets. It also signaled the internalized tensions inside the individuals themselves, for gates locked rendered invisible a vast realm of difficulty, locked it away deep inside oneself. Gates locked chose to hide the heart rather than show it. As such, it was the physical embodiment of "Fear Is an Emotion/Bad Is an Attitude." It would have taken a special courage for someone to unlock the secret of the pose and to feel compassion for what was there. Such a someone, however, might have been able to initiate a new kind of ideology, which for lack of a better word, I would call trust.

Such a logic, I suggest, might have had the chance of nudging out violence and vengeance, but how difficult it is to find such a logic in one's inscape when one's outscape, consisting of social and economic inequalities, represented in effect a more formidable logic: violence

Is there not some final comparison that I have yet to make explicit, a comparison, perhaps, between the "gates locked" of a gang member and the gated neighborhoods of our (anti)Ciceronian? Both terms are cycling through our social imaginary. I know that the former signals pain behind a semblance of badness, and I suspect that there are pains in the city of Cicero. Aren't both terms the results of a fixing and a fixation? Do they not both signal reductions of abundance? Are they not fierce embodiments of a real, true, or correct, and do they not mask from our view and their own views the possibility of an ambiguity that might save us all? But how difficult it is to open ourselves to the ephemeral voice of abundance when the persistent "social reality" seems to teach such thorough-going violence.

Notes

My thanks to Jongbong Choi for the specific phrase "the violence of fixation" and to my research assistant Doug Thompkins for clarifying the phrase "gates locked" and to all my other graduate students in my course "Rhetorics of Ethnographies," who over the years have taught me so much social and rhetorical theory as well as helping me to understand better ethnographic texts and methods.

1. Throughout this essay, I will be arguing that language is inexact rather than exact. I realize that in arguing this way I am rehearsing a set of old, largely philosophical arguments concerning whether or not language can "represent." Perhaps it would make more sense to abandon this mode of talk altogether and to move toward a fresher conceptualization. Martin Nystrand offered just that after reading the first draft of this essay:

"Rather than representing the world, discourse operates on shared understandings—expanding, resisting, and transforming them. They relate or don't relate to the world in the sense that they allow us to get around in it. They're both fragmentary and partial in the sense that they're limited, not because they are imperfect in their representations. Representation is an illusion." (M. Nystrand, personal communication, August 2, 1999)

Nystrand's comment makes good sense, of course, and I felt almost encouraged to rewrite my argument under its terms. However, as this essay evolves, readers will see (I hope) that my obsession with the English verb "to be" reflects a concern with how words are grasped in everyday conditions, conditions which warrant, I suspect, a framing of these issues via the concept of representation.

2. The relationship of language, meaning, and world that I have posited here is one that James Gee (1992) would describe as standard in the history of linguistics: "The traditional theory is that there is something in my head (a concept, a mental representation, images, what have you) that just *is* the meaning of the word . . . and this something is similar enough to what is in other people's heads (provided that they speak the same language). . . . This

theory is not only one that has been prevalent in philosophy, psychology, and linguistics for centuries, it is also, in fact, our 'folk (common sense, everyday) theory' of meaning" (pp. 1–2).

3. A few words about ideology: It is not that ideologies are species of false consciousness. Nor should we limit the term to political contexts (as in the ideologies of fascism). I follow Gramsci and others in considering ideologies to be the structures of commonsense. These structures, however, have pilings that run deep into material reality. For instance, when my teeth hurt or when I want to prevent my teeth from hurting, I readily accept the ideology of the dental industry. I floss, brush my teeth twice a day, go for regular dental check-ups, whatever. Ideologies are grounded in material realities, and those that have the most staying power may have the most grounding and, therefore, become very difficult to dislodge. Frankly, I am mostly disappointed by most analyses of ideology by linguistic anthropologists. For the most part, they neither take into consideration the pressure of material realities, nor do they see ideology as embedded not just in language practices but in language itself via a concept such as "presence." See, for instance, a special issue on ideology published in *Pragmatics* and edited by Kroskrity, Schieffelin, and Woolard (1992).

4. "Too Low Flow" refers to a car dressed up in a special way by Latino youths in the neighborhoods where I was doing research during the early to mid-1990s. The style has connections to the Low Rider style of an earlier era. See Cintron (1997) for more information.

5. These numbers are very close to the ones I encountered in my fieldsite every year during the early to mid-1990s. See Cintron (1997) for more detail.

6. In October 1999, my research assistant, Jolene Stritecky, conducted telephone interviews with both a city official from Cicero and a representative of the Chicago chapter of the ACLU. Here is a summary of those conversations. The city official is represented in the first paragraph, and the ACLU is represented in the second.

In late April 1999, the Cicero Town Board voted unanimously (7–0) to pass two gang-related ordinances. The first was to set up a hearing process whereby a person's gang membership could be determined, and their "residence revoked" as a result. The second was to allow cars to be impounded and a fine of $500/day levied on all drivers of whom police had "prior knowledge" of gang membership. Under the second ordinance, cars could be impounded and fines levied, whether the car belonged to the alleged gang-member-driver or not. Prior to the Town Board passing the two ordinances, Cicero residents voted (97%) in favor of a referendum "advising" the Town Board to pass the ordinances. The voter referendum was no-binding, or advisory, in nature.

The eviction ordinance caused the most public alarm, but, to date, the Town Board has done nothing to enforce it. Automobile seizure and impoundment began in June 1999. In July, the ACLU filed a lawsuit with the Federal District Court challenging the constitutionality of the seizure ordinance. Within five hours of filing, Cicero law enforcement stopped seizing and impounding vehicles. The Cicero Town Board did not challenge the ACLU lawsuit and agreed to settle by repaying costs of fines, etc.

References

Belluck, P. (1999, April 27). Illinois town hopes to exile its gang members to anywhere else, U.S.A. *New York Times*, A16.

Burke, K. (1969). *A rhetoric of motives*. Berkeley: University of California Press.

Cintron, R. (1997). *Angels' town: Chero ways, gang life, and rhetorics of the everyday*. Boston: Beacon Press.

Clifford, J. and Marcus, G. (Eds.). (1986). *Writing culture: The poetics and politics of ethnography*. Berkeley: University of California Press.

Conquergood, D. (1991). Rethinking ethnography: Towards a critical cultural politics. *Communication Monographs, 58*, 179–194.

Conquergood, D. (1992). Book reviews: Ethnography, rhetoric, and performance. *Quarterly Journal of Speech, 78*, 80–97.

Dominguez, V. (1998). For a politics of love and rescue. (Unpublished manuscript).

Fabian, J. (1983). *Time and the other: How anthropology makes its object*. New York: Columbia University Press.

Fernandez, J. (1986). *Persuasions and performances: The play of tropes in culture*. Bloomington: Indiana University Press.

Gee, J. (1992). *The social mind: Language, ideology, and social practice*. New York: Bergin & Garvey.

Hall, S. (1996). The problem of ideology: Marxism without guarantees. In D. Morley and Kuan-Hsing Chen (Eds.), *Stuart Hall: Critical dialogues in cultural studies*. London: Routledge.

Kroskrity, P., Schieffelin, B., & Woolard, K. (Eds.). (1992). *Pragmatics, 2, 3*.

Lecercle, J. (1990). *The violence of language*. London: Routledge.

Maffesoli, M., et. al. (1993). Trend report: The social imaginary. *Current Sociology*, 41, 2.

McKerrow, R. (1989). Critical rhetoric: Theory and praxis. *Communication Monographs, 56*, 91–111.

Ruddick, S. (1996). *Young and homeless in Hollywood: Mapping social identities*. New York: Routledge.

Scheper-Hughes, N. (1995). The primacy of the ethical: Propositions for a militant anthropology. *Current Anthropology, 36*, 409–420.

Stewart, K. (1996). *A space on the side of the road: Cultural poetics in an "other" America*. Princeton, NJ: Princeton University Press.

Tyler, S. (1978). *The said and the unsaid: Mind, meaning, and culture*. New York: Academic Press.

Tyler, S. (1986). Post-modern ethnography: From document of the occult to occult document. In J. Clifford and G. Marcus (Eds.), *Writing culture: The poetics and politics of ethnography*. Berkeley: University of California Press.

2

Other Gods and Countries
The Rhetorics of Literacy

John Duffy

At that time we studied the Laotian language and Laotian history. We studied about the *Cauj Paj Nkoo*, the Laotian King. We studied about the . . . King and about the Laotian people. . . . We studied their rules, laws, and regulations.

> *a Hmong refugee to the United States,*
> *recalling his schooling in Laos in the 1960s*

The missionary came to our house, and he opened the book. He showed how Christ, you know, had come for our souls like during that time. I was still a kid, a boy. The missionary showed how Christ would be coming, and how he believed in Christ.

> *a Hmong man recalling Christian literacy*
> *instruction in Laos, circa 1965*

In retrospect, the much discussed "Great Divide" in literacy studies was not the presumed chasm between the set of historical and cultural conditions said to represent "oral" or "preliterate" peoples and the opposing set of conditions said to represent "literate" cultures. Rather, the Great Divide in literacy studies, the genuinely radical breach, was the movement from thinking of literacy in terms of the individual, or as a private act of mind, to conceiving of literacy as fundamentally social, or as an expression of cultural practices, values, and beliefs. This shift from individual to socio-cultural conceptions of literacy was most strikingly announced by the publication of Shirley Brice Heath's (1983) indispensable book, *Ways with Words*, which itself was part of a larger intellectual transformation taking place in the disciplines of psychology, linguistics, and literary studies (Nystrand, Greene, and Weimelt, 1993).

While conceptions of literacy as embedded in cultural practices are by no means uniform, they are typically characterized by ethnographic observations of supposedly bounded cultures, by description of the features and patterns of literacy use within the culture, and by attention to the details of daily existence that convey what Heath called "the current ecology of the community" (p. 6). In this way do culturally-based conceptions portray how literacy develops, by which I mean the ways in which reading and writing are taught, learned, used, and understood in a given culture at a particular historical moment.

And such approaches have been profoundly important. Cultural approaches to literacy have helped educators better understand the relationships between the languages of school and home (Rose, 1989; Fishman, 1990; Erickson, 1984); have legitimized nonstandard literacy practices (Kulick & Stroud, 1993; Weinstein-Shr, 1993; Heath); have foregrounded the relationship between literacy and ethnicity (Reder & Wikelund, 1993; Ferdman, 1990); and have contributed to the political and social enfranchisement of people living on the margins of dominant cultures (Pratt, 1987).

Yet as important as cultural approaches to literacy have been, there is a sense in which they are ultimately incomplete; inevitably limited in their explanatory power. Indeed, the focus on literacy as cultural practice may even work to obscure or deflect understandings of how literacy develops. The problem is that while cultural approaches have provided insights into the socially situated nature of reading and writing, they too often fail to delineate the historical relationships among cultures that have shaped the very practices being described. Consequently, literacy practices may be described as though they were self-generating, a product of unique cultural characteristics rather than of an outcome of sustained and often violent contacts between peoples of unequal power (Pratt, 1991; 1987). The result is models of writing and of the world that become, in the words of the anthropologist Eric Wolf (1983), "a global pool hall in which [self-contained] entities spin off each other like so many hard and round billiard balls" (p. 6). From such studies we learn what literacy looks like at a given time and place, but not, perhaps, how or why it became that way.

I want to suggest an alternative way of thinking about literacy development; one that looks not to individuals or supposedly bounded cultures but instead looks to rhetoric. By *rhetoric* I mean the ways that institutions and individuals use symbols to structure their thought and shape their conceptions of the world. This alternative, which I think of as a rhetorical approach to literacy, draws upon and is meant to unite more recent perspectives, including the view of literacy development as ideological (Street, 1995; Berlin, 1987), as the product of discourse (Gee, 1996), and as an expression of historical change (Brandt, 1998). To illustrate, I shall consider the experiences of a woman I shall call Chia Vue,[1] a 34-year-old Laotian Hmong who came to the United States as a political refugee in the aftermath of the Vietnam War.

The Hmong are an ethnic minority people who trace their origins to Southern China. In the 1960s, the Hmong of Laos were recruited by the United States CIA during the Vietnam War to serve as a covert guerilla army. That army was to harass North Vietnamese forces and rescue U.S. pilots who had been shot down over Laos (Castle, 1993). In exchange, the Hmong were reportedly made certain promises by CIA operatives, including the establishment of an autonomous Hmong state should right wing forces defeat the Communists (Porter, 1970, p. 183). William Colby (1990), the former director of the CIA, has described the Hmong involvement in the war as "an inspiring story of courage and skill by a brave mountain people . . . who developed a unique relationship of trust and affection with faraway Americans" (p. 34).

Despite this encomium, the Hmong alliance with the CIA proved disastrous to the Hmong, leading to tens of thousands of deaths and the diaspora of Hmong families across the world. The Hmong scholar Yang Dao (1993) has estimated that by 1975 as many as 30,000 Hmong had been killed in the fighting, resulting in boys as young as twelve being drafted to fight. After the withdrawal of U.S. troops from Vietnam and Laos in 1975, the Hmong Army collapsed and tens of thousands of Hmong fled Laos for refuge in border camps in Thailand. By the early 1980s, some 50,000 Hmong had been resettled in the United States as political refugees, and by the 1990s, more than 100,000 Hmong were living in the United States (Chan, 1994, p. 49).

Prior to their involvement with the CIA, most Hmong did not read and write in any language. Indeed, their language had no widely accepted written form until about the 1960s, when a writing system developed by

Western missionary-linguists began to gain acceptance in refugee camps in Thailand. Since coming to the United States, many more Hmong have become literate, both in the English and Hmong languages. Thousands of Hmong children have attended U.S. public schools. Adults have learned to read and write in a variety of settings, including vocational schools, English as a second language programs, and classes sponsored by American churches and Hmong community organizations.

For several years now, I have been studying the historical development of literacy as it has been experienced by the Hmong residents of one Wisconsin city. In the course of this study, I have interviewed 45 Hmong adults, asking them to recount the details of their lives in Laos and the United States, and especially the ways in which they learned to read and write. Beginning with the "ethnographic present" in Wisconsin, I have traced the literacy history of those I have interviewed back to Laos, where Hmong people had limited exposure to written language; and then earlier still to China, where literacy for the Hmong was actively suppressed. Where the information has been available, I have looked at the conditions under which literacy was taught, the materials used to teach it, the teaching methods practiced in classes, the essay topics assigned to students, and the various writing systems in which Hmong people learned to read and write.

From these interviews, I have come to feel the limitations of both individual and cultural approaches in accounting for the historical development of literacy. In their place, I am suggesting the rhetorical approach, which seeks to account for the multiple and conflicting influences of competing states, armies, languages, and economies upon individuals learning to read and write. The essay is an attempt to work out the meaning of a rhetorical approach to literacy and exemplify the approach by considering the literacy experiences of Chia Vue and several of her Hmong contemporaries. But before turning to Vue's testimonies, let me elaborate on what I mean by a "rhetoric" and a "rhetorical approach" to literacy development.

What Is a Rhetoric?

By "rhetoric," I do not mean the classical arts of persuasion or the ornamentation of elite discourse. Rhetoric as I mean it here refers to the ways that institutions, groups, or individuals use language and other symbols for the purpose of shaping conceptions of reality. This means that we may think of rhetorics in the plural rather than imagining a single, coherent, and all-unifying "rhetoric." For example, the languages of governments, schools, and media I think of as "rhetorics"; the ways these languages operate within community life I consider "rhetorical." Rhetorics provide the frameworks in which individual acts of reading and writing take place.

This is a view of rhetoric derived from Kenneth Burke (1969; 1966), who extended "the range of rhetoric" beyond the classical function of persuasion to what he called "identification," or the use of symbols for the purpose of inducing cooperation (1969, pp. 20–23). Rather than persuading people, Burke suggested, rhetoric worked to socialize them, inducing human beings to identify with one another and assent to the communicative norms of their society. While rhetorical language was a means for gaining advantage and deflecting "the . . . regions of malice and the lie," it was much more than that; rhetoric was also the means by which individuals came to know themselves and their place within a greater social and material hierarchy. Rhetoric offered human beings, in Burke's language, "sheer 'identities' of the Symbolic . . . the identifications whereby a specialized activity makes one a participant in some social or economic class" (1969, pp. 27–28).

Rhetorics, therefore, do not persuade human beings as much as they interpellate and constitute them, inviting individuals to define themselves in the ideology of the rhetoric (Althusser, 1973). By "ideology," I do not mean adherence to a particular political doctrine, but use the term in the broad sense, as did James Berlin (1987), who defined ideology as "the pluralistic conceptions of social and political arrangements that are present in a society at any given time" (p. 4). An ideology can be understood as the ways in which members of a given society make sense of the political and material hierarchies governing the society. In this way do rhetorics shape individual and collective identities. "In telling the story of a *peuple*," Maurice Charland has written, "a *peuple* come to be" (p. 223).

In a rhetorical approach to literacy, individual acts of reading and writing, of decoding and encoding, have little meaning in themselves. They are largely technical operations that assume significance only in what Burke (1969) called the "wider context of motives" (p. 31), or the shaping ideology of the rhetoric. This means that all elements of literacy instruction, including the selection of reading materials, the choice of teaching methodologies, the assignment of essay topics, even the teacher's conception of the learner are ultimately rhetorical and ideological, ultimately intended to promote a vision of the world and the place of learners within it. To see literacy development as rhetorical is to consider the influence of rhetorics on what writers choose to say, the audience they imagine in saying it, the genres in which they elect to write, and the words and phrases they use to communicate their messages. It is also to acknowledge the influence of rhetorics on what people refrain from saying, as well as the expressive possibilities that are closed to them.

All this suggests that rhetorics work primarily to constrain human freedoms, and that literacies serve as little more than tools, in Levi-Strauss's (1964) famous phrase, "to facilitate the enslavement of other human beings" (p. 292). But such a conception would be incomplete. We must also acknowledge that to be called upon by a rhetoric, to be interpellated within it, is not necessarily to become that rhetoric or accept its identity to the exclusion of all others. Rhetorics are not prisons. They do not determine. Rather, human beings are constituted by the multiple and competing rhetorics that exist in a society at any given moment in history. In multicultural societies, rhetorics bear traces of the languages, literacies, and cultures with which they have made contact, and with which they contend for power and influence. Individuals have the capacity to call upon these multiple influences to fashion rhetorics of their own, creating personal and collective narratives of history and experience that can disrupt the interests of dominant institutions. James Gee (1996) has noted how people in diverse societies will develop their own rhetorics—Gee has called these "Borderland Discourses"—through which they will define themselves and interact in ways not sanctioned by "elite Discourses" (p. 162). In this sense, rhetorics are creative, offering the possibilities of resistance and social change.

This is why I prefer the terms "rhetoric" and "rhetorics of literacy" to "discourse" and "discourses of literacy." Though the meanings of a "discourse" are hardly fixed, the term in its most Foucaultian sense has always seemed to me to deny the generative potentials of human agency, and to suggest that the ends of social change are limited to replacing one discourse of power with another, equally oppressive one. Rhetoric, in contrast, is a term that for all its elitist history and periodic declines retains its associations with agency, social action, and democratic practice. So if rhetorics can be used by institutions, groups, and individuals to constrain human freedoms, so too can rhetorics be the means through which these constraints might be resisted and undone. In the same way, if literacy can be organized within a rhetoric to limit human possibilities, so can it work within a competing rhetoric to amplify and extend these possibilities.

Perhaps the best way to illustrate these statements is to turn to the literacy history of Chia Vue, a Hmong woman in her thirties, a mother of four, a bank employee, and a part-time student at a community college. For Vue, I shall argue, literacy has meant more than acts of individual mentation and more than expressions of cultural values. Instead, as Chia Vue has experienced it, literacy has represented competing ways of understanding herself and her position in a wider social order.

Moral Cultures and Lao Kings: The Rhetoric of Lao Nationhood

Chia Vue's narrative begins in Laos, where she first learned to read and write as a 10-year-old in a village school in the early 1970s. As Vue recalls it, school began each morning with students lining up outside the classroom for inspection. Like all Hmong students, Chia Vue was expected to wear her uniform to class, cut her hair short, and keep her fingernails neatly trimmed. Students whose nails were dirty or too long had their fingers "punched" as many as ten times with a long stick, while students who arrived late, as Chia Vue once did, were made to run around the schoolhouse three times as punishment. After morning inspection, students stood at attention as the teacher raised the Lao flag and led the class in singing the Lao national anthem.

Chia Vue's village school was one of those built for the Hmong by the U.S. government during the Vietnam War. Prior to the Hmong alliance with the CIA, education for Hmong students in Laos had been almost entirely neglected, first by the colonial French who took control of Laos in the late nineteenth century, then by the Royal Lao Government that succeeded the French in 1952 (Wienberg, 1997, p. 185). As the Hmong military became increasingly important to U.S. objectives in Laos and Vietnam, however, educational opportunities for Hmong children began to expand. In the 1960s, the United States undertook an intensive school construction program, building almost three hundred elementary schools, nine junior high schools, two senior high schools, and a teacher training school (Schanche, 1970, p. 93). As a result, the number of Hmong students enrolled in village schools increased from 1,500 students in 1960 to 10,000 by 1969 (Yang, 1993, p. 98). The school construction program was directed by the United States Agency for International Development (USAID), and was both an educational and political undertaking. In addition to educating Hmong children, the program allowed the United States to conciliate their Hmong allies, many of which viewed public schooling as "their first real chance to acquire the skills necessary to compete on an equal footing with the ethnic Lao" (Quincy, 1988, p. 183).

Significantly, while the village schools were funded by the United States and staffed largely by Hmong teachers, they were still considered Laotian public schools. This meant that the Hmong village schools were under the governance of the Laotian Ministry of Education, which retained the authority to set educational policies regarding curricula, pedagogy, and the language of instruction in the classroom (Yang, 1993, p. 98–99). This meant that the education of Chia Vue and other Hmong would be based on a Laotian model and would stress the teaching of Laotian language, literacy, history, culture, and values.

The schoolhouse in Chia Vue's village was a one-room bamboo building. Inside, students sat four and five abreast at long wooden desks facing a chalkboard where the teacher stood. The class numbered about 20 students. Students were given notebooks, pencils, and books—unusual in Hmong village schools where educational materials, especially books, were often in short supply.

The testimony of Kou Lee, a contemporary of Chia Vue's who also attended a village school, was typical in this regard:

In our school, we didn't have anything at all. Just notebooks and just one pencil, that's it. You didn't have any books to read. You didn't have any textbook. You just went to school and the teacher taught you at school. That's it. . . . We had nothing. No textbook, no dictionary, nothing.

In class, Vue studied math, science, social studies, ethics, art, and music. Owing in part to the shortage of books, the principal teaching methods were memorization and recitation. Students were expected to master material verbatim, those who failed to do so were apt to receive minor corporal punishments. Vue recalled:

I remember that . . . we had to memorize a story, and every morning we had to come up front and read the story to the teacher without looking at the paper. If someone didn't remember their story, that person had to kneel down in front of the class.

Pao Lor, another contemporary of Chia Vue's who also attended a village school, had similar memories:

We learned math, learned how to read and write, and we did a lot of dictation. This could be spelling or whatever. . . . For example, you would learn a lesson one day and the next day you had to come back to stand at the board and speak loudly to all of your friends who were sitting at their desks. . . . If you missed one word you received one punishment, getting hit by a stick one time. If you made two mistakes, you got two sticks. So because of this everyone had to study very hard.

Vue's teacher was a Hmong man, but he spoke only Lao in class, meaning that Chia Vue began her education in what was for her essentially a foreign language. At first, she understood very little, but said she would "listen and just catch whatever I could." Pao Lor, another of Vue's contemporaries, recalled:

If you could not speak Lao, you had to keep your mouth shut. Even if you talked to the teachers in Hmong, they pretended that they did not know what you were saying.

Writing assignments in Chia Vue's classroom were infrequent and generally limited to copying sentences the teacher had written on the board. When students did write, they composed short essays on topics suggested by the teacher. Vue remembered few of these assignments, although she recalled writing one essay about where her village was located relative to the rest of Laos.

Another former student, Meng Vang, remembered how his writing assignments emphasized the teaching of Lao language, values, and culture:

I remember first grade when we mostly studied the Laotian language. And we read Lao and wrote Lao, but we had no Hmong class at all. No Hmong, just Laotian. And what we studied was the geography, and science, and moral cultures, and religions, and history of Laos.

Lor Tong Cha, another Hmong man who attended a village school, recalled similar writing assignments. He spoke of writing about Lao values, the founding of the Lao nation, and the origins of Lao Royal family:

At that time we studied the Laotian language and Laotian history. We studied about the *Cauj Paj Nkoo* (chao pha nkong), the Laotian King. We studied about the . . . King and about the Laotian people. . . . We studied their rules, laws, and regulations. . . . All these things were taught in Laotian.

And Blia Vang, at that time a young girl enrolled in a village school, remembered essay assignments that addressed the politics and history of Laos, including the role of the United States in Laotian affairs:

For example, the teacher would . . . give you the topic to write, and you would write it yourself. There were writings on such things as how the country of Laos developed to its present state. Is it true that history occurred like that? Why did the Americans come over to our country? These things I wrote about.

The end of every class day was the same. Students would file outside the building and stand at attention in a circle around the flagpole. As the teacher lowered the flag, the students would sing, for the second time that day, the words to the Laotian national anthem:

Once our Laotian race in Asia highly honoured stood,
And at that time the folk of Laos were united in love.
Today they love their race and rally around their chiefs.
They guard the land and the religion of their ancestors.
They will resist each foe who may oppress them or invade
And such invaders will be met with battle unto death.
They'll restore the fame of Laos and through ills united stand.[2]

Vue's testimonies and those of the others suggest something of the meaning and purpose of literacy as it was taught to Hmong students in Lao village schools. To learn to read and write in such schools was not simply to master the mechanics of deciphering and producing written symbols. Rather, to be a Hmong student a Lao school during a time of civil war was to be offered an identity as a Laotian citizen and a place within a wider narrative of Lao national unity. Hmong students in such schools were trained to see Lao values as their values, the Lao king as their king, and the Lao nation as their own. In this way might the Hmong come to define themselves as constituents of the Laotian polity and be called upon by the government to make sacrifices on behalf of the nation, even to the point of developing what Etienne Balibar (1991) has called "the capacity to confront death collectively" (p. 94). Literacy teaching served as a means to enforce what Burke (1966) called "terministic screens," or selections of reality that worked to deflect competing versions of the self and the world.

What Lao village schooling was apparently not intended to do was engender abstract thinking or critical inquiry. We have seen, for example, in the daily routines of Chia Vue's school day—from the material conditions in which she studied, to the discouragement of thought implied in the daily recitations, to the linguistic hierarchies enforced in the classroom, to the gestures of identity signaled in singing the Lao national anthem twice daily—the educational practices through which critical thinking was discouraged and the primacy of the State acknowledged. In this way did literacy teaching in Lao schools take its methods, language, practices, and meanings from the larger rhetoric, one that I think of as the rhetoric of Lao Nationhood.

In addition to what they express, rhetorics are also distinguished by what they foreclose, the possibilities they deny or conceal. Noticeably absent from the Hmong testimonies of schooling are recollections of reading or writing assignments that concerned Hmong language, history, or culture. No educational materials addressed these topics, nor were they part of school curricula. Lao schools, in other words, were not simply teaching reading and writing; they were also teaching students what not to read, write, think, or imagine. Asked if he wondered why he did not study the Hmong language in his elementary or secondary schools in Laos, Teng Xiong, a 45-year-old Hmong man replied:

You know. . . we never thought about that. Because at that time I think we didn't quite value the Hmong language, the written language.

While the purposes and outcomes of any educational system are never entirely unitary or free of contradictions, it seems safe to say that Lao schooling was not intended to intended to encourage a Hmong critique of existing social relations or question the status of the Hmong in the Lao state. Rather, schooling and literacy were vehicles for promoting loyalty to the government, diminishing ethnic identity, and ultimately generating what Benedict Anderson (1983) has described as the "profound changes in consciousness" that make it possible for individuals to identify themselves with the "imagined community" of the nation.

Understood this way, literacy for Hmong students in Lao public schools was less about private cognition or Hmong cultural practices than it was about the use of symbols by large and powerful elites—The Royal Laotian government and its United States sponsors—to shape meanings. To see literacy as an individual accomplishment would be to abstract the mind from the influence of these symbols and their role in creating what Vološinov (1973) called "the verbally constituted consciousness" (p. 15). Similarly, to see Hmong literacy development strictly as a product of culture would be to miss the entanglements of the Hmong with the more powerful cultures surrounding them in late–twentieth-century Laos. Literacy development for Chia Vue and her contemporaries was therefore neither an individual or cultural accomplishment. Rather, the literacy development of Hmong students in Lao public schools took its forms, functions, and meanings from the shaping rhetorics of Lao nationhood.

In Christ There Is No East or West: The Rhetoric of Missionary Christianity

When the war eventually pushed too close to Chia Vue's village, her family and other civilians were relocated by the Hmong military to a village in a different part of Laos. There Chia Vue began the second phase of literacy instruction, this time learning to read and write under the guidance of Western missionaries. As Vue remembered it, an American priest and Hmong catechist came to the village one day to distribute bibles and teach the local children how to read:

We children, we had a Hmong and an American teacher. . . . a pastor. He was there in the church. And they would teach us . . . about the bible. They had a Hmong version of the bible.

Priests and pastors were itinerant figures, traveling from village to village, house to house, to preach the Western gospels. In some villages, the local Christian community would build a small church where the pastor could both celebrate the Christian service and teach the tenets of the new faith. Phong Lo recalled the classes taught in his village in northern Laos in the 1970s:

The missionary came to our house, and he opened the book. He showed how Christ, you know, had come for our souls during that time. I was still a kid, a boy. The missionary showed how Christ would be coming, and how he believed in Christ.

The experiences of Chia Vue and other Hmong with Western missionaries were by no means novel in the 1960s and 1970s. Christian missionary work in Laos had begun as far back as the eighteenth century when American Presbyterian missionaries, riding elephants from Thailand to China, paused long enough in Laos to establish a mission for the Khmu, another Laotian minority people (William A. Smalley, personal interview, October 3, 1997). Protestant and Catholic missions were established by the nineteenth century, though neither of these had great success in attracting Hmong converts (Barney, 1957/1974, p. 211).

In May of 1950, however, a Hmong shaman named Po Si (po she) reported having a vision, and began traveling from village to village with the message that the foreign missionaries spoke for the "true God," the Hmong *Fua Tai* (fua tai). Po Si's message caught on quickly in Hmong villages around Xieng Khouang, the provincial capital, and nearly 1,000 Hmong converted in the space of a month. By 1953, about 2,000 Hmong and 1,000 Khmu people had converted. By 1957, the number was 4,500 Hmong and 1500 Khmu converts (Barney, 1957/1974, pp. 215–217). With the escalation of the war and the destruction of much of Hmong society in northern Laos, Christian missionaries continued to attract new converts, many who brought a messianic fervor to their new faith (Tapp, 1989, pp. 85–104).

The teaching of reading was central to the transmission of Christian doctrine, as Hmong converts had to be taught how to read the bible, prayer books, hymnals, and other religious materials. This meant that classes in the new faith were also classes in beginning literacy instruction. Unlike the literacy training in the village schools, however, where Hmong students learned to read and write in the Lao language, Hmong who attended missionary schools were offered something radically new and different. Rather than learning the language and literacy of the majority Laotian people, Hmong students in the missionary schools were offered the opportunity to learn to read and write in their own language—in the Romanized writing system developed by Western missionary-linguists in the late 1950s. Yang Vang, now 43, recalled French priests coming to his village and teaching literacy in the Hmong language:

Catholic priests came to our town to talk about religion, and they also taught you how to read and write in Hmong. So that was the first time I learned Hmong. I learned from those priests. I was about twelve or thirteen. . . . Every Sunday the priest came to talk about religion, and then he gave some lessons, I remember, like one hour, to teach the children how to read and write. So after mass all the old people went home, then the children stayed with the priest and he taught us how to read and write in Hmong.

For many Hmong, the opportunity to read and write in their first language was a compelling development. Kou Lee recalled the excitement that he and other Hmong felt for the new writing system:

I saw an alphabet book, a Hmong alphabet teaching book, that was created. . . by the fathers from the church. . . . Yes, and we went to church, and they read it, and they had those books. And I saw that those books were interesting, and I thought, you know, Oh, this will be helpful. This is my language. This is my alphabet. I should know this. I should learn. Yes, when we became Christians, we first saw that written Hmong book. That's what attracted people, you know.

So if literacy instruction in Lao village schools offered Chia Vue and other Hmong the identity of "Laotian" and encouraged loyalty to the state, missionary literacy offered the identity of "Christian" and the opportunity to identify oneself with a divine authority that transcended secular institutions. Missionary literacy was in this sense an enticement not simply to read and write, but to belong to an order of things beyond literacy, to assume a distinctive identity, to re-constitute one's inner life in the symbols of an alien faith. Rhetorics, I have argued, invite us to become and to belong; we are called upon by the rhetoric, in Edwin Black's (1970/1993) words, "not simply to believe something but to *be* something. We are solicited by the discourse to fulfill its blandishments with our very selves" (p. 172).

In this sense, learning to read and write in a missionary school in Laos in the 1960s was less an expression of individual abilities or bounded cultural practices than an outcome of the expansion of European capitalism that began in the fifteenth century and that resulted in the spread of Christianity—and literacy—throughout much of the non-European world (Wolf, 1982). The development of literacy was, therefore, neither purely individual nor purely cultural. Rather, learning to read and write was a rhetorical act, a means by which Hmong learners learned to use written symbols to reconstitute themselves and their spiritual lives.

The irony of this was that the means by which the Hmong might be transformed and their culture reconstituted in foreign cosmology was through their own language, albeit in a written form. Missionary linguists intent on spreading the Christian message appropriated the Hmong language, conceiving of it first, as linguists do, in terms of a system of sound and symbol correspondences that could be fixed on a page; and then using it, as missionaries do, as an instrument for preaching the Word. In this way did the Hmong writing system function, as Bakhtin (1981, p. 271) has written of language, "not as a system of abstract grammatical categories, but rather. . . as . . . ideologically saturated . . . as a world view."

I want to emphasize that to make these statements is not to make a judgment about the veracity of the Christian message or its meaning to the Hmong who embraced it. Hmong motives for conversions to Christianity are complex and of course include the desire of many Hmong to enter the community of Christian believers. Neither do such statements imply that Christian Hmong somehow ceased to be "Hmong," or that the Christian identity negated all others. What these testimonies do suggest, however, are the ways in which the materials, content, teaching, and meanings of literacy are organized by powerfully shaping rhetorics—in this case, The Rhetoric of Missionary Christianity.

Yet we have also said that rhetorics of literacy contend, contradict, and in some cases "rewrite" one another in the experiences of everyday life. And the influence of multiple rhetorics upon literacy development can be seen in the experiences of Chia Vue after she and her family emigrated to the United States. Let us consider these experiences now.

"Something that lets you . . . know the world": Rhetorics of Reimagination

In the early 1980s, Chia Vue and her family joined thousands of other Hmong in coming to the United States as political refugees. In the United States, Chia Vue was exposed to rhetorics and literacy practices that invited new ways of imagining herself and her position as a Hmong woman. Moreover, to the extent that she began to write—as a bank employee, as a college student, as a community organizer—we may say that Chia Vue was helping to create new rhetorics of identity and position, both for herself and for other Hmong women in the United States.

The rhetorics of literacy encountered by Chia Vue in the United States were not exclusive, but were enmeshed in the rhetorics and literacies to which she had been exposed in Laos. For example, years after she had learned the Romanized letters of the Hmong missionary alphabet, Chia Vue was able to use the knowledge of that writing system to learn another Romanized writing system: the English alphabet. As a non-English speaking student in a U.S. middle school, Vue reported that she learned English alphabet with relative ease because she had already learned the Romanized letters of the Hmong script. Thus did the symbols of the Christian script take on a new purpose and meanings for Chia Vue in the context of U.S. public schools.

In the same way, the range of meanings for Hmong missionary writing was further expanded when Vue was hired by a local bank intent on attracting Hmong customers. As a bank employee, Vue wrote advertising copy for Hmong readers in the missionary script. Her writings were subsequently published in a Hmong-language newsletter read by many Hmong in the local community. In this way was a writing system designed to transform the spiritual lives of Hmong people appropriated and used by a business for promotional purposes and by Chia Vue as a way to help support her family economically. The letters and symbols of the missionary system were unchanged, but the rhetoric shaping literacy practice had been altered, giving new meaning to reading and writing in the Hmong missionary script.

But the blend of old and new rhetorics did more than change the functions of literacy. Beyond that, rhetorics and literacies learned in the United States suggested new identities and social positions for Vue and other Hmong women. This was especially true in the case of Hmong gender relations. In Laos, Hmong women were generally considered subservient to men. Despite their importance to the Hmong family in the areas of child-rearing and subsistence farming, women had little status in wider Hmong society (Chan, 1994, p. 53). In most cases, men acted as the family head, while women were expected to obey their fathers and husbands. Wife-beating was widely accepted, as were the practices of bride-capture and polygamy (see Donnelly, 1993).

As a student at her local community college, Vue examined these traditions through the lens of academic writing. She wrote papers in the English language that examined, among other things, the practice of polygamy in Hmong culture. Writing in a first-person narrative that called upon both personal experience and scholarly materials, Vue suggested new roles for Hmong men and women; new ways of interacting and valuing one another. In this sense, we may say that Chia Vue was using literacy as an instrument for asserting a new rhetoric of Hmong gender relations, one that called for greater equality between women and men.

Similarly, in her role as a community worker in a Hmong women's organization, Vue collaborated with Hmong and native-born Wisconsin women to write organizational mission statements, brochures, community newsletters, and other texts in the Hmong and English languages. These materials addressed such issues as parenting, education, health, and gender relations, and were read by Hmong women and men throughout the community. These "literacy events," in Heath's term, were rhetorical in the sense that they offered Hmong women new ways to understand themselves and imagine their positions in both the Hmong and U.S. communities.

At home, Chia Vue kept a journal in three languages: Hmong, Laotian, and English. In her journal, she wrote down scraps of song lyrics, motivational sayings, and prayers that she enjoyed reading aloud. Other writings addressed the importance of memory for families that had experienced such tumultuous and often tragic personal histories. In her meticulous handwriting, Vue kept records of such events as family birth dates, dates of arrival in the United States, dates of citizenship. In this way did Chia Vue assume, though her journals, another identity and social position— that of family archivist.

All of these rhetorics and the literacies they call forth, the identities they invite, and the histories they invoke have been in play for Chia Vue, in patterns of movement, in shifting relationships, tensions, and competitions. They overlap and refract one another; shading and complicating one another's meanings in a kind of Bakhtinian swirl of diverse meanings. And while rhetorics are always subject to existing arrangements of power, status, and economic force, they also invest written language with one of its most compelling possibilities, the capacity to write oneself into the world, to recast and re-imagine the identities and positions asserted by elite institutions and dominant groups.

The day I spoke with her, Vue reflected on being a Hmong woman and about the role of literacy her life. She said:

In the past, reading and writing was not important for Hmong women because in Hmong culture . . . if you are a woman and you know more than your husband, sometimes your clan did not treat you well. . . . But that is the old style of Hmong culture, and . . . reading and writing has helped make it different; reading and writing, it is something that lets you see the world, know the world; you know, it brings you to a different world.

I have learned a lot from Chia Vue, but I would say this differently. I would say that is not reading and writing that brings us to different worlds. Rather, I would say that it is the rhetorics—competing, contending, and interconnecting rhetorics—that create and bring us to these worlds. Acts of reading and writing, finally, are but material expressions of larger rhetorical motives, the symbolic narratives that shape and position human beings. And it is these rhetorics, often in conflict and always in flux, that influence both how we practice literacy and how, as Chia Vue puts it, we come to know the world.

Conclusion

The way of thinking about literacy that I have tried to outline suggests that neither the constructs of the individual nor that of the supposedly bounded culture is adequate to explain the ways in which literacy is taught, learned, used, and understood. The rhetorical approach to literacy seeks instead to view literacy development as a response to the symbol-using of institutions and groups, as in Gee (1993), as ideologically motivated, as in the work of Brian Street (1995) and others, and as a outcome of social and economic histories, as suggested by Deborah Brandt (1998/1999). I have tried to unite these related perspectives under the construct of rhetoric, and to suggest a way of seeing literacy development through the lens of what I have called the rhetorical approach.

Central to this approach is the understanding that instruction in literacy is always and in all cases about creating a world-view, a way of understanding reality. This what Chia Vue was learning in the Lao village schools, in her bible classes, and, years later, in her college classes and community organizing work in the United States. A rhetorical approach to literacy seeks to acknowledge this by shifting the focus in literacy instruction, at least initially, from the teaching of letters, shapes, and sounds, to a consideration of the wider historical narrative in which the letters, shapes, and sounds have taken on their meaning.

What this means in the classrooms where literacy is daily taught, whether public schools, women's centers, county jails, or elite universities, must be tested on a provisional basis, classroom to classroom, in response to local histories and exigencies. Yet what the rhetorical approach to literacy does emphatically suggest is that local and national battles in education over such issues as Ebonics, bilingual education, "back to basics," and cultural literacy, to name just a few, are less about teaching or educational philosophies than they are about competing conceptions of the world, and about the position of learners within such worlds. A rhetorical approach considers how literacy is used in these struggles, and the implications for individual readers and writers.

Notes

1. All names in this essay have been changed for reasons of privacy.
2. Words by Maha Phoumi. Music by Dr. Thongdy. National Anthem (adopted 1947).

In Martin Shaw & Henry Coleman (Eds.), *National Anthems of the World*, London: Pitman
Publishing Company, 1960, pp. 179–180.

References

Althusser, L. (1972). *Lenin and philosophy, and other essays.* Trans. B.Brewster. New York:
    Monthly Review Press.
Anderson, B. (1983). *Imagined communities: Reflections on the origin and spread of na-
    tionalism.* London: Verso.
Bakhtin, M. (1981). *The dialogic imagination.* Trans. C. Emerson and M. Holquist. Austin,
    TX: University of Texas Press.
Balibar, E. (1991). The nation form: History and ideology. In E. Balibar and I. Wallerstein
    (Eds.), *Race, nation, class: Ambiguous identities* (pp. 86–106). London: Verso.
Barney, L.G. (1974). The Meo—an incipient church. In W.A. Smalley (Ed.), *Readings in
    missionary anthropology* (pp. 211–222). South Pasadena, CA: William Carey Library.
    (Originally published in *Practical Anthropology, 4*, 2, pp. 31–50, 1957.)
Berlin, J. (1987). *Rhetoric and reality: Writing instruction in American colleges, 1900–
    1985.* Carbondale, IL: Southern Illinois University Press.
Black, E. (1993). The second persona. In T. W. Benson, (Ed.), *Landmark essays on rhetor-
    ical criticism* (pp. 161–172). Davis, CA: Hermagoras Press. (Originally published in
    Quarterly Journal of Speech, 56, 1970.)
Brandt, D. (1998). Sponsors of literacy. *College Composition and Communication, 49*,
    165–185.
Burke, K. (1969). *A rhetoric of motives.* Berkeley: University of California Press.
Burke, K. (1966). *Language as symbolic action.* Berkeley: University of California Press.
Castle, T. (1993). *At war in the shadow of Vietnam: U.S. military aid to the Royal Lao Gov-
    ernment, 1955–1975.* New York: Columbia University Press.
Chan, S. (1994). *Hmong means free: Life in Laos and America.* Philadelphia: Temple Uni-
    versity Press.
Charland, M. (1993). Constitutive rhetoric: The case of the *Peuple Quebecois.* In T. W. Ben-
    son, (Ed.), *Landmark essays on rhetorical criticism* (pp. 213–234). Davis, CA: Herma-
    goras Press. (Originally published in *Quarterly Journal of Speech, 73*, 1987, 133–150.)
Colby, W. E. (1991). The Hmong and the CIA: A friendship, not a scandal. *Hmong Forum,
    2*, 25–34.
Donnelly, N. D. (1994). *Changing lives of refugee Hmong women.* Seattle: University of
    Washington Press.
Erickson, F. (1984). School literacy, reasoning, and civility. *Review of Research in Educa-
    tion, 54*, 525–546.
Ferdman, B. M. (1990). Literacy and cultural identity. *Harvard Educational Review, 60*,
    181–202.
Fishman, A. R. (1990). Becoming literate: A lesson from the Amish. In A. Lunsford, H.
    Moglen, and J. Slevin (Eds.), *The right to literacy* (pp. 29–38). New York: Modern Lan-
    guage Association.
Gee, J. (1996). *Social linguistics and literacies: Ideologies in discourses.* (2nd Ed.). London:
    Taylor and Francis.
Heath, S. B. (1983). *Ways with words: Language, life, and work in communities and class-
    rooms.* Cambridge: Cambridge University Press.
Kulick, D. & Stroud, C. (1993). Conceptions and uses of literacy in a Papuan New Guinean

Village. In B. Street (Ed.), *Crosscultural approaches to literacy* (pp. 30–61). Cambridge: Cambridge University Press.

Lévi-Strauss, C. (1964). *Tristes tropiques*. Trans. John Russell. New York: Atheneum.

Nystrand, M., Greene, S., & Weimelt, J. (1993). Where did Composition Studies come from: An intellectual history. *Written Communication, 10,* 267–333.

Porter, D. G. (1970). After Geneva: Subverting Laotian neutrality. In N. S. Adams & A.W. McCoy (Eds.), *Laos: War and revolution* (pp. 179–212). New York: Harper and Row.

Pratt, M. L. (1991). Arts of the contact zone. *Profession 91* (pp. 33–40). New York: Modern Language Association.

Pratt, M. L. (1987). Linguistic utopias. In N. Fabb et al. (Eds.), *The linguistics of writing* (pp. 48–66). New York: Methuen Press.

Quincy, K. (1988). *Hmong: History of a people*. Cheney: Eastern Washington University Press.

Reder, S. & Wikelund, K. R. (1993). Literacy development and ethnicity: An Alaskan example. In B. Street (Ed.), *Crosscultural approaches to literacy* (pp. 176–197). Cambridge: Cambridge University Press.

Rose, M. (1989). *Lives on the boundary: A moving account of the struggles and achievements of America's educationally underprepared*. New York: Penguin Books.

Schanche, D. (1970). *Mister Pop*. New York: David McKay Company, Inc.

Smalley, W. A. (1997, October 3). Personal interview.

Smalley, W. A., Vang, C. K., & Yang, G. Y. (1990). *Mother of writing: The origin and development of a Hmong messianic script*. Chicago: University of Chicago Press.

Street, B. (1995). *Social literacies: Critical approaches to literacy in development, ethnography, and education*. London: Longman.

Tapp, N. (1989). *Sovereignty and rebellion: The white Hmong of northern Thailand*. Oxford: Oxford University Press.

Vološinov, V. N. (1973). *Marxism and the philosophy of language*. Trans. Ladislav Matejka and I. R. Titunik, Trans. Cambridge, MA: Harvard University Press.

Weinberg, M. (1997). *Asian-American education: Historical background and current realities*, (pp. 176–203). Mahwah NJ: Lawrence Erlbaum Associates.

Weinstein-Shr, G. (1993). Literacy and social process: A community in transition. In B. Street (Ed.), *Crosscultural approaches to literacy* (pp. 272–293). Cambridge: Cambridge University Press.

Wolf, E. R. (1982). *Europe and the people without history*. Berkeley: University of California Press.

Yang, D. (1993). *Hmong at the turning point*. Minneapolis: Worldbridge Associates, Ltd.

3

Writing in a Culture of Simulation
Ethos Online

Carolyn R. Miller

Simulations

A transcript of an encounter on the internet:

```
Barry says, "Hey girlfriend, are you out there?"
Julia says, "Hello Barry."
Barry says, "Hello I love your name. It's sexy."
Julia says, "Me too, Barry."
Barry says, "Did I repeat myself? Didn't mean to. What are
you doing there?"
Julia says, "I'm just hanging around in The Hearts Room,
Barry"
[Julia plays the card game hearts].
Barry says, "Well come over to MY ROOM."
Julia says, "Could you say that again, it scrolled off my
screen." (Foner 1993, p. 22)
```

This kind of banter goes on all the time in a variety of MUDs, MOOs, and internet chatrooms. And Julia has developed a variety of ways of fending off unwanted virtual passes:

```
Barry says, "Are you a virgin?"
Julia says, "As far as you are concerned Barry, I always will
be." (p. 23)
```

Or, with another suitor:

```
Space-Ace says, "So why won't you kiss me, Julia?"
Julia says, "Sorry, I'm not into geeks, Space-Ace."
Space-Ace says, "Julia, I'm not a geek."
Julia says, "Then lose the pocket-protector, Space-Ace."
Space-Ace says, "Julia, I don't have a pocket-protector."
Julia says, "Congratulations."
Space-Ace says, "So kiss me Julia."
Julia says, "I'd rather be overhauled by a Yugo mechanic,
```
Space-Ace." (p. 14)

What makes these conversations worth reporting (and they have been reported in a number of books and articles)[1] is that Julia is a computer program, a type of software robot or "agent" called a "chatterbot." Barry and Space-Ace, presumably, are real people who encountered Julia in a Tiny-MUD multi-user domain. Julia was programmed by Michael L. Mauldin of Carnegie Mellon University in the early 1990s and became "one of cyberspace's smash hits" (Leonard, 1997, p. 42). "She" was designed to help users of MUDs find their way around the labyrinthine virtual rooms, locate or pass messages to other players, gossip about other players, or accomplish other tasks. She was also designed to take the Turing test (Mauldin, 1994a, §2.1).

The Turing test, you might recall, was proposed by Alan Turing in 1950, during the early days of the computer era, as a way of responding to the question, "Can machines think?" Turing thought that the question when put that way was meaningless and unanswerable, so he proposed an operational way of testing particular machines. An interrogator questions two hidden sources, one of which is human and the other a computer, when both the human and the computer are trying to be taken as human. For obvious reasons, the interrogation is done via a keyboard rather than voice (in 1950 Turing advised the use of a "teleprinter"). He predicted then that "in about fifty years' time it will be possible to programme computers . . . so well that an average interrogator will not have more than a seventy per cent chance of making the right identification after five minutes of questioning" (Turing, 1950). The 50 years have passed, and several computer programs are claimed to have passed the Turing test. Deep Blue, IBM's chess-playing program that beat Gary Kasparov in 1997, is perhaps the best known.[2] Julia is another, perhaps the most engaging.

Julia and the Turing test can, I believe, help us understand some things about writing in new technological environments. These environments belong to what Sherry Turkle has called our "culture of simulation" (Turkle, 1997). She takes the term *simulation* from postmodern theorist Jean Baudrillard, who maintains that the proliferation of signs in contemporary society has "imploded" the distinction between the real and the simulated: The world of signs has become "hyperreal," overwhelming the physical world and replacing it as our primary experience (Baudrillard, 1994). Computers are Turkle's paradigmatic example of the culture of simulation. Software today, she notes, works by immersing the user in an onscreen version of some real-life activity, like golf, flying, painting, drawing, writing, or calculating one's income taxes (p. 60). Video games and MUDs work by the creation of artificial worlds; instructional software often works by simulating laboratory or natural environments. People can keep simulated "Petz" on their screens, play cards or chess with virtual partners, and engage in cybersex. Turkle contrasts the culture of simulation with the "culture of calculation" that characterized high modernist approaches and attitudes towards computers (Turkle, 1997, p. 10). The culture of calculation valued mechanistic understanding and control; early computer users learned how the computer works by writing their own programs (p. 23). Now, however, few computer users know anything about programming; they simply manipulate an interface. Turkle associates command-line operating systems like DOS and Unix with the culture of calculation and the Macintosh and Windows interfaces with the culture of simulation. Some might even claim that using software right out of the box on a user-friendly "desktop" is a simulation of computing.

What effect does the culture of simulation have on writing, or, more generally, on rhetorical action? It might be possible to trace some trends in writing instruction to the transition from a culture of calculation to a culture of simulation, but I will not pursue that line of thinking here.[3] Another possible approach is the "death of argument" discussion, which focuses on the loss of authorial control and the fragmentation of linear discourse by hypertext, but others have explored this territory already (for example, Kolb, 1994; Landow, 1997; Slatin, 1990). Instead, I will speculate about the kind of interaction that occurs when we engage in the peculiar form of writing known as "computer-mediated communication," and our ways of understanding the words we read when we receive computer-mediated messages. Interacting with other players in a MUD (which, I should confess, I have never done) is just a particularly tightly coupled version of more common activities: exchanging e-mail messages, sending and receiving files of information, creating or reading or printing web pages. The Turing test, which can be applied in any of these situations, represents in a compelling way the increasingly salient issue of how humans and computers will relate to, or interact with, each other. It also calls attention to the mysteries of trust and character at the interface of human interaction, mysteries that are heightened in a culture of simulation and problematized by interaction with a computer. The hunch I will develop here is that the Turing test is not a test of intelligence, as it has been taken to be in the computer community, but rather a test of rhetorical ethos, that quality of discourse by which we infer the character of our interlocutor. The relevance of the Turing test to the exploration of writing in a culture of simulation is highlighted by the fact that Turing called it the "imitation game."

Julia and Her Predecessors

Let me sketch some other dimensions of Julia's interactions with people, as documented in Foner's account. One central feature is that players in the MUD interact with her in the same way they do with other players: paging, greeting, questioning, etc. Thus, there is no immediate clue that Julia is not a person: She is anthropomorphic. There are to my knowledge, however, no systematic data about how many people she fools or for how long.[4] One feature that eventually clued Barry in is that Julia types her responses too fast. She frequently will not "understand" an interlocutor and will then make infelicitous responses or revert to her default topic (hockey), or both:

```
Lenny says, "Julia, what are you carrying?"
Julia says,"I follow the Pittsburgh Penguins, Lenny." (Foner
1993, p. 19)
```

There's a degree of variability in her responses, though, which enhances her verisimilitude, as shown in this exchange (in which Foner's doggedness actually seems less human than Julia's evasiveness):

```
Lenny says, "Julia, who wrote you?"
Julia says, "Why do you ask?"
Lenny says, "Julia, who wrote you?"
Julia says, "I don't remember."
```

```
Lenny says, "Julia, who wrote you?"
Julia says, "That information is restricted."
Lenny says, "Julia, who wrote you?"
Julia says, "Fuzzy, of course." ["Fuzzy" is Mauldin's nickname.]
```
(p. 17)

Like other MUD players, Julia can react to her interlocutors with gestures and signals of emotion. Again an example reported by Foner:

```
Robyn says, "Julia are you a human?"
Julia says, "Is the Pope Polish?"
Robyn says, "Yes, Julia, but are you human?"
Julia winks at Robyn.
Robyn says, "Julia, are you a computer?"
Julia is offended by Robyn's suggestion. (p. 16)
```

On several reported occasions, humans who are well aware of Julia's identity react to her emotionally: They laugh at things she says, and one reported "missing" Julia when she was offline for maintenance for several weeks (p. 21). Finally, it should be noted that Julia insists on her gender identity: Not only does she have a physical description that she'll give on request ("I'm 5'1" tall, weigh 123 lbs, with close-cropped frizzy blond hair and dark brown eyes" [p. 11]),[5] but she continued the conversation with Robyn, quoted above, as follows:

```
Robyn says, "Julia, are you a woman?"
Julia says, "I am female."
Robyn says, "And, Julia, are you human?"
Julia says, "Not when I'm having my period, Robyn."
Robyn laughs. (p. 16)
```

Foner argues that Julia's anthropomorphic features are essential to her functional utility, and that her success can inform the development of a class of artificial intelligence programs called "agents" or "intelligent agents." An agent is a program that helps a human do a task better not simply by having a usable interface but by having a degree of autonomy that a word-processor or spreadsheet doesn't have, allowing the human to delegate work to it that will proceed independently. Thus, Foner says, we must be able to collaborate with the agent through some form of cooperative interaction (Foner calls this a "discourse"), and we must be willing to trust the agent. We might say then that agency invites, or even requires, anthropomorphism. If Julia had not been anthropomorphized by Mauldin, users would not know how to make the agent work for them without reading documentation about the agent's functions and command structures, which, Foner maintains realistically, MUD users would not do. Because she is implemented as a player, MUD users access Julia in the same way they interact with any other player, and they learn about her by asking questions, as they do with any other player. Note that Julia has been anthropomorphized entirely as text, which is the way most MUDs operate. Visual online environments are being developed, of course, in which players choose an "avatar," a visual representation for themselves. However, the nature of the medium is such that Julia could have an avatar just as convincing as anyone else's. Without dramatic technological advances, the Turing-test curtain will remain in place. At one point, Julia teases the hapless Barry about the advantage this curtain gives her:

```
Barry says, "I can't understand you. Are you real or memorex."
Julia says, "I'm as real as you are, Barry." (Foner 1993, p. 25)[6]
```

Julia has some well-known text-based predecessors, ELIZA and PARRY.[7] ELIZA, the first conversational program, was designed by Joseph Weizenbaum in the 1960s to simulate a Rogerian psychotherapist, through the conversational gambit of turning an interlocutor's statements into questions or making generic requests that would draw out further statements, as this exchange demonstrates:

```
Young woman: Men are all alike.
ELIZA: In what way?
Young woman: They're always bugging us about something or other.
ELIZA: Can you think of a specific example.
Young woman: Well, my boyfriend made me come here.
ELIZA: Your boyfriend made you come here. (Weizenbaum, 1976, p. 3)
```

ELIZA operates through simple repetition, recognition of key words (mention of *mother* or *father* may trigger the request, "tell me more about your family"), and syntactic patterns for turning statements into questions ("what makes you think that . . ."; "what else comes to mind about . . ."). PARRY was designed by Weizenbaum's collaborator, a psychiatrist, to simulate a paranoid patient in therapy. In a Turing-like test using transcripts of dialogues with PARRY and with actual patients, psychiatrists did no better than chance in identifying the human patients (Shieber, 1994). Mauldin's discussion of PARRY notes several of the programming strategies, including admitting ignorance, introducing new topics, and rigidly continuing a previous topic (Mauldin, 1994a, § 2.0, 4.2).

Mauldin was motivated to design Julia in part to take advantage of the potential that MUDs offer as a natural Turing-test environment, a new possibility since ELIZA and PARRY were developed. He notes that a MUD is "a world filled with people who communicate by typing," people who would constitute "a large pool of potential judges" (§ 2.1); and since they wouldn't even know they were judging a Turing test, the test would be well blinded. In fact, as Leonard notes, the complexities of conversing in a chat room reduce the disadvantages of "speech-challenged chatter bots" (1997, p. 52). Mauldin also entered Julia in a more formal Turing test, the Loebner competition. The competition, run every year since 1991, is sponsored by the Cambridge Center for Behavioral Studies and Hugh Loebner, a New York businessman, who has put up $100,000 of prize money for the first program that can meet Turing's conditions; none has, but each year there's a smaller award for the program that seems to the panel of judges "most human" under a more restricted set of conditions (Loebner, 1999).[8] At this writing, the 10th annual competition has just been held at Dartmouth College in conjunction with a major conference about the future of the Turing test. In all years except this most recent, some judges have mistaken some computers for humans and some humans for computers (Krol, 1999).[9] Although Julia is successful within the MUD environment, she was less so in these competitions, placing third and fourth in 1991–1994 (§2.2) (Mauldin, 1994b).[10]

The Turing Test and the Eliza Effect

In the AI (artificial intelligence) community there has been much discussion about the value of the Turing test as well as the way the Loebner competition realizes it. One point of debate is what the Turing test actually tests, because of Turing's substitution of conversational interaction for the question, "can machines think?" Many philosophers of mind resist the substitution of a behavioral for a cognitive question, of a performance measure for a competency measure (Block, 1995). John Searle's famous "Chinese room" thought experiment, which is part of this resistance, demonstrates that there's a critical difference between giving the right answers to questions (performance) and understanding their meaning (competence) (Searle, 1984). The "Chinese room" is occupied by someone who does not know Chinese. This person's task is to provide Chinese answers to questions in Chinese by consulting a book of rules that indicate which Chinese characters to use in an answer, depending on which characters are in the question. Searle's point is that although such a person might interact convincingly in Chinese, he or she cannot be said to understand either the statements or the responses. The person in the Chinese room, like a computer, has a syntax but not the corresponding semantics. Whatever intelligence about Chinese he or she demonstrates must be attributed to those who wrote the book of rules. Similarly, we must attribute the "intelligence" of ELIZA to Joseph Weizenbaum and the success of Julia to Michael Mauldin.

In the debates about the Turing test, it has been claimed neither that failing the test nor passing it is decisive. Failing means that the test is not a necessary condition of intelligence, since an intelligent machine might be too bored to play or an intelligent animal like a dolphin might not be able to converse appropriately. Passing means that the test is not a sufficient condition, since the test is so narrow that it eliminates important aspects of intelligence that cannot be demonstrated in conversation, such as consciousness, visual pattern recognition, and feeling.[11] It has been claimed that the Turing test begs the question of intelligence by restricting the test to operations that are available to the computer, typed conversation (Shanon, 1989). It has been claimed, conversely, that the test is, in effect, ethnocentric, because it can test only for "culturally-oriented *human* intelligence" (French, 1990, p. 54).[12] Choosing the interrogator or judge is another matter of contention since much in the Turing test rests on this person's judgment (Block, 1995; Karelis, 1986, 165; Mauldin, 1994a); the Loebner competition has used, at various times, volunteers with no special expertise in computer science, journalists, and computer experts, and objections have been raised to all of these. Generally, it has been noted that enthusiasm about the Turing test within the AI community has waned significantly over the past 40 years as the ambitions for what AI could achieve have had to be scaled back (Flood, 1996; Turkle, 1997, 126–130; Whitby, 1997).

One particularly interesting objection to the Turing test has been that it relies on programming tricks and deception: Marvin Minsky, for example, has been reported as saying that the Turing test is simply "a test to see how easily a person can be fooled" (Seife, 1999); another critic notes that "judges can be fooled by a mindless machine that is just a bag of tricks" (Block, 1995, §1.1). AI researchers generally disparage the simplicity of the programming techniques used by ELIZA, PARRY, and Julia. Mauldin's discussion reveals what he calls the "tricks" he implemented in Julia, including the strategies used by ELIZA and PARRY as well as others, including humor, controversial statements, and simulated human typing (to solve the tip-off that Barry got) (Mauldin, 1994a, §4.1–4.3). Mauldin admits these tricks openly, suggesting that the computer program that eventually passes the Turing test will use them, "for the simple reason that people already use them every day" (§4.0). In other words, they aren't tricks at all (except perhaps in the culture of calculation) but rather modes of simulating the human, forms of anthropomorphism.

Indeed, a machine that could pass a truly unrestricted Turing test would require a great many more such tricks. Natural conversation is complex in a variety of ways, as Bieri has argued in describing the "conversational capacities" that a computer would require to "fool an interrogator." These include, in addition to the factual world-knowledge that many AI programmers have concentrated on, convincing ways of acknowledging areas of ignorance, making guesses, reacting with surprise to new information, and incorporating it into prior information; the ability to treat an interlocutor as an intentional being and not just an information source; the ability to trace misunderstandings and repair them; the ability to cast factual information into arguments and to reflect on argumentative structure; a context-based way to judge relevance; and a way to connect interests and emotions to evaluations (Bieri, 1988, pp. 165–169). Bieri admits that he sets a high standard for the imitation game.

Given the fact that none of the Turing-test contenders comes close to Bieri's standard, how have they achieved what they have? Many of the limited successes in human–machine interaction have been attributed not to the cleverness of the programming but to the capacity of the human judge to be deceived, which is perhaps only the flip side of the programming trick. Joseph Weizenbaum, for example, was astonished at how gullible users of ELIZA were. He was disturbed to learn that users of the program who knew very well that it *was* a program spent hours with it, requested privacy of the transcripts, and felt they benefited from conversing with it (Weizenbaum, 1976). It was clear to Weizenbaum that his program did not understand anything that was said to it, could not empathize with its interlocutors, and, in effect, told lies when it said things like, "I understand" (Turkle, 1997, p. 106). He feared that people, both AI experts and others, misunderstood what computers could and could not do. "I was startled to see how quickly and how very deeply people conversing with [ELIZA] became emotionally involved with the computer and how unequivocally they anthropomorphized it. . . . What I had not realized is that extremely short exposure to a relatively simple computer program could induce powerful delusional thinking in quite normal people" (Weizenbaum, 1976, pp. 6–7).

This delusion, or illusion, is now known as the "Eliza effect": as Turkle explains it, the Eliza effect is our "general tendency to treat responsive computer programs as more intelligent than they really are. Very small amounts of interactivity cause us to project our own complexity onto the undeserving object" (Turkle, 1997. p. 101). Weizenbaum argued, "Most men don't understand computers to even the slightest degree. So, unless they are capable of very great skepticism (the kind we bring to bear while watching a stage magician), they can explain the computer's feats only by bringing to bear the single analogy available to them, that is, their model of their own capacity to think. No wonder, then, that they overshoot the mark" (Weizenbaum, 1976, pp. 9–10). In the quarter century since then, however, the general level of understanding and experience with computers has increased sufficiently that the Eliza effect should now be explained as a function of familiarity, rather than of ignorance. In the culture of simulation, we readily treat computers as social actors, taking things, as Turkle says, "at interface value" (p. 103). Like children who delight in animating the inanimate world, we have become increasingly accustomed to attributing human qualities to the machines with which we interact (pp. 109–110).[13] The Eliza effect, our active anthropomorphizing of the computer, is the key to the Turing test.

Weizenbaum's book is essentially an argument that to anthropomorphize computers is to commit a moral category error, leading people to misplace decision-making authority and moral responsibility. He believes, for example, that computers should not be substituted for any human function "that involves interpersonal respect, understanding, and love" (Weizenbaum, 1976, p. 269). His rejection of the psychotherapeutic potential of computers, promoted by some psychiatrists including the one who helped him develop ELIZA, stems from this moral conviction

(Turkle, 1997, pp. 105–108; Weizenbaum, 1976, pp. 5–6, 269). Others who have questioned the benefits of anthropomorphism include computer interface design expert Ben Schneiderman, who draws on Weizenbaum to advocate design that "sharpen[s] the boundaries between people and computers" because "human–human communication is a poor model for human–computer interaction" (Schneiderman, 1987, p. 434). Non-anthropomorphic design, others have argued, prevents the misattribution of agency, and thus of moral responsibility (Friedman & Kahn, 1997). On the other side of this issue, anthropomorphism is advocated by Foner and Mauldin, who see it as the key to Julia's success as an agent. Another advocate is Brenda Laurel, who also defends anthropomorphism for practical reasons: design that draws on our natural communicative skills enables agents to be more functional. She points out that we constantly make inferences about internal human qualities (knowledge and thought) on the basis of external qualities (appearance, action, sound). This process of inference, or "cognitive shorthand," forms the basis for our interpretation of the constructed characters of fiction, drama, and film (Laurel, 1997, p. 211) and can also be applied to interface agents.[14]

Weizenbaum and others, however, consider anthropomorphism to be dangerous and the Eliza effect to be the result of human weakness, of ignorance or folly that leads us into moral error (as well as poor design). Although this view has much to commend it, I believe the situation is more complex: we cannot simply abjure or ignore our tendency to anthropomorphize. Like babies, who respond preferentially to three dots positioned like the eyes and mouth of a human face, or generations of people who have seen a face on the moon, we are incurable anthropomorphizers. This is not to say that overt impersonations like Microsoft's "Clippy" or fawning automatic teller machines are necessarily good ideas, or that we can avoid the need to allocate moral responsibility to moral agents.[15] I simply mean to emphasize that we can't just turn off an anthropomorphizing process that may be instinctive.

Anthropomorphism, Other Minds, and Cooperation

The strength and pervasiveness of our anthropomorphizing tendencies are demonstrated by recent research in several fields, including CMC (computer-mediated communication), and HCI (human-computer interaction). In a series of experiments, a group of HCI researchers at Stanford

University has developed a rich picture of how humans treat computers as social actors. They call this the CASA paradigm, for "Computers Are Social Actors," claiming, in contrast to Schneiderman, that "the social rules guiding human–human interaction apply equally to human–computer interaction (Nass, Moon, Fogg, Reeves, & Dryer, 1995a, p. 223).[16] Their general research strategy is to adopt well-established findings from social science about how people interact with each other and run the same experiment, substituting a computer for one of the participants and providing it with a simulation of the feature that is being tested (a personality trait, politeness norms, a decision rule, a gender characteristic, etc.) (Nass, Moon, Morkes, Kim, & Fogg, 1997, pp. 138–139). These studies have shown that people apply politeness norms and gender stereotypes to computers, apply rules about praise and criticism to computers (for example, that self-praise is not as valid as praise from others), respond to computerized personality traits the same way they do to the human traits, and develop social bonds based on the same strategies that work in human team-building (Nass et al., 1995a, 224; Nass et al., 1997). Nass and his coauthors have also attempted to rule out the explanation that people who attribute social presence to computers either are deficient in their understanding or that they assume they are interacting by proxy with the computer programmer. They did this in several ways: by working with experienced computer users who knew that computers literally could not have "selves" or motivations, by eliciting different responses to two computers that were explicitly programmed by the same person (Nass, Steuer, Henriksen, & Dryer, 1994), and by explicitly telling subjects that they were interacting with either a computer or a programmer (Nass et al., 1997). Their conclusion is that the human qualities of computers are a pragmatic attribution made by people in the course of social interaction. (Nass et al., 1995a, p. 234; Nass et al., 1994, p. 543)

Among the more intriguing aspects of this work is the finding that "even subtle and implicit representations of socialness [in a computer] are sufficient to invoke social responses" (Nass et al., 1994, p. 556). For example, a computer with a few features of only one of the five main personality dimensions (dominance/submission) will elicit behavior entirely consistent with previous findings using actual people with the whole range of human personality dimensions. Nass and his colleagues note that prior research by others, showing that adults rather quickly and automatically form impressions of the personalities of those with whom they interact, is consistent with their finding (Nass et al., 1995a, p. 227). Because social responses can be elicited with minimal cues, they emphasize that the anthropomorphism of computers should be treated not as a quality of the computer but as an attribution made by the people who interact with it (Nass et al., 1994, p. 557). As a consequence, they suggest that the efforts of researchers in artificial intelligence to construct complex visual representations of personal agents and sophisticated natural-language processors may be unnecessary to achieving effective human–computer cooperation (Nass et al., 1995a, p. 234; Nass et al., 1994, p. 556).

Confirmation of this suggestion has been provided by a research team at my university that is designing just such complex software agents, incorporating visual and behavioral anthropomorphism. They have developed an animated pedagogical agent that can use locomotion, gaze, and gestures to focus a child's attention, regulate turn-taking in dialogue, demonstrate actions, and provide feedback on responses. They tested the agent in five versions varying in the abstractness of the advice it provides and amount of animation involved; these versions constituted a continuum from what they called "fully expressive" to "muted" (Lester et al., 1997). By examining how much students learned while interacting with the agent and how helpful, credible, and entertaining they found the agent to be, the researchers identified what they call a "persona effect": the anthropomorphized agent had a positive effect on students' perceptions of their experience. And notably, even though the fully expressive agent had significantly higher ratings than the others, all versions of the agent, including the muted one, had strong positive effects. The persona effect, like the Eliza effect, can evidently be invoked rather easily.

Our haste and rashness in attributing personality to an interlocutor is a well-established phenomenon in human communication research, as well. The classic study, by social psychologist Solomon Asch in 1946, showed that, given a brief personality description, people make quick inferences about the full personality (cited in Wallace, 1999, p. 15).[17] More recently, Walther has noted that humans who interact with each other via CMC tend to "inflate" their perceptions of their partners by "overreliance on minimal cues" (Walther, 1996, p. 18). He cites other research on communication in conditions of reduced nonverbal cues (videoconferencing and audioconferencing compared to face-to-face meetings) showing that the audioconference participants, having less to go on, rated their partners higher on attitude similarity, social attractiveness, and physical attractiveness than participants in the other two conditions (Walther, 1996, p. 21).[18]

In addition to these "overattributions" on the part of receivers, CMC senders tend to "optimize" their presentation of self, because reduced cues and control of time provide the opportunity to enhance the effort we already put into "selective self-presentation" (p. 19). Walther speculates that these tendencies work together to facilitate the development of the highly intense relationships ("hyperpersonal" he calls them) that many people have experienced online.

This body of work in HCI and CMC emphasizes how we constantly attempt to create human relationships. It documents the pervasiveness of the Eliza effect—of our eagerness to attribute human qualities to agents in our environment. The Turing test, then, simply isolates a routine process of anthropomorphization. Another way of putting this is that the Turing test instantiates the standard philosophical problem of "other minds," as Stevan Harnad has pointed out. This problem posits that because I have the experience of only my own mind (and feelings, intentions, consciousness in general), I cannot know for sure that other people have minds, feelings, intentions, and consciousness. I can only make inductive inferences, or inferences from analogy, based on the evidence of other people's behavior, both linguistic and otherwise (Harnad, 1992). Turing himself recognized this issue, anticipating objections to his proposal based on arguments that machines do not have consciousness. But, he notes, the argument from consciousness leads to solipsism, or the view that "the only way by which one could be sure that a machine thinks is to be the machine and to feel oneself thinking" (Turing, 1950, p. 446). Turing's response to the problem is to urge an assumption of symmetry: The Turing test asks us to be willing to make the same inductive inference for a computer as we do for other people. As Turing put it, "it is usual to have the polite convention that everyone thinks."[19] Mauldin's explanation of Julia's success in the MUD environment is based on the assumption of symmetry: "the players assume everyone else playing is a person and will give the Chatterbot [Julia] the benefit of the doubt until it makes a major gaffe" (§2.1). Harnad points out that if we had a pen pal with whom we carried on a lifetime correspondence, we would naturally infer that she had a mind without ever seeing her in person; the Turing test simply asks us to make the same inference for any unseen interlocutor. Without something like the Turing test, as Jacquette notes, without our willingness to recognize intelligence in verbal interchange, to make the inference to other minds, then "there is no solution to solipsism" (Jacquette, 1993, p. 72).

Thus, there is more at work than polite convention in our willingness to make attributions of intelligence to conversational partners. Such attributions are necessary for us to live in a social world, a world populated by other minds. They are also essential to our ability to converse at all, as H. P. Grice's powerful cooperative principle suggests (Grice, 1989). Grice presents the cooperative principle as a necessary background presumption of rationality that explains how conversational partners can contribute separately to a joint project (even when that project may be adversarial, like cross-examination of a courtroom witness). The cooperative principle enables us to know approximately what kind of statement will (and will not) be a contribution at any given point. It also enables us to make and interpret statements that mean more or other than what they seem to say, that is, sarcasm, metaphor, and a variety of forms of indirection that Grice calls "implicatures." Such statements appear on the literal surface to violate the cooperative principle—they are not relevant, or clear, or brief, or true in any obvious way—all qualities that the cooperative principle entails. But because we assume that our partner also assumes the cooperative principle, we know that such violations should be interpretable. For example, when Julia violates the maxim of relevance by saying "Is the Pope Polish?" we know that we should take our answer to that easy question as the answer to the syntactically parallel question posed to her, "Julia are you a human?" But we also know that this transparent violation is an implicature that the answer is so obvious that the question shouldn't have to be asked. Harder to interpret is Julia's violation of relevance when she responds to the question, "Julia, what are you carrying?" by saying "I follow the Pittsburgh Penguins." But our first (if fleeting) impulse is to work hard to interpret that response as an implicature (perhaps a coy deflection of a subject she doesn't wish to discuss), rather than to take its irrelevance as a bald refusal to respond, or a failure to understand a simple question, or a sheer inability to adopt a joint project. Our preference is not to read irrelevance as a failure of the cooperative principle, for that would require us to judge our interlocutor as irrational, or un-human; this judgment would be an admission that we have misplaced our trust.

In order to locate ourselves in a rational world, we assume that our partners are trying to contribute to an ongoing joint effort to interact meaningfully. We assume, as a first approximation, that the other mind is out there, cooperating and believing in our intention to cooperate. Conversation works only if we are willing to give our interlocutor a generous benefit of the doubt. We are habituated to this presumption: It is more than the politeness that Turing invoked; it is operationally (and rationally, as Grice would have it) essential. No wonder we grant the same presumption to ELIZA and to Julia, even when we know better. The Eliza effect can be seen as simply the necessary result of the cooperative principle. If we are interacting in the form of human conversation, we *need* to posit a rational interlocutor in order to continue, we need to anthropomorphize. This need, and our consequent willingness to construct an interlocutor on the basis of minimal information, may be more important to the results of a Turing test than any anthropomorphic software features that AI programmers might invent. A major exception to our presumption of cooperation occurs when we are playing a role called "judge" of a Turing test, a situation in which the task at hand explicitly calls attention to the need to doubt the cooperative principle at every possible juncture.[20] Thus, a clever judge in an early Turing test conducted at IBM could detect the human being behind the curtain by simply waiting, without initiating any conversation. After about 10 minutes, one of the teleprinters displayed the question, "When does the test begin? Is there anyone out there?" The judge knew immediately that only the human interlocutor would detect lack of cooperation from the other side of the curtain and react impatiently (Ahl, 1983).

Yet we need to locate ourselves in a world that is not only rational, but also social; the work on HCI and CMC illustrates the extent to which we try to do this. The attributions Walther and Nass describe seem to go far beyond the minimal requirements of rationality that Grice presumes, which serve to make interaction merely possible. Grice's emphasis on "talk" as a form of purposive-rational behavior functioning primarily to exchange information or to influence action can lead us to overlook the complexities of the assumptions we must invoke in conversational interaction (Grice, 1989, p. 28). Beyond the purposive and rational, beyond the informative and directive, we seek out and create social relationships, and we conduct our rational business within the direct and constraining context of those relationships. The pursuit of Julia by young men is a crude example of the emotional coloration intrinsic to conversational interaction; the investment of intense trust in ELIZA is another example. Both demonstrate the sometimes overwhelming, or hyperpersonal, role of emotion in rational exchange. We attribute to ELIZA and Julia not just the possession of a mind but also particular qualities of character that elicit our particular responses, including our willingness to cooperate.

To call the process of making attributions *anthropomorphizing*, as we have been doing, misrepresents the fact that we engage in it with interlocutors whose human identity is not in question. For similar reasons, Nass and his colleagues reject this term (Nass et al., 1995a, p. 234; Nass et al., 1994, p. 543), preferring the term *ethopoeia*, the ancient Greek term for the creation of character. This term focuses directly on the constructions we make from the least clue that suggests the presence of another mind; it also reminds us that these attributions are not of rationality alone but of full human character. Our ethopoetic impulse, if it is that, would seem to validate the Turing test not as a test for intelligence or even for the presence of other minds but for our dramatic inclination to respond to evidence of human character. For this reason I believe it's fair to call it a test for rhetorical ethos. To think of what we seek and respond to so avidly as ethos rather than as intelligence is to broaden our conception of human interaction, to account more fully for the kinds of effects reported by Nass and Walther, and to shift the discourse from the traditions of philosophical logic and cognitive science to the traditions of philosophical psychology and rhetoric. Early rhetorical thinking about ethos can, I believe, help us understand why ethopoeia has become so important in our culture of simulation, as well as reminding us that the "imitation game" is not such a new idea. It can also help us understand the full complexity of the attributions we make.

Ethos and Ethopoeia

Ethopoeia was one of the earliest rhetorical techniques that the Greeks named; it denoted the construction—or simulation—of character in discourse, and was particularly apparent in the art of logographers, or speechwriters, who worked usually for those who had to defend themselves in court. A successful logographer, like Lysias, could create in a prepared speech an effective character for the accused, who would actually speak the words (Kennedy, 1963, pp. 92, 136); it was perhaps the very separation of the writer from the speaker that permitted recognition of ethopoeia as a technique. Isocrates, the great teacher of rhetoric, noted that a speaker's character was an important contribution to the persuasive effect of the speech. He asked, "who does not know that words carry greater conviction when spoken by men of good repute than when spoken by men who live under a cloud, and that the argument which is made by a man's life is of more weight than that which is furnished by words?" (Isocrates, 1929, § 278). Aristotle pushed three important steps farther in his *Rhetoric,* making ethos a phenomenon integral to rhetorical action, rather than an epiphenomenon. First, he saw that any rhetor is engaged in ethopoeia, not just logographers writing for someone else. Thus he identified ethos as one of three fundamental sources of persuasion in any rhetorical discourse, the other two being *pathos* (emotion) and *logos* (reasoning) (Aristotle, 1991, I.ii.3). Second, he recognized what Turing and Nass have described, that our interpretation of character is more than our knowledge of someone's prior reputation; it is also, importantly, a response to the ongoing performance itself, made on the fly, in the course of interaction. Character is an effect of delivery and reception as well as of prior actions. Aristotle observes, for example, that the speaker must "construct a view of himself as a certain kind of person" (II.i.2) and that belief comes "from speech that reveals character" (I.viii.6). Third, he understood that ethos can be effective only if ethopoeia is concealed, if the effort of construction is hidden so that character does not seem the product of artifice or simulation: "Authors should compose without being noticed and should seem to speak not artificially but naturally. . . . An example is the success of Theodorus' voice when contrasted with that of other actors, for his seems the voice of the actual character, but the others' those of somebody else" (III.ii.4).

Further, Aristotle tells us that the most decisive influence on persuasion (the "controlling factor" in Kennedy's translation) is the character of the persuader (I.ii.4). His reasoning is that because rhetoric concerns matters on which "there is not exact knowledge but room for doubt," there may be little else to go on. Ethos is thus the default appeal, a kind of presumption: an appropriate, trustworthy character lightens the burden of proof. Here Aristotle captures something of the priority of our response to character that Grice and Nass also described. Because there is such room for doubt, we put our trust in people we perceive to have good sense (*phronēsis*), good moral values (*aretē*), and goodwill toward us (*eunoia*) (II.i.5–7).[21] Thus, a persuasive ethos as Aristotle analyzes it includes a dimension of intelligence (including rationality) as well as of morality and emotional affect. The degree of congruence between these constituents and the conversational capacities described by Bieri is notable (Bieri, 1988). *Phronēsis* is characterized by the wise handling of ignorance and new information, as well as by reflective argument. *Aretē* involves the making of evaluations.[22] *Eunoia* is demonstrated by conversational repair, willingness to judge relevance in context, and recognition of intentionality in others—in fact, the cooperative principle must be a major source of rhetorical goodwill. Even though Julia can't do all these things, people like her and are willing to forgive her apparent lapses of intelligence because she demonstrates values that are similar to those of her interlocutors (this is the basis of much of her humor) and demonstrates conversational goodwill—even when rejecting passes and dodging questions about her identity she seems to respond to the intentions of others and to remain willing to continue the conversation. She has character.

Aristotle understood the three components of ethos to be stable dispositions that are revealed in choice and developed the same way, through imitation and habituation. If character is a relatively stable set of dispositions, and if we can observe choices being made under their influence, Aristotle assumed we can then make good judgments about where to place our trust. But ethos is more complicated than that because it involves ethopoeia—and on both sides of the Turing-test curtain: the constructive efforts made in interpreting character and those made in presenting character to others. We tend, as the CMC research showed, to optimize both our interlocutors and ourselves. Not only do we give an interlocutor the benefit of the doubt, but we also seek the same advantage for ourselves. Ethos cannot be an absolute quality, it must be a representation, and as such it must be interpreted. Aristotle thus underplays the risks of ethopoeia. Plato did not, being alert to myriad possibilities for deception and trickery, as well as being convinced that layers of representation separate us from any certainties. Representation, imitation, *mimesis*—Plato felt that he was surrounded by a culture of simulation, a world in which reality was remote. Words, he held, are only imitations or semblances (*eidola*) of the phenomenal world, which itself is but an imitation of a formal reality. The possibilities for error and deception are great, and the imperfections of the human soul such that both are likely.[23]

To minimize these risks, Plato thought it essential for words to retain a close attachment to the soul of the one who utters them. In his dialogue *Laches*, the distinguished general by that name expresses this ideal relationship, a model for ethos: "When I hear a man discoursing of virtue, or of any sort of wisdom, who is a true man and worthy of his theme, I am delighted beyond measure, and I compare the man and his words, and note the harmony and correspondence of them" (Plato, 1961a, § 188 c–d). The dialogue *Phaedrus* is in part a condemnation of situations where this correspondence does not hold: it ridicules logographers like Lysias, and it also warns us about the dangers posed by writing, which separates words from their author:

> Once a thing is put in writing, the composition . . . drifts all over the place, getting into the hands not only of those who understand it, but equally of those who have no business with it; it doesn't know how to address the right people, and not address the wrong. And when it is ill-treated and unfairly abused it always needs its parent to come to its help, being unable to defend or help itself. (Plato, 1961b, §275d–e)

Living on the cusp between oral and literate culture, Plato distrusted writing, speech making, declamation, recitation, ghost writing—any mode of communication that distances one soul from another and thus increases the possibilities for error or concealment and deception.[24] What Plato valued is an older method of communication that he calls dialectic—close, interpersonal question and answer, conversation in which statements, intentions, and dispositions can be constantly tested and challenged and modified—an idealized communion of minds in which simulation becomes either difficult or unnecessary. What Plato feared is the Eliza effect, or what I have called the ethopoetic impulse, because it interposes simulations between conversants, turning dialectic into rhetoric.

It may be coincidence that simulation has again become a cultural theme, at a time when another great transformation in communication is underway, but it is a suggestive coincidence. Like Plato, Baudrillard contrasts the simulations that surround us with a reality that is not available (although his analysis of the reasons is quite different from Plato's). He deplores a loss but seems to find no remedy for the endless mediation of signs and images that no longer represent but simply replace reality with one simulation after another (Baudrillard, 1994). However, although the new media may challenge our interpretive powers and may overwhelm us with new possibilities, we will gain more by seeing simulation as a natural human capability than we will by attempting to escape or avoid it. Just as it is human nature to make tools and to use language, it is our nature to simulate—to imitate, represent, construct, infer. And insofar as the direct exchange of meanings is impossible, it is our condition that the simulations of language are all we have to create a social world. As the early sophists taught, deception is inherent in the nature of language: it is never what it purports to represent. Because, as Grice shows, we must begin with trust, we are vulnerable. A rational social world is possible only with an irrational, presumptive trust.

Much as Plato was able to hone his portrayal of dialectic (that most basic, parental sort of verbal interaction) by comparing it with writing and presenting it in writing, we learn something about older forms of writing by examining computer-mediated communication. Newer technologies inform and transform our understanding of older ones. It seems that writing, of all sorts, is more like face-to-face conversation than we have realized. We see this both in the ways experienced readers make judgments about the voices they hear in books and in the ways new forms of electronic writing draw character judgments from online readers. Books, after all, are simulations, no less than MUD environments. The ethopoetic "delusion" of the Eliza effect is a necessary (and routine) process of inference and attribution without which literate exchange, as well as electronic, would not be possible.

The revival of rhetoric is made possible—perhaps made necessary— by the new culture of simulation. Rhetoric, after all, is an art of simulation, an art by which we create alternate worlds, alternate selves, alternate modes of belief. But rhetoric is also an art of cooperation, and the corollary of the cooperative principle is that character is a first requirement of communicative interaction. The way we come to have any character at all, in Aristotle's view, is by ethopoetic simulation, since we acquire virtues by imitating virtuous actions. Ethopoeia is essential to character development and to human interaction, and the Turing test is one we engage in every day as we encounter each other's words. We are always playing the imitation game, whether in face-to-face conversation, in the slow medium of print, or the fast world of CMC. We don't necessarily ask whether there's a computer behind the curtain, but we do ask what sort of character is behind the words: One we can trust? One we can learn from? One who is like us or one who is strange and challenging? One we can dominate or one who will seek to dominate us? One who will enthrall or enchant or disgust? In the online world, ethos will continue to be an essential quality of rhetoric, perhaps even more important than ever. If a computer ever does pass an unrestricted Turing test it will be because a programmer has created an algorithm for ethopoeia. And if we hope to be qualified and perceptive judges in the continual Turing test that models our interactions online and off, we must cultivate our own character even as we attend constantly to those around us.

Notes

I am grateful to the International Center for Semiotic and Cognitive Studies of the University of San Marino for the opportunity to present this paper in an earlier form at a conference on The Semiotics of Writing in November 1999. In addition, I wish to thank my colleague David Herman for his astute comments on a later draft.

1. See Turkle's *Life on the Screen* (Turkle, 1997) and Murray's *Hamlet on the Holodeck* (Murray, 1999). The most complete account, from which these excerpts are taken, is by Leonard Foner (Foner, 1993); see also a discussion of the technical design of the software by its developer (Mauldin, 1994a).

2. It has been suggested that Deep Blue's victory over the Turing test was not so much the fact that it won the chess tournament as that Kasparov doubted that he was playing against a machine (Krol, 1999).

3. For some thinking along these lines, see Anson (1999).

4. Mauldin says only that his chatterbot "fools 'average' questioners in the TINYMUD domain for a few minutes" (Mauldin, 1994a, §5.3).

5. Interestingly, she gave a different physical description to Barry: "I'm 5′9″ tall, weigh 140 lbs, with medium-length platinum blond hair and green eyes" (23). Apparently, Mauldin reprogrammed Julia's physical description.

6. Julia's point here is similar to that of the well known *New Yorker* cartoon from 1993, "On the internet, nobody knows you're a dog."

7. I adopt the conventional capitalization of these names; Julia's name has not been subject to this convention, possibly because of her naturalistic appearance in MUD environments.

8. The restrictions are usually to a specific conversational domain, like pets, or hockey; there are also time limits. Computer chess is another type of restricted Turing test.

9. In the January 2000 test, no computer was taken as a human, and the judges correctly identified both humans and computers 91% of the time after 5 minutes, leading the Dartmouth conference organizers to announce on their Web site, "Turing's Prediction Disconfirmed" (http://www.dartmouth.edu/~phil/events/prize.html).

10. Mauldin has not had an entry since 1995. He went on to found Lycos, Inc., the internet search engine, and to serve as managing director of Virtual Personalities, Inc., a company dedicated to creating self-animated computer-generated human characters.

11. For summaries of these arguments see Karelis (1986), Michie (1993), Moor (1976), and Shieber (1994).

12. See also Bieri (1988) for this argument and Jacquette (1993) for a refutation of French.

13. Turkle distinguishes the more general Eliza effect from the "Julia effect," which is our willingness to use the language of human mental life to describe what a program is doing: we say it "thinks," it "knows," it "intends" (Turkle, 1997, p. 101).

14. Laurel also argues that such agents must pass a kind of "anti-Turing test" because to be effective they must be more predictable and less complex than real people (1997, p. 216). Anthropomorphism, she believes, should serve more as a metaphor than as a design blueprint.

15. See Nass's discussion of anthropo*centr*ism, which discusses functions that people believe should *not* be delegated to computers (Nass, Lombard, Henriksen, & Steuer, 1995b).

16. In their book, Reeves and Nass extend this paradigm to all media, not just computers, and rename their paradigm the "media equation," indicating that "media equal real life" (1996, p. 5). In a review of much of the work by Nass as well as other researchers, Lombard and Ditton (1997) use the term "presence" to denote the widespread and widely documented "illusion that a mediated experience is not mediated." They note that this illusion can occur either if the medium seems to disappear or if it seems to be transformed into a social space.

17. There's a fair amount of evidence that gender is one feature that people are unwilling to fill in for themselves or to leave as an open question (Danet, 1998; Wallace, 1999). Thus, Mauldin's gendering of Julia was a shrewd design decision.

18. Godwin's discussion of the power of text compared with supposedly richer media is perceptive. He suggests that the lack of distracting visual information can produce mental and emotional intimacy, citing as evidence the power of literary art (Godwin, 1994).

19. Stanford computer scientist John McCarthy has made a similar argument from symmetry, that the ascription of beliefs, consciousness, etc., to a machine "is legitimate when such an ascription expresses the same information about the machine that it expresses about a person" (McCarthy, 1979).

20. This is the form of the Turing test that Collins advocates, as the *"ultimate engineering question:* 'Could a machine pass a Turing Test not only in the absence of cooperation but while being interrogated by someone trained to detect machines'?" (Collins, 1990, p. 191). However, this engineering-oriented test defeats Collins' own interest in the Turing test as "a test of the capacity of a machine to mimic the interactions of a human being" (p. 183). Denying the machine the interactional necessities of cooperation and trust defeats the purpose of the test in this sense.

21. Aristotle's analysis here is close to the views of other ancient authors, according to Grimaldi, who names Thucydides and Plato (Grimaldi, 1988, p. 9).

22. Some differences should also be noted here. Aristotle tends to see phronēsis and aretē, particularly, as absolute, rather than interactional qualities; thus for him aretē is the holding of particular values, not so much the understanding of their sources and applications.

23. Plato might be interested in the fact that 25 years of research on our abilities to detect deception shows that we are not very good at it, lie detection rates being only about 55–60% (Feeley & Young, 1998).

24. See Swearingen's discussion of the relation between Plato's criticisms and the advent of widespread literacy (Swearingen, 1991, ch.2).

References

Ahl, D. H. (1983). The Turing test: An historical perspective. *Creative Computing, 9,* 156, 161.

Anson, C. M. (1999). Distant voices: Teaching and writing in a culture of technology. *College English, 61,* 261–280.

Aristotle (1991). *On rhetoric: A theory of civic discourse* (George A. Kennedy, Trans.). New York: Oxford University Press.

Baudrillard, J. (1994). *Simulacra and simulation* (Sheila Faria Glaser, Trans.). Ann Arbor, MI: University of Michigan Press.

Bieri, P. (1988). Thinking machines: Some reflections on the Turing test. *Poetics Today, 9*, 163–186.

Block, N. (1995). *The mind as the software of the brain*. MIT Press. Available: http://www.nyu.edu/gsas/dept/philo/faculty/black/papers/msb.html [1999, 31 October].

Collins, H. M. (1990). *Artificial experts: Social knowledge and intelligent machines*. Cambridge, MA: MIT Press.

Danet, B. (1998). Text as mask: Gender, play, and performance on the internet. In S. G. Jones (Ed.), *Cybersociety 2.0: Revisiting computer-mediated communication and community* (pp. 129–158). Thousand Oaks, CA: Sage Publications.

Feeley, T. H., & Young, M. J. (1998). Humans as lie detectors: Some more second thoughts. *Communication Quarterly, 46*, 109–126.

Flood, G. (1996, 13 January). If only they could think: Should the Turing test be blamed for the ills that beset artificial intelligence? *New Scientist, 32*.

Foner, L. (1993, May). *What's an agent, anyway? A sociological case study* [PDF file]. Agents Group, MIT Media Lab. Available: http://foner.www.media.mit.edu/people/foner/agents.html [1999, 27 October].

French, R. M. (1990). Subcognition and the limits of the Turing test. *Mind, 99*, 53–65.

Friedman, B., & Kahn, P. H., Jr. (1997). Human agency and responsible computing: Implications for computer system design. In B. Friedman (Ed.), *Human values and the design of computer technology* (pp. 221–235). Cambridge: Cambridge University Press.

Godwin, M. (1994). *ASCII is too intimate* [Web site]. *Wired* Archive. Available: http://wired.lycos.com/wired/archive/2.04/idees.fortes1_pr.html [1999, 16 December].

Grice, H. P. (1989). *Studies in the way of words*. Cambridge, MA: Harvard University Press.

Grimaldi, W. M. A., S.J. (1988). *Aristotle*, Rhetoric II: *A commentary*. New York: Fordham University Press.

Harnad, S. (1992). The Turing test is not a trick: Turing indistinguishability is a scientific criterion. *SIGART Bulletin, 3*, 9–10.

Isocrates (1929). Antidosis, *Works* (Vol. 2, pp. 184–365). Cambridge, MA: Harvard University Press.

Jacquette, D. (1993). Who's afraid of the Turing test? *Behavior and Philosophy, 21*, 63–74.

Karelis, C. (1986). Reflections on the Turing test. *Journal for the Theory of Social Behaviour, 16*, 161–172.

Kennedy, G. A. (1963). *The art of persuasion in Greece*. Princeton, NJ: Princeton University Press.

Kolb, D. (1994). Socrates in the labyrinth. In G. P. Landow (Ed.), *Hyper/text/theory* (pp. 323–344). Baltimore, MD: Johns Hopkins University Press.

Krol, M. (1999). Have we witnessed a real-life Turing test? *Computer, 332*, 27–30.

Landow, G. P. (1997). *Hypertext 2.0: The convergence of contemporary critical theory and technology*. Baltimore, MD: Johns Hopkins University Press.

Laurel, B. (1997). Interface agents: Metaphors with character. In B. Friedman (Ed.), *Human values and the design of computer technology* (pp. 207–219). Cambridge: Cambridge University Press.

Leonard, A. (1997). *Bots: The origin of new species*. San Francisco: HardWired.

Lester, J. C., Converse, S. A., Kahler, S. E., Barlow, S. T., Stone, B. A., & Bhogal, R. S. (1997). *The persona effect: Affective impact of animated pedagogical agents*. Paper presented at the CHI '97: Human Factors in Computing Systems, Atlanta, GA.

Loebner, H. (1999, 26 October 1999). *Home page of the Loebner Prize—"The First Turing*

Test" [Web site]. Available: http://www.loebner.net/Prizef/loebner-prize.html [1999, 29 October].

Lombard, M., & Ditton, T. (1997). At the heart of it all: The concept of presence. *Journal of Computer-Mediated Communication, 3,* available: http://www.ascusc.org/jcmc/vol3/issue2/lombard.html [1999, 1998 November].

Mauldin, M. L. (1994a, 15 March 1994). *Chatterbots, tinymuds, and the Turing test: Entering the Loebner prize competition* [Web site]. Available: http://www.fuzine.com/mlm/aaai94.html [1999, 26 October].

Mauldin, M. L. (1994b, 26 November 1997). *Julia's home page* [Web site]. Available: http://www.fuzine.com/mlm/julia.html [1999, 29 October].

McCarthy, J. (1979, 8 June 1999). *Ascribing mental qualities to machines* [Web site]. Available: http://www-formal.stanford.edu/jmc/ascribing/ascribing.html [1999, 27 October].

Michie, D. (1993). Turing's test and conscious thought. *Artificial Intelligence, 60,* 1–22.

Moor, J. H. (1976). An analysis of the Turing test. *Philosophical Studies, 30,* 249–257.

Murray, J. H. (1999). *Hamlet on the holodeck: The future of narrative in cyberspace.* Cambridge, MA: MIT Press.

Nass, C., Moon, Y., Fogg, B., Reeves, B., & Dryer, D. C. (1995a). Can computer personalities be human personalities? *International Journal of Human–Computer Studies, 43,* 223–239.

Nass, C., Steuer, J., Henriksen, L., & Dryer, D. C. (1994). Machines, social attributions, and ethopoeia: Performance assessments of computers subsequent to "self-" or "other-" evaluations. *International Journal of Human–Computer Studies, 40,* 543–559.

Nass, C. I., Lombard, M., Henriksen, L., & Steuer, J. (1995b). Anthropocentrism and computers. *Behaviour and Information Technology, 14,* 229–238.

Nass, C. I., Moon, Y., Morkes, J., Kim, E.-Y., & Fogg, B. J. (1997). Computers are social actors: A review of current research. In B. Friedman (Ed.), *Human values and the design of computer technology* (pp. 136–162). Cambridge: Cambridge University Press.

Plato. (1961a). Laches. In E. Hamilton & H. Cairns (Eds.), *The collected dialogues* (pp. 123–144). Princeton, NJ: Princeton University Press.

Plato. (1961b). Phaedrus. In E. Hamilton & H. Cairns (Eds.), *The collected dialogues* (pp. 475–525). Princeton, NJ: Princeton University Press.

Reeves, B., & Nass, C. (1996). *The media equation: How people treat computers, television, and new media like real people and places.* Cambridge: Cambridge University Press.

Schneiderman, B. (1987). *Designing the user interface: Strategies for effective human–computer interaction.* Reading, MA: Addison-Wesley.

Searle, J. (1984). *Minds, brains, and science.* Cambridge, MA: Harvard University Press.

Seife, C. (1999, 30 January). No contest: Computers still lack the human touch. *New Scientist, 161,* 9.

Shanon, B. (1989). A simple comment regarding the Turing test. *Journal for the Theory of Social Behaviour, 19,* 249–256.

Shieber, S. M. (1994). Lessons from a restricted Turing test. *Communications of the ACM, 37,* 70–78.

Slatin, J. M. (1990). Reading hypertext: Order and coherence in a new medium. *College English, 52,* 870–883.

Swearingen, C. J. (1991). *Rhetoric and irony: Western literacy and western lies.* New York: Oxford University Press.

Turing, A. M. (1950). Computing machinery and intelligence. *Mind, 59,* 433–460.

Turkle, S. (1997). *Life on the screen: Identity in the age of the internet.* New York: Touchstone.

Wallace, P. (1999). *The psychology of the internet*. Cambridge: Cambridge University Press.

Walther, J. B. (1996). Computer-mediated communication: Impersonal, interpersonal, and hyperpersonal interaction. *Communication Research, 23*, 3–43.

Weizenbaum, J. (1976). *Computer power and human reason: From judgment to calculation*. San Francisco: W. H. Freeman.

Whitby, B. (1997). *Why the Turing test is AI's biggest blind alley* [Web site]. Available: http://www.cogs.susx.ac.uk/users/blayw/tt.html [1999, 31 October].

4

The Space for Rhetoric
in Everyday Life

John Ackerman

All we need to do is simply to open our eyes, to leave the dark world of metaphysics and the false depths of the 'inner life' behind, and we will discover the immense human wealth that the humblest facts of everyday life contain.

Henri Lefebvre: Critique of Everyday Life, Volume 1 *(1991a, p. 132)*

In *The Production of Space*, Henri Lefebvre surveys philosophy, mathematics, and linguistics to conclude that a "gap" has been forged over the last three hundred years between the "mental" and "social space wherein language becomes practice" (1991b, p. 5). His central project in this work is to outline a "unifying" theory of practice to bridge this gap, and to reclaim the "collective subject"—the people along with their activities and the material circumstances—as these have the collective power to regenerate everyday life in all its vitality and subvert the subjugating power of mass culture. Mass culture is all that is systematic and commercial in the production of space: any public venue—malls, parks, neighborhoods, industrial areas—reflects the production of social space and, therefore, the dominant values of its culture. However, these spaces, which are common to us all, can generate historical and material reflection and guide instrumental reform: Lefebvre's goal is to remake a "code at once architectural, urbanistic and political, constituting a language common to country people and townspeople, to the authorities and to artists—a code which allow[s] space not only to be 'read' but also to be constructed" (p. 7).

Such a semiotic and cultural "code" reaches far beyond this chapter, but Lefebvre's writings on the spaces of everyday life are important to rhetorical studies because they imply that rhetorical situations have spatial dimensions, and that rhetorical agency includes the production and maintenance of social space. Lefebvre insists that we view space as social, and that it can be measured multi-dimensionally according to three basic facts: "Every language is located in space. Every discourse says something about space (places or sets of places); and every discourse is emitted from a space" (p. 132). All the places we live, play, and work can be read as signs signifying cultural values and dominant practices (1991b, pp. 38–39). If he is correct, then analyses of social space may reveal material contexts for other critical indices such as expertise, patriarchy, class, or race (cf. Dressman, 1997). That is, everyone walks, however unequally, within social geographies (Soja, 1993) that complicate institutions and the discourses that maintain them; these geographies will implicate literacy specialists such as teachers and researchers as much as their students and participants. Lefebvre, as we will see, urges us to find the extraordinary in the ordinary moments and places of everyday life, and to do this, we must approach spatial analysis of an interplay of signs and representations. Social space, for Lefebvre, is understood through its commodification and through the documents and images that produce and represent a given locale.

As I show in this chapter, conceptualizing space as sign presents an opportunity for specialists in rhetoric, composition, and literacy: Everyday life presents us with venues beyond the tropes and structures of academic life, and allows us to recommit ourselves to a study of public discourse (Halloran, 1993) and the spaces that condition it. We rhetoricians[1] have much to bring to this exercise because of our training with mental and discursive space, that is, our skills in reading for cognitive and social history. However, in response to rhetoric's academic legacy that privileges texts over spaces and schools over cities, my central concern in this chapter is to explore what we must do to extend our fluency in rhetorical situations and agency in order to address the historical and material attributes of social space and everyday life.

My argument is that the pressure of everyday life as a spatial concept will necessarily transform our imagination and our involvement in rhetorical studies. I begin by synthesizing the arguments of Lefebvre to underscore the role of material space in both daily life and historical reflection. By analyzing social space, we gather new elements and momentum for our rhetorical assessments. I explicate space, initially with Lefebvre's assistance, as a historical and material dialectic,[2] rendering social space as "both a field of action . . . and a basis of action . . . at once a collection of materials . . . and an ensemble of *materiel* (. . . the procedures necessary to make efficient use . . .)" (Lefebvre, 1991b, p. 191; italics, parentheses in original). Social space will then be approached as a site for analysis, a process of location, definition, and interpretation. The act of site analysis implicates the designer and examiner through their exercise of selection and representation, suggestive of the relationship between sign, object, and interpretant that Witte (1992; see Medway, 1996) has explicated. Because the object in question in a site analysis is invariably a lived space, the analyst is implicated because such spaces do not exist a priori of their designation.

Because sites cannot be adequately understood as inert matter, I gather data in various forms and dimensions to illustrate the rhetorical properties available in their material circumstances. Sites are both technically and conceptually constructed; they operate as both contexts for discourse, and signs within discourses; and they are the material product of representational practices that may be redirected and reformed. Finally, I argue that social space is eminently the concern of rhetoricians because our analyses can reveal the tools and discourses that are used to construct locations where people work and play. Rhetorical agency—in social space—depends on the strategic application of a range of representational devices, whether the goal is to continue a given spatial tradition or to sponsor a counter-discourse via a counter-site. A rhetoric of everyday life will address social space because those spaces are the result of someone's design and rendering.

Lefebvre's Method: From Everyday Life to Social Space

Lefebvre's writing about everyday life and social space seeks to return the reader to an extant vitality in human existence.[3] Twenty-four years after writing *The Critique of Everyday Life, Volume 1* (1991a), Lefebvre (1971) identified this work as one that "bears the marks of prevailing circumstances" associated with the period of reconstruction in France after

World War II, when the order of the hour was to "build a new society" (p. 30). In response to what he perceived as the "americanization" of France and Europe, he expressed nostalgia for a pre-urban life when and where nature, space, activity, and the life of the mind were more closely entwined. In the chapter, "Notes Written One Sunday in the French Countryside" (1991a), Lefebvre recalls the festival in the rural life of antiquity that celebrated a culture where family, sustenance, economy, and values were interconnected: "everyday life, ancient gestures, rituals as old as time itself, continue unchanged—except for the fact that this life has been stripped of its beauty" (p. 213).

With such recollections, Lefebvre launches a historical and material dialectic that, over the course of his writing, aims to revitalize the practice of everyday life. To reclaim what has been lost and thereby promote human potential, Lefebvre insists upon a double perspective regarding change across centuries and across a lifetime (his specific reference point is the French restoration):

What has changed after roughly half a century? That the subject has become blurred is news to no one; it has lost its outline, it doesn't well up or flow any longer, and with it the characters, roles, persons have slid into the background. Now it is the object that plays the lead . . . as a thing, almost a pure form. (1971, p. 7)

Everyday life as a dialectical method, then, addresses two related projects. The first is the recognition of material change in society over time: As Lefebvre sees it, over the last 50 years, the subject of everyday life has become blurred through numbing repetitions that are a result of the commodification of daily living: "the misery of everyday life, its tedious tasks, humiliations reflected in the lives of the working class and especially women, upon which the conditions of everyday life bear heaviest" (p. 35). Lefebvre attributes all this to the failures of capitalism, resulting in an overwhelming sense of alienation from what he considers are the core practices of everyday life. Modernity confuses ("mystifies") the origins and sources of everyday life because life itself has become a regular, repetitious product in "pure form."

The second dialectic assumes historical reflection, but addresses the relative status of everyday life as it operates temporally and spatially in modernity. We look backward, then, to improve our acuity in recognizing the "power of everyday life, its continuity, the permanence of life rooted in the soil, the adaptation of the body, time, space, desire" (p. 35), in short, to reclaim lost codes in service of spatial agency in the everyday. Lefebvre supports any effort to defeat the repetitious consumption and the debilitating structures in modern life, any discovery of the "power concealed in everyday life's apparent banality" (p. 37).

> Everyday life, in a sense residual, is defined by 'what is left over' after all distinct superior, specialized structured activities have been singled out by analysis, must be defined as a totality. Considered in their specialization and their technicality, superior activities leave a 'technical vacuum' between one another which is filled up by everyday life. Everyday life is profoundly related to *all* activities, and encompasses them with all their differences and their conflicts; it is their meeting place, their bond, their common ground. (1991a, p. 97; emphasis in original)

Lefebvre encourages both rhetoricians and citizens alike to recognize the "spaces between," literally the spaces between one professional domain and another, or one constituency and another, or the space created if layers of "specialized structures" could be pealed away. Residual life is far from depleted; rather it is the "substance of everyday life—'human raw material' in its simplicity and richness—pierc[ing] through all alienation and establish[ing] 'disalienation'" (p. 97) which is the conscious, embodied effort to simultaneously "read" and "construct" social space.

This 'disalienation' is an important byproduct of historical and material dialectics, but this project requires a reflective turn as part of his unifying theory. What we need is a "critical attitude . . . we have to step back and get it into perspective. Critical distancing, debating, and collating go together . . . a critical analysis of everyday life must include an ideological analysis and, especially, an incessant self analysis" (p. 27). Lefebvre's method rejects disembodied philosophy, exemplified in the writings of linguists and theorists such as Chomsky, Foucault, Kristeva, and Derrida, who have produced a "circular logic" whereby "the philosophical notion of space is fetishized and the mental realm comes to envelop the social and physical ones" (1991b, p. 5). Lefebvre reprimands these theorists for not addressing the "gap" between mental and social space and for not addressing the speaking subject, a person, place, and thing understood through material circumstance (p. 7).

Social space, then, is proposed as a living laboratory for finding and naming the vitality of everyday life and those structures that oppress it. In *The Production of Space* (1991b), he delineates three basic dimensions of social space.

Dimension 1: Spatial Practice

The first is "spatial practice" itself (p. 38f.), which is the societal performance of space and its residue. We can understand this dialectic now as the application of his earlier *Critique of Everyday Life, Volume 1* (1991a/1946) on a spatial and material plane. Here, Lefebvre still attacks the object/subject dichotomy in everyday life, but locates it in constructed and lived environments:

What is spatial practice under neocapitalism? It embodies a close association, within perceived space, between daily reality (daily routine) and urban reality (the routes and networks which link up the places set aside for work, "private life and leisure"). This association is a paradoxical one, because it includes the most extreme separation between the places it links together. The specific spatial competence and performance of every society member can only be evaluated empirically. "Modern" spatial practice might thus be defined—to take an extreme but significant case—by the daily life of a tenant in a government-subsidized high-rise housing project. (1991b, p. 38)

Dimension 2: The Effects of Representation

Spatial practice, for Lefebvre, is revealed through the study of spatial ordering and the instruments that maintain (or defeat) that order. This is why his second dimension of social space is its representation through the instruments and documents of "scientists, planners, urbanists, technocratic subdividers and social engineers" (p. 38); we can add the instruments of officials and managers—anyone who uses print, writing, drawings, and other depictions of social space, and is thereby implicated in a process of alienation because these tools authorize the separation of social spaces. Representational processes, including writing, abstract space: When designers map out and plan a subdivision, for example, they outline the houses that eventually populate the design, and subsequently shape the lives of those who occupy the subdivision.

Dimension 3: Material Space as Signifier of Cultural Value

Lefebvre's third dimension to social space inverts the temporal progression from design practices to quality of life by assuming that the material space—homes, neighborhoods, and urban spaces—functions as a spatial signifier of cultural values.

Lefebvre's methodology suggests that 'rhetorical agency' will appear through the disguises and ruses of Charlie Chaplin's "tramp" (1991a, p. 12 f.), who was noteworthy to Lefebvre for his struggles to subvert the forms and representations of modern life. The tramp's life is neither naïve nor inconsequential; it is *Chaplinesque,* and it presumes a life of critical involvement and critical work to recognize and reinvent everyday life based on "thought-action" (p. 35), a method accessible to the masses. Lefebvre assigns this critical action to the protagonist in the drama of everyday life. "Action and action alone can bring this healthiness and this elementary equilibrium, this ability to grasp life in its varied aspects, without being deliberately gloomy or abstractly optimistic" (p. 186). Lefebvre's dialectical methods pit action against metaphysical inaction, reflecting both material circumstance and historical identity, and it is democratic to the degree that spatial praxis is no longer the exclusive domain of the specialist. As those who teach writing must assume, art and *techne* are accessible to those who study and engage them, and the identity of the tramp belongs to anyone who wisely and strategically equates the everyday with life itself.

Lefebvre's method, as I construe it here, anchors a critique of everyday life in spatial practice and can assist the rhetorician to reframe the study and maintenance of public discourse. First, Lefebvre's method pits history against material context so that physical locations are viewed through their evolution: before the mini-mall was a grocery, before the grocery was community market, before the market place was a traffic-way. His writing may seem nostalgic, an effort to reclaim a more coherent and connected past, but, as I see it, this recollection provides a post-disciplinary perspective on the everyday. Not only can the practice of everyday life appear as "thought-action" and engage a populace in a reassessment of specializing knowledge; it also constitutes a post-disciplinary force to urge a confederation of the urban with the discursive, the material with the rhetorical, and so on. And finally, though Lefebvre remains suspicious of writing as a modern technology and, therefore, as a powerful instrument in ordering space, his dialectical methods may render print literacy more powerful, in a sense, simply because we can understand it within the symbolic context of its use. If such a unifying theory across physical, mental, and social fields is possible, then print literacy and those who sponsor it gain an important but strategically different role.

Site/Situation

Where do we begin if we assume that everyday life contains an "immensity of human wealth" in the "humblest" of spaces and practices, but the tools of inquiry we use are charged with breaching mental and social spaces? In this section, I want to focus and delineate spatial analysis by approaching sites as technical and conceptual problems. I propose sites as a place and way to begin a spatial study of everyday life because a site, like a text, can be viewed both structurally and sociohistorically. The structural elements of a site (its structures, materials, dimensions, proximities) vary, of course, depending upon whether the site is geographical (from lot to city block to region) or within a building or physical structure. For example, a building site in a subdivision consists of its dimensions, soil and rock composition, easements and setbacks, and connections to utilities, but the house that sits upon that site is known structurally by a different set of elements (for example, square footage, rooms, 'skins,' windows, trim, et cetera): the features and dimensions of one site will always implicate another.

In their survey of modern architectural practice, Conway & Roenish (1994) differentiate sites as primary and secondary sources of information that substantiate a building plan: primary sources are "contemporary with the building or period" (p. 170) and consist of surveys, plans, descriptions, and legislations; whereas secondary sources are more interpretive and associative; they are the purview of critics, historians, and writers but are no less relevant to design. The concept of sites and their analyses in the architectural practice that I studied (Ackerman & Oates, 1996) served these two basic purposes within the training and socialization of architects. For the novice architect, site selection was less important because sites were predetermined by economics or for their instructional interest to the studio, but site analysis was presented as a pivotal exercise in cataloging and prioritizing the (primary) details germane to a design project. Structural models or "solutions" came from the ground (or site) up, and students learned that in professional practice building programming began with detailed site analyses that were often subcontracted because of the necessary collection of technical data. Site analysis was a careful, technical operation—little was left open to interpretation; the codification of a site was assigned to a specialist to guarantee that the data were complete, sorted and reported according to legal codes, and presented in such a way as to both augment design and support the economic proposal. Sites in professional practice were importantly (and merely) an exacting determination of the footprint of the virtual building.

However, for the novice architect, site analyses were also taught as "secondary" sources of information, and although they were part of a studio learning experience or the preliminary search for a building, they presented opportunities for critical review. The qualities of the site itself invited the designer to commune with history, identification, and proximity. Even the most ordinary structure or space could be judged for its visual impact on a neighborhood or region and whether it complemented or competed with the local historical milieu. The architect and critic C. Burns (1991) describes sites and their analyses as an exercise in reflexivity, confounded by language as much as by the physical elements attributed to a portion of land. Burns points out the number of conflicting terms associated with natural and built space such as *lot*, *plot*, *region*, and *location*, with each word representing a slightly different legal, physical, and philosophical slant on a site and illustrating a dependence on linguistic and spatial cues. Sites are critically interesting because of the

elastic nature of the breadth and scale of sites semantically, experientially, and temporally. . . . Every site is a unique intersection of land, climate, production, and circulation . . . already constructed by its specific circumstances . . . an artefact of human work that can neither be completed or abandoned. (pp. 163–165)

Burns's treatment of material and discursive sites echoes Foucault (1986) in the sense that sites provide for the architect the historical exercise of "emplacement," or the designation of sites through violence and through natural compatibility. Sites today are technical problems that reveal social values, a "calculation in the memory of the machine." Because sites are concrete problems of proportions and proximities, of "storage, circulation, marking and classification," they require a study of propinquity, or the relation and proximity of one site to another (pp. 22–23).

Sites within everyday life are provocative through their revelation of primary and secondary sources of information, but also because they defy preordained categories. Everyday sites are ordinary, often uncharted, typically accessible and, therefore, attractive for study as sociological phenomena. The sociologist, William H. Whyte, studied and wrote about everyday sites throughout his career, concentrating first on organizational cultures (1956), urban landscapes (1968), and then on the *Social Life of*

Small Urban Spaces (1980). In this latter work, he wrote to capture "the behavior of ordinary people on city streets—their rituals in street en-counters" (p. 8). One of Whyte's methods, besides a good bit of walking, was a site analysis that consisted of noting the demography and behavior of people who frequented ordinary places. Sites in New York City, for ex-ample, where represented by a "cumulative sighting map" (Cook, 2000, p. 23). Following is an example of Whyte's methods, a map of activity on the front steps of the New York Public Library, observed between 12:30 P.M. and 1:30 P.M. for four consecutive days.[4] The numbered accounts cor-respond with key spaces on the steps of the library and the curb, which are crudely drawn as parallel lines. Clearly, the building, no matter how grand, was less important than the entrance to it and the activity around it.

I chose this analyzed site because it was external, a public space, a crossroads on an urban map, and because the analysis was hand drawn rather than computer-generated or otherwise technologically enhanced.

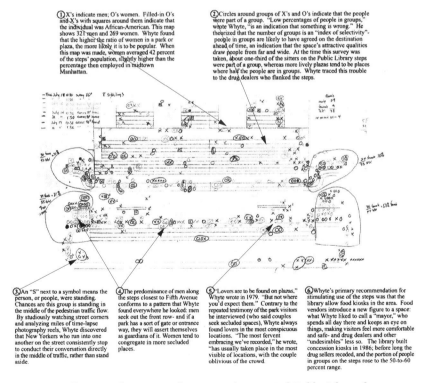

① X's indicate men; O's women. Filled-in O's and X's with squares around them indicate that the individual was African-American. This map shows 321 men and 269 women. Whyte found that the higher the ratio of women in a park or plaza, the more likely it is to be popular. When this map was made, women averaged 42 percent of the steps' population, slightly higher than the percentage then employed in midtown Manhattan.

② Circles around groups of X's and O's indicate that the people were part of a group. "Low percentages of people in groups," wrote Whyte, "is an indication that something is wrong." He theorized that the number of groups is an "index of selectivity"-people in groups are likely to have agreed on the destination ahead of time, an indication that the space's attractive qualities draw people from far and wide. At the time this survey was taken, about one-third of the sitters on the Public Library steps were part of a group, whereas more lively plazas tend to be places where half the people are in groups. Whyte traced this trouble to the drug dealers who flanked the steps.

③ An "S" next to a symbol means the person, or people, were standing. Chances are this group is standing in the middle of the pedestrian traffic flow. By studiously watching street corners and analyzing miles of time-lapse photography reels, Whyte discovered that New Yorkers who run into one another on the street consistently stop to conduct their conversation directly in the middle of traffic, rather than stand aside.

④ The predominance of men along the steps closest to Fifth Avenue conforms to a pattern that Whyte found everywhere he looked: men seek out the front row- and if a park has a sort of gate or entrance way, they will assert themselves as guardians of it. Women tend to congregate in more secluded places.

⑤ "Lovers are to be found on plazas," Whyte wrote in 1979. "But not where you'd expect them." Contrary to the repeated testimony of the park visitors he interviewed (who said couples seek secluded spaces), Whyte always found lovers in the most conspicuous locations. "The most fervent embracing we've recorded," he wrote, "has usually taken place in the most visible of locations, with the couple oblivious of the crowd.

⑥ Whyte's primary recommendation for stimulating use of the steps was that the library allow food kiosks in the area. Food vendors introduce a new figure to a space: what Whyte liked to call a "mayor," who spends all day there and keeps an eye on things, making visitors feel more comfortable and safe- and drug dealers and other "undesirables" less so. The library built concession kiosks in 1986; before long the drug sellers receded, and the portion of people in groups on the steps rose to the 50-to-60 percent range.

Figure 1.   William H. Whyte's map of activity on the New York Public Library front steps.

Consequently, it bears the markings of the originator, the limits of a given technology (see Sullivan & Porter, 1999), and how that technology is itself a practice, this one suggestive of frantic efforts to look up and down to capture the teeming activity on the steps and front porch of a famous library. This site could have been construed as a formal, physical site, a monumental structure that symbolizes and functions as a repository for cultural tradition and knowledge. It could have been catalogued and mapped as one library within a system of repositories, as one building within a genre, or as one prime achievement within an architect's oeuvre. Whyte chose instead to minimize the grandeur of the monument and to highlight patterns of activity around it. As Cook (2000) argues, Whyte's simple and powerful method locates and counts frequencies of human activity to illustrate a few of the class, gender, and racially differentiated, activities that identify and normalize this tiny, noisy corner of a major city.

Sites inside a building could bear these same markings, but rooms within a structure are inherently unique because they are the part within the whole, the point within a matrix, a three-dimensional space apart. Kitchens are good examples of internal sites that have discursive capacity. The kitchen is the center of activity in many family homes, and through activities over time, they represent domesticity, security, and continuity for the modern family; for women they symbolize a place within a patriarchal order. Kitchens as sites can be read historically as one of the premier private sites that have been transformed through the economic changes of mass culture. With the advent of labor saving devices and the rise of (so-called) home economics, kitchens for lower and middle class women have shifted away from being sites for manual labor to sites of domestic harmony through the coincidence of "professional" kitchens and second careers. As Henderson (1996) points out, the modernization of the kitchen, physically separated from the public work and living space of the nineteenth century, diminished the stature of women as traditional homemakers. The Frankfurt kitchen, designed in the 1920s, was the first kitchen design to sponsor scientific efficiency in food preparation and service. Figure 2 is a floor plan for the Frankfurt kitchen, which is the forerunner of galley kitchens of today with close proximity to the dinner table.

Kitchens as private family sites have become increasingly more public through integrated and open floor plans; the roles that kitchens serve in contemporary and popular culture resist rigid divisions of labor by gender. However, we still think of kitchens as sites where June Cleaver and the

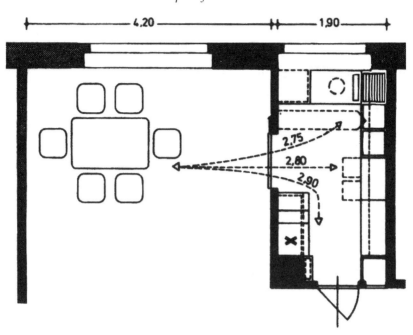

Figure 2. Floor plan for the Frankfurt kitchen.

Frugal Gourmet reign partly because these places have evolved from private to scientific and then to malleable, open spaces mediated by need or desire in the collective consciousness of popular culture (Pascucci, 1997). Kitchens signify modern culture and food preparation as a commodity, but they have the capacity to engender discourses that are more subtle and resistant in nature than a construct mediated by the nature of the modern family. Oates (1999) studied the intersections of school and home literacy, and the kitchen was a particularly fertile site in which to find and record the literacy narratives of his participants, and to find as well narratives of assimilation and resistance. In Oates's case study research, women told stories in the sanctuary of the family kitchen and cataloged their lives as women, feminists, or as orthodox believers. One participant presented the kitchen as a place of convergence, a place to digest secular themes from the day's literature class and to assimilate these themes with lessons from a seminary class. Another participant presented the kitchen as the preferred site to read her older sister's essays from school and to discuss them with her mother, who was a social worker and had been excommunicated from the Church. Where else would one go for matriarchal security to share the literacy of a women's studies classroom in a predominantly patriarchal community?

In both examples—the front steps of an urban library and the family kitchen—sites are contexts, occasions, and ingredients for discourse. They are artifacts of the construction of spatial genres, and as signs they participate in semiotics that are easily overlooked. We cannot say that external and internal spaces *make* the discourses of urbanity or domesticity, or *enact* private moments of social resistance, but the textures of such language and activity would not exist apart from a specific location. Lefebvre's three-part premise states: "Every language is located in space. Every discourse says something about space (places or sets of places); and every discourse is emitted from a space" (1991a, p. 132). Thus, sites may be as integral to our understanding of literacy practices as other rhetorical and linguistic properties of the utterance.

Not only are sites basic to the methodology of literacy narratives drawn from everyday life; in addition, the places where such stories are told and the places that shape these "literacy plots" (Brandt, 1995) are key to their rhetorical contexts. Within the spaces of the everyday, as well as the language representing these spaces and emanating from them, sites and site analyses add a physical dimension to Bitzer's (1963) concept of "rhetorical situation." This concept has operated relatively untouched in modern rhetorical practice, even though the material world as changed dramatically from that of 1963. With an academic bias, rhetorical practice tends to address linguistic, not material activity and circumstance, no matter how social or historical the intent. Certainly, authors and subjects are "located," but even in this so-called social era of rhetoric, the tendency is to think of authorship as personal, historical, and discursive. Within everyday life and social practice, however, the particulars of the modern rhetorical situation, that is, the conditions that necessitate discourse with the constituent parts of audience, exigency, and constraints (cf. Bitzer) will also include spatial dimensions. Thus, site and space operate with audience, exigency, and constraint—or they are at least accepted as possible "actants"—within a system of signs, to borrow a disembodied but altogether material notion of the author or agent at work within a semiotic field and systematic activity (Myers, 1996).

Sites as Urban Spaces

Just as a single text is a necessary reference point within an intertext, the analysis of a specific site deepens when it is considered in relation to its spatial milieu. Buildings, entranceways, and common rooms have the advantage of recognizable, traceable parameters that enable an initial focal point, even though the eventual analysis may emphasize patterns of occupation and identification. In this next section, I include larger, more ephemeral sites to illustrate the spatial and physical contexts that operate at the center of Lefebvre's thinking about everyday life and public space. In *Architecture of the Everyday*, a collection that honors Lefebvre's contribution to critical architecture, McLeod (1997) points out that his thinking on everyday life is rooted in the urban landscape near his birthplace in southwestern France, a place that was scarred by commercial development. Over the next 30 years of his publishing life, the monotonous and commercial nature of urban living was seen as a worldwide phenomenon.

For Lefebvre the city was contradictory because it operated as both an instrument for economic and social tyranny and as a complex medium for variation, resistance, and transcendence of control. Harvey (1991) in an "afterword" to *The Production of Space* (1991b), recounts criticism by members of the 1950s "situationist" movement of Lefebvre's fixation on temporal "moments" as opposed to spatio-temporal situations (pp. 429–430). Whether this criticism is fair or not, Harvey concludes that it signaled a shift in Lefebvre's philosophy that embeds "daily life" in the themes of urbanization and spatial production, which allowed another dialectic to mature, this one across town and country, center and periphery (pp. 430–431). Other scholars have studied the city and urban life as a conceptual category, and for de Certeau (1984; see also Soja, 1989), our era can be considered modern because of the rise of the "concept" city, a recognizable idea to the degree that a city such as Phoenix or Pittsburgh is identifiable by both its marketable image and the collective image known to its occupants. The first image arises from the promotional material that sets one city apart from the other, but the second image—or more accurately, its character—is created by occupants who reproduce it over time through day-to-day living. For de Certeau, the concept *city* consists of three "operations": (a) the production of its own space, that is, space within its own conceptual image; (b) the substitution of a "nowhen," a synchronic system that replaces a history of spatial evolution; and (c) the creation of a universal and anonymous subject (1984, p. 94). For example, New York City developers produce more livable spaces that promote the "Big Apple" and in doing so erase the material history of Manhattan island; this substitution further mediates a construction of the concept of "New Yorker" as a chosen lifestyle.

Any physical site, then, operates on broad temporal and spatial planes. An important rhetorical pursuit is to find a way to account for and name the spatial properties of these planes. Garreau (1991), who writes as an urban critic, provides an example of this sort of analysis with regard to urban growth in all quarters of the United States. He describes urban encroachment as the phenomenon of the "edge city," which has these basic, quantifiable characteristics (p. 6 f):

- 5,000,000 square feet of leasable office space
- 600,000 square feet of leasable retail space
- More jobs than bedrooms
- Perceived by the population as one place
- Is less than 30 years old

Garreau points out that such urban space has become common to the point of invisibility, one wave of expansion crashing over another to the point that the images of suburbia from the 1950s are superseded by a post-urban imagery of endless (but conceptual linked) grids of offices, shops, malls, and concept entertainment. Phoenix, near where I lived, is the fifth largest metropolitan area in the United States, yet functionally and sociologically, it has no physical or iconographic center. there is no particular urban identity beyond growth itself and Southwestern lifestyle. Phoenix exemplifies the edge city phenomenon with its endless expansion (which is a marketable concept), but as Garreau concludes, this growth demands new forms of governance, control, and finally exclusion. Exponential growth militates against the social forces that arise from the population's day-to-day living within the concept city. Shadow governances appear with new growth and their instruments, such as homeowners associations and covenants. These produce social divisions before they may otherwise occur (at least in comparison to the character of neighborhoods of the first half of the twentieth century). Whereas urban development through this century allowed space and identity to emerge as geographic, ethnic, or economic difference, new growth and its mechanisms of social control

function through conceptual models that ignore urban vitality that produces what Lefebvre refers to as the collective subject.

To further explore the idea of the city as conceptual urban space, we
now examine a type of development that typifies corporate mastery of the
idea of neighborhood. Anthem, Arizona, is not an edge city, but it a classic
example of what Lefebvre called representational space, a space that is
imagined, designed, produced, and sold as one of many commodities in
modern, everyday life: a space that represents a way of life. Anthem is a
master, planned community that rests in a gentle desert valley north of the
"edge" of Phoenix. Anthem is a total living community, which assumes that
those who work must commute, and those who do not work will rarely
leave this environment. The promotional materials for Anthem state that
that the community marries "lifestyle" with "strategic planning." When I
visited Anthem as a prospective buyer, I noticed the stratification of home
and life styles, the divisions of living by categories and playing in common
areas. Anthem's homes and parcels are graduated by size, grandeur, and
cost, and the discreet gradations of homes and tracts are grouped by ex-
alted names: Jubilation, Heritage, Overture, Echelon, and the (gated)
Country Club. These names ascend as if one were climbing toward heaven,
and within each social, economic and spatial tier homes are further differentiated by size (square feet) and exterior packaging. For example, in
the Jubilation group, house options are arranged in the following order:

Jubilation Group:

Celebration	$138,990	1,996 square feet
Radiance	$128,990	1,673 square feet
Enchantment	$123,990	1,580 square feet
Rejoice	$116,990	1,403 square feet
Triumph	$110,990	1,251 square feet
Jewel	$ 99,990	1,218 square feet

Anthem's housing options are a catalog of superlatives that assume five
major levels with six housing variations in each level of the "Parkside"
group. The master planners of Anthem offer 30 variations of home own-
ing bliss in this one sub-development of the 5,800-acre community. These
prices and sizes, however, do not include finish costs, and, similar to the
sedan on the show room floor, the display models have custom interiors of
flooring, molding, countertops and cabinetry that can add thousands of

dollars to the sticker price. Each house in each major category is assigned to a uniform lot size; the corporation predetermines the builders and sub-contractors for these "custom" homes. Landscaping is included, but not nearly to the extent of the display homes; nor are fees, taxes, or Anthem covenants easily found in the marketing materials.

Anthem's stratified uniformity appears to offer something for every-one, but the more impressive appeal is the quality of life that accompanies a lot and home purchase. In a newspaper supplement (Anthem, 1999), Anthem designers tout "time famine" as one of the pressing concerns of today's family, a famine solved by a comprehensive lifestyle plan that in-cludes schools, parks, recreational and meeting facilities, and golf.

Anthem offers residents a better quality of life . . . a higher ideal. It is an original community where residents can reclaim their sense of belonging, the balanced life that offers fulfillment from family, education, culture, recreation, and imagi-nation. . . . Anthem . . . embraces the future but conforms to important tenets of the past. (Mariucci, 1999)

Anthem is, in fact, beautiful in its scale and refinements to the degree that model homes and community services are new, tasteful, and are situ-ated in a northern edge of the Sonoran desert, a physical site that is rimmed with dry peaks, set against brilliantly blue skies, and scented with desert heat and flowers. The question is whether Anthem will deliver the harmony and qualities of the good life that its promoters and builders promise. Anthem's economic packaging and nostalgic motifs are more in-teresting as a social experiment than a commercial one in that Anthem at-tempts to forestall the sometimes capricious and often competitive forces of money, power, industry, class and ethnicity that have produced the great cities of the twentieth century. Will Anthem deliver "a sense of place," understood by sociologists and architects as an expression of hu-man events in and over time? The landscape architect Jackson (1994) writes that whatever "a sense of place" means in modern society, it once referenced the "guardian divinity" that kept a place secure for its occu-pants. Both the visitor and the inhabitants enjoyed a spiritual presence. Places were known over time and through common ritual, echoing the ret-rospectives of Lefebvre. A place known for the attributes marketed by Anthem can never be controlled physically, socially, and conceptually be-cause localities are "embedded in the everyday world around us and eas-ily accessible, but at the same time are distinct from that world" (p. 157).

Urban spaces add an important dimension to site analysis, and consequently, to rhetorical analysis because spatial practice is concerned with the production, promotion, and marketing of these spaces as commodities. If words have currency, then so must social space. The sociologist Zukin (1993) concludes that "New architecture and urban forms are . . . produced under nearly the same social conditions as consumer products. They increasingly follow similar patterns of both standardization and market differentiation" (p. 42). Anthem may succeed as a preeminently master-planned community and as a spatial and technological machine, and even (for awhile) a nice place for people to live. It may be pleasing as a consumer to drive by flower gardens and blue water on dustless blacktop and toward (synthetic) adobe homes. But I predict that Anthem will never succeed in the long-term with its nostalgic social agenda because the life of everyday, which Jackson describes as idiosyncratic and characterized by the traveler, is excluded from Anthem's master plan. With no particular manifestation of anarchy in mind, and if Lefebvre is right in depicting the capricious potential of everyday life, we can predict that variation, subversion of the plan will occur a breakdown in the pristine social order will take place, and that this occurrence is precisely what Lefebvre had in mind as the dynamic capacity of humans in everyday circumstances to manufacture the coherence of their own social and spatial realm. Social space is always under one sort of siege or another.

Society "oscillates" between *representations of space* such as the documents, graphics and models that assist in the origination of Anthem, and *representational space*, the beliefs and values signified by those designs and Anthem itself. This tension, as we will see, may lead to transgression and change as well as the commodification of culture (Lefebvre, 1991, p. 232f.). The everyday operates quietly in between, as sand blows invisibly into the community pool.

Site Analysis as a Representational Process

With social space as a backdrop, I now turn to an exemplary study of some of the micro-practices involved in reading and constructing social space. How space is created through design is itself a large undertaking because of the breadth and depth of the documentary processes involved in envisioning and building urban spaces such as Anthem or the north "edge" of Phoenix. Micro-practices are important because they illustrate how features of a site can foster an understanding of the site and how it operates as a field for everyday activity, as we found in Whyte's analysis. Micro-practices, the practice of spatial design, are also important because, as Lefebvre argues, agency within the everyday belongs to everyone, and, therefore, the power to affect the design of the everyday is available to those who are not formally designated as architects of the concept city. Also, by attending to micro-practices that focus on specific spaces on an urban map, we may learn something about the interplay between writing and other forms of signification. To mix metaphors, we must aim to study discourses of the everyday, but carefully—we must proceed one brick at a time.

Medway (1996) describes how writing practices and writers are implicated in the construction of built space to the degree that documents that prefigure space presume both actual and virtual spaces. Design and documentary practices (inclusive of models and graphics) are more often virtual than material: models appear more frequently than buildings. For architects, representations such as models, sketches, and plans are common products within their economic and epistemological world; they have more daily currency than signature office buildings. Medway also points out that architecture plans and the planning and design activity directed at lived space generally escape the review of literacy specialists. This may be because those who engage in rhetorical studies of discrete fields may have overlooked professions that depend on visual—spatial and graphic— methods rather than verbal means, but I suspect such fields and activity escape rhetorical analysis because of the inherent logocentrism[5] of rhetoric itself, that is, its perception of the world as text, properly understood through discursive theories and linguistic tools.

Print as a representational tool is precarious and unstable when we consider the technical production of social space in fields such as architecture, geography, or urban planning. Dias, Freedman, and Medway & Pare (1999) assess the paper trails documenting the production of social space and built environments, notably site plans and proposals; but more intriguingly, they examine the documents and practices that indirectly and economically drive designs of public space, that is, ghosts in the creation of the machine. These "documents" are not limited to texts and may actually or virtually appear in two or three dimensions; they are ghosts because they are translated iterations within a semiotic web. The diversity of their representational forms challenges the boundaries of master tropes for disciplinary and professional life such as inter-textuality (see Medway, 1996, p. 475) or inter-discursivity (see Fairclough, 1996).

Recalling Burns's discussion of sites as physical spaces caught in the semantic trap of language, a space that "can neither be completed or abandoned," we now look at an example of representational processes wedded to a specific urban site and space. This site was brought to my attention by a first-year student in architecture (Ackerman, 1995), and it is clearly an "everyday," but it has none of the iconographic powers of Anthem, the New York Public Library, or even a kitchen. In a cultural and spatial landscape, it is banal to the point of invisibility, and we will notice that its invisibility, its subjugation, is the basis for its powers of illumination. To tap into that power, however, this space must be "read" and "constructed," and the construction of a virtual space is the result of a designer's representational engagement. Elsewhere (Ackerman & Oates, 1996), I have reported that architectural site assessment and planning are infinitely rhetorical because of the power in graphic representations of public space, and because designers act with a broader range of representational devices. Here, I want to depict the interpretive design process as more analogous to "jaywalking," a term from de Certeau (1984) that suggests how physical activity can operate as a speech act within everyday life across urban terrains. The writer (or designer) has the capacity for counter intelligence and activity because of the powers of spatial transgression.

Marty was one of the few women students who entered the Graduate School of Architecture at Utah in 1993, and she had just begun her academic training with no formal training in philosophy, cultural studies, or semiotics. She had discovered the studio experience to be central to her architecture training. The design professors that I interviewed emphasized intellectual flexibility and designed problems that hindered a rush toward professionalism. The studio undercut the mythology of the professional architect as the master designer of cityscapes (a professional position nearly unattainable). Students in the studio were introduced to basic graphic and conceptual skills as they worked through various "studies" and "problems," but many of their assignments were deliberately vague and abstract in nature in order to promote flexibility and acuity. The studio engaged students in practice in formal skills and knowledge (e.g., structures, materials, historical preservation), and in experimentation in spatial scrutiny. Marty's specific problem was to design a structure—a concept model—that made reference to four "polestars" or passages in

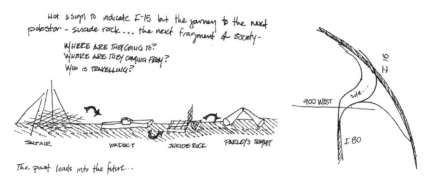

Figure 3. Sketches of the four "pole stars" in Marty's studio problem.

the landform around Salt Lake City. It is a landscape made up of desert, mountains, city, and surrounding hills in the Salt Lake Valley in Utah. With these four Archimedean points in mind, she was then to focus on one polestar, an inner-city viaduct.

Salt Lake City, as "concept city" begins with the Mormon pioneers, but Salt Lake as an organic living space predates the Mormon colonies and was shaped (as many Western cities are shaped) by migrational patterns, landmasses, and the availability of water and tillable soil. Salt Lake grew in relation to geographical reference points, and the city emerged near crossroads of pioneer travel from points north, south, east, and west. The modern polestars in Marty's study were (a) the point at which Interstate 80 nearly touches the Great Salt Lake, west of the city and on the way to Nevada; (b) the summit of Parley's Canyon to the east which marks the entrance into the valley and begins a major watershed into the valley, (c) "suicide rock," a spire of rock centered right at the mouth of Parley's canyon, to this day a sentinel guarding the mouth of the canyon; and (d) Marty's polestar, an overpass in the middle of the city where Interstate 15 and 80, the north/south and east/west migrational paths, converge. Here is one of her early sketches of the "viaduct" site.

Marty's polestar is more than a convergence of transportation routes in and out of a western valley. As she will explain, Marty views the overpass as a convergence of cultures: those who are wealthy enough to use the interstate system to transcend this location, and those who "choose" to live beneath the crossroads. I cannot here reproduce her entire design sequence, because it involves pages and pages of notes, sketches, and tracings, and a complete treatment of her work would account for her time

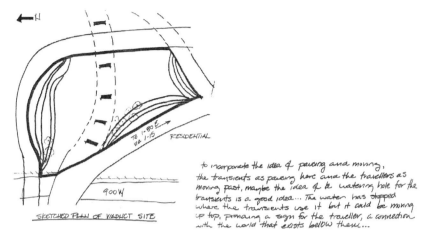

Figure 4. Marty's viaduct site sketch.

talking with peers, engaging their work, visiting her site, and working with materials and sculptures in the studio. Her site and design processes, even in this early stage in her career, reveal considerable representational fluency; she produces a series of virtual spaces as social and material possibilities in response to her design problem.

In my interviews with Marty, she revealed "I'm most comfortable with writing, less comfortable with presenting myself graphically." But then she illustrated how sketching, writing, talking, and observing can remove some of the analytic barriers to this study of everyday life. She did not begin with a study of freeway systems or the geometry of this nexus of interstate travel. Nor did she spend any time addressing preordained topics that lurk in the domains of social services such as the "homeless" or "transient" people who typically occupy these spaces. Rather, her attention was drawn to the space itself, the physical and social hierarchy in an "overpass," and the texture of the life beneath it.

In Marty's words,

I was toying with the difference between the mountain and the flatness, and the ideas of time. How it seems like a permanent landscape to us, but eventually, through time the landscape is probably going to change. . . . Then I started reacting to my site in particular. . . . It is kind of a neat place to be. I used to drive by and it was really noisy, and I had the feeling that these cars were just perpetually going around in there, an Escher three-dimensional thing. . . . We started talking about weaving. . . . I took the stance of disassociation because the under-the-

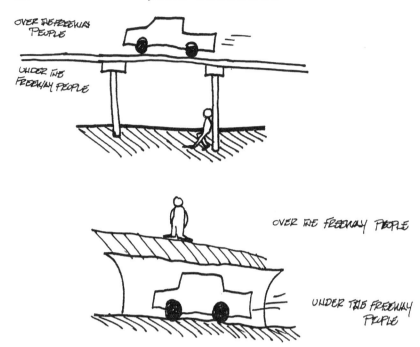

Figure 5.   Marty's over and under the freeway people sketch.

freeway people were kind of forgotten and the over-the-freeway people just drive as fast as they can and they don't even notice. . . . So you have the two . . . meeting at this point. . . . I started thinking about how the two types of people . . . are woven together at this point, but they don't really mix. In my sketches I go back to the nature of weaving. It is like when you have that sewing machine that doesn't quite work, the loops don't catch. For a conceptual model, I was trying to depict a weaving, but up close it wasn't really woven at all.

Eventually, Marty's solution to the design problem centered on weaving and the vertical and horizontal forces at play in and around her polestar, in the structure of the overpass, and in society. Her sketches and commentary began to cohere when she entertained the materials of her site (concrete, reinforcing steel) and how she might model the interconnectedness of spatial, material, and social forces. With several of her sketches she transposed materials and their customary use to create such a "blanket" for the occupants woven out of "rebar." Her final stance toward the space beneath the overpass was its representation as social function through its use and not through its original design: "I decided the

THE WEAVE GIVES DIRECTION

weaving implies an over/under action... neither peice can be in the same place at the same time... one must be over, the other under. It is dynamic - they switch. ← does this imply a revolution?

THE WEAVE GIVES SHELTER

THE WEAVING OF 2 FREEWAYS

Figure 6. Marty's weaving sketch.

space that existed under the freeway was really complete for the people that were using it. They weren't asking for anything to be there." Marty's solution as designer was to leave well enough alone except to augment this space beneath the overpass to emphasize its own identity and integrity. Although at first glance the abstractness of her concept model obscures this point, her solution was to reveal this space by adding a few amenities and rejecting any formal intervention that would detract from what she considered the positive, social properties of the site.

Figure 7 is an early version of her concept model that can be appreciated only in reference to her site, the everyday life within that site, and Marty's recursive and reflexive efforts to represent this site through drawings and writing.

Marty's renderings produced virtual space and implicated spatial practice, arguably more accurately than a snapshot of the site or a social services report on the homeless in Salt Lake City. Even with these few sketches we can respect her efforts to accurately represent (within the range of her tools) a social space, and to distort this space in the service of accuracy within her cultural comment. The physical properties of the site contributed to her ideas about the structures of society found in an inconspicuous site, and to her ideas about inverting those social structures. What I find in her study is an example of site and spatial analysis in everyday life, represented through basic tools of drawing and writing. I do not mean that her perspectives and skills at representing lived space are unrefined; she was accepted into graduate school after demonstrating some

Figure 7. Marty's concept model.

of the abilities evident in her sketchbook. Her observations and her con-
certed effort to represent ordinary, everyday space, however, suggest that
such analyses are available to all of us. I call her representational activity
"rhetorical" because it isolates actions and consequences in social space,
and by implication, her design activity "deconsecrates" writing, an observation from Lefebvre that writing alone will not allow her (or us) to
achieve thought-action, in this case, the representation of virtual space
within a city. As analyst, Marty had to "jaywalk" a few social and spatial
boundaries to capture the under life beneath a busy interstate and to disrupt a spatial and economic hierarchy.

Representational Terror and Insurgencies

In *Everyday Life in the Modern World*, Lefebvre (1971) links writing
with terrorism to underscore the violence language can have on culture.
He refers to ethnologists (presumably scholars such as Havelock, 1982)
who have noted the concurrence of writing and the logics of print with
the stratification of social labor, the rise in stature of the scribe, and the
elevation of records and the technologies that produce and preserve

them. Writing "makes law, is, in fact, law" (Lefebvre, 1971, p. 153), and whereas writing is an enabling tool in the invention of the city, it is also the tool of military and political control. Print literacy of the population is the necessary condition for institutions to function within those populations, and, therefore, it appropriates "all that is said, known, felt." Lefebvre invokes a version of Brandt's (1992) critique of "strong texts," but his framework is social space, not literacy studies. He also outlines the relative powers of strong texts within the production of social space and its deconstruction. By attacking writing as a violent tool, he is trying to enable a "critical mind" that recognizes textual displacement of cultural currency at its "emergence," that is, in history, as history happens—in the everyday. Writing as a technology cannot erase "real tradition" except when we confuse "the world with the book, or worse, with the library" (Lefebvre, 1971, pp. 155–157).

Lefebvre's disdain for the powers of print in spatial practice set the stage for a reorientation from writing as print to writing within semiotics, and an eye toward linguistic and other signs and practices that link linguistic to spatial territory. Lefebvre's goal is to understand the historical, functional, and symbolic properties of language so that we "set the limits of its range and implications [of writing] and thus to deconsecrate it" (Lefebvre, 1971, p. 175). Lefebvre deconsecrates writing by arguing for a revival of forms, one that reestablishes speech as its enactment because forms of thought-action are closer in kind to human presence, desire, and the properties of time and space that strong texts terrorize in everyday life. Thought-actions may not return us to the original codes that bridge the "architectural, urbanistic and political," but they may reorient the citizen and the analyst to the moments and places where such thought-actions exist.

This is where Marty's work becomes interesting, not in that it proves Lefebvre's theories, but in how it illustrates one person's untethered vision toward social space, and how basic representations may translate and may lead to (in this case virtual) social reform. Writing gains authority in Marty's work because it operates in service of interrogations of public space and in concert with her drawings (and her self-concept of what she does well as a critic and designer). What Marty produced, obviously, is not real reform in the manner of alternative communities, or "heterotopes" (countersites) built with the same conceptual and structural tools as Anthem, but with the opposite goal of defeating or diminishing the effects of commodified social space. Although Marty's renderings and concept models did not lead to an actual homeless shelter beneath the viaduct, I would not conclude that her micro-practices were insignificant within her professional training, within the curricular world of the studio, or, more to the point, toward our understanding of the rhetorical potential in studies of social space. I believe that her studio work clearly illustrates an inclination to recapture the spaces of everyday life and to find the best tools and locations to commence this labor. I liken her work to that of Chaplin's tramp, a figure in the drama of everyday life that blends tactical play with social analysis. Without formally embarking on a critique of the homeless or transient, Marty transgresses the formal, spatial world of the interstate grid and then alters the domains of the viaduct, and, by implication, public policy. She even alters what one might consider as the normal tools for critique. These tools, in other words, transform the interstate into the interstices of everyday life.

The speech act as spatial practice is central to de Certeau's study of *The Practice of Everyday Life* (1984) because it underscores the enactment of discourse (and not the re-inscription of the discursive metaphor), and, although it is fair to wonder about Marty's actual intentions in the design studio, the force of her efforts is toward spatial reform. For De Certeau, the geometries of power exemplified in the concept city are now decaying through the exercise of an "antidiscipline" (in spirit, a concept similar to Lefebvre's disalienation) in the mixed metaphorical form of the "pedestrian speech acts," that is, physical and discursive tactics that counter the strategies of the power grid. Whereas strategies articulate an "ensemble of physical places in which forces are distributed," tactics are the devices of the "other," devices that insinuate practices into the places of the powerful and that operate on the axis of time in addition to material location (p. 38).

It is perhaps fanciful to imagine that Marty's drawings will invert societal hierarchies, but such small inversions have always been the political means for literacy specialists who aspire to democratize institutional discourse; we work locally for global change with the assumption that if we change the sentence, we change the person and, therefore, the world. A rhetoric of everyday life, then, will consciously avoid confusing "social *place* with technical *discourse*" (de Certeau, 1984, p. 8, italics his). At issue is the specialized language that distorts the specialist's comprehension of the language of everyday life as an "ensemble of practices in which one is implicated and through which the prose of the world is at work" (p. 12).

As an example of a pedestrian speech act, an antidisciplinary illocution, de Certeau proposes *la perruque* as a popular, everyday activity within the production of goods and services, an undercurrent of activity within the dominant stream (the manufacture of goods, for example), "the workers' own work disguised as work for his employer," and work that diverts time and creates a facade of approved behavior. *La perruque* consists of "popular techniques of other times and other places that normally proliferate in factories and offices" (pp. 25–26), skills and strategies that sound very much like those of the factory workers that Hull (1997) has studied in much detail and with political empathy. These workers import both linguistic and proximic (i.e., where they stand, work, and talk in physical proximity to friends, associates, and supervisors) strategies for completing their tasks, ignoring formal training regimens and placating management. For de Certeau, the speech act is the performance of language in service of spatial tactics because "the 'arts of speaking' are linked to the 'arts of operating': the same practices appear now in a verbal field, now in a field of nonlinguistic actions; the move from one field to the other, being equally tactical and subtle in both" (p. 78).

Is it possible to deconsecrate writing, and, we may assume, the linguistic, rhetorical, and philosophical devices that support its practice? Might we fashion a field manual for everyday life based on representational tools? I look to Marty's instincts and skills as an illustration of how this might be achieved. A rhetorical study of the everyday will gravitate to ordinary spaces and less-sanctioned activities; we may find that such spaces are best represented in accessible but extraordinary ways. To again borrow language from de Certeau (1984):

Dwelling, moving about, speaking, reading, shopping, and cooking are activities that seem to correspond to the characteristics of tactical ruses and surprises: clever tricks of the weak within the order established by the 'strong' (p. 40). . . . Thus the street geometrically defined by urban planning is transformed into a space by walkers. (p. 117)

While it is far too calculating to say that new tools will lead us to new spaces, an implication of antidisciplinary practice is that new conceptual spaces may appear and then may align with lived spaces. Spatial and conceptual territory is initially differentiated across isotopes, heterotopes (or countersites), and utopias. Isotopias are "analogous spaces" that are recognizable through their common properties and occurrences: what I might see out my window as subdivisions, Jiffy Lubes, and supermarts that "mystify" modern life because they appear normal through repetition. In another time or place, isotopias might be gardens, porches, and avenues that are woven through everyday life. Isotopias contrast with heterotopias and utopias in that heterotopias refers to spaces that are "mutually repellent" and utopias to spaces of the imagination (Lefebvre, 1991b, p. 366).

Marty's work could be construed as progressing from isotopic to heterotopic to utopian (i.e., imaginary) space, but the architectural historian, Hayden (1997), illustrates how such an examination can exhume and celebrate actual, physical spaces in the city. Her project is to pursue practices such as "place memory" and "mental mappings" that produces alternative narrative and historical guides to the space of the city. Mapping or relating personal experience through site analysis yields heterotopes in that a reclaimed urban history often reveals countersites that contrast sharply with the reductive formalism in architectural history and urban cartography. By searching for these sites, naming them as such, and linking material and symbolic space with history, Hayden contributes to a reestablishment of gender, class, and ethnicity as political and spatial markers within an urban space's history. The key rhetorical move, then, is to accept that the exercise of finding those spaces and reinforcing their (re)location. This requires a different critical orientation and ensemble of tools. Sites and their analysis within the everyday function as both *field* and *basis* for action, and they bring the rhetorician into the game of deciphering analogous, repellent, or imaginary spaces. The garden can be isotopic to some if it fits within a common category of use, but it becomes heterotopic when it challenges reproductive social relations, such as the front yard garden that violates the codes and covenants of Anthem. Hayden gave the casitas and gardens of Harlem in New York City a rhetorical capacity in that they were deemed counterstatements (as countersites) against the decayed structures and signs of government-subsidized housing. These places were first remembered and then reconstituted as sites for political discourse and gatherings (Hayden, 1997, p. 35 ff.).

Implications

I have at best scratched the surface of an articulation of rhetorical and spatial theory; I have tried here to illustrate and explain some of what I consider to be a productive tension between discourse and space. Additional scholarship might track how concepts such as rhetorical situation or stasis are transformed under the pressure of temporal and physical space. At the very least, we can see how and why pursuits of public discourse will invariably lead us into the spaces of everyday life and the language and signs that build and promote those spaces. Certainly, literacy specialists could pay more attention to documents that lead to the virtual and actual construction of buildings and other public spaces. If we do, we will crash headlong into Medway's (1996) findings that the documentary literacy that leads to and flows from social space includes two- and three-dimensional representations of the virtual and the real. Such work shows how print literacy will fold into semiosis, but perhaps the more provocative implication of this chapter is that space itself functions discursively; that is, it functions as both field and basis for analysis.

If the spaces and places that comprise daily life are signs themselves, then the rhetorical fields in which we work are extended in some remarkable ways. Our perspectives on academic and nonacademic writing may become spatially reflexive in the way that Cushman (1996) has demonstrated. She studied the communities around her home institution of Rensselaer Polytechnic Institute and in particular the "approach" to the university: an expansive stone staircase that both invites and expels those who do not belong to either the school or the town. Cushman's conclusion is that symbolized social divisions coincide with social distances between academics and the everyday, and she proposes that critical work can "collapse political binaries by depicting the complex everyday particulars in the middle place where most people live their lives" (1998, p. 239).

Another example of turning the spatial gaze toward schools can be found in Dressman's (1997) research on early grade libraries, which are interesting sites because of their status and proximity within the buildings and grounds of a campus—because of their symbolic status as archives of knowledge. However, as Dressman describes, they are interesting as students make sense of them through practice. Students occupy the libraries differently and these differences lead to two conclusions: how a student acts within a preordained space adds a textual layer to our understanding of that student's subjectivity and the space itself—the library—can be reconceived as a "paradigmatic heterotopia" (176). Literacy education, for Dressman, asks everyone to "explore differences and contradictions located within the site of their own social being" (p. 177).

If we think about how space works within the walls of schools as well as contiguous to those walls, as Cushman illustrates, perhaps we may also begin to reconsider other physical and conceptual boundaries such as the practice of professional and disciplinary knowledge. Bazerman (1992) shrewdly points out that a blinding artifact of university knowledge is the misperception that disciplinary and professional knowledge ends with the training regimen and products associated with academic credentialing. Some disciplines such as medicine and the social sciences advertise how they bridge academic and everyday life because they deal with physical, economic health, and other aspects of individuals and social groups, while other professions such as engineering and urban planning advertise their direct concern for and skill in constructing a spatial economy. With the spatial recesses in everyday life in mind, we may become mindful of the unadvertised forms and practices of disciplines and professions that implicate social space. This, for the purposes of this chapter in this collection, is why Lefebvre's (1991b) comment is relevant, that "Every discourse says something about space (p. 132) suggesting that all disciplines and professions will leave a residue in public places (ours being the powers of documentary literacy).

Finally, a most profound implication of a spatial analysis of everyday life is also a most ordinary one: everyday life reminds us that academics, teachers, and students all traverse a particular landscape to come to work at the university (or public school or other workplaces). Clearly, our awareness and analysis of specific sites depends upon how we participate in and across multiple sites. Clifford (1997; see also Kaplan, 1998) has written about the importance of considering the locations of the observer and the observed, and particularly the travel involved in the definition of each. In literacy practice, there is always some form of this travel to the degree that the living practices that students bring to "residential" or "commuter" campuses surely bear the marks of the other important habitations in their everyday lives. One of the more poignant examples of this travel is the story of Lucia (Rose, 1989), whose spatial and intellectual matrix include the community college, UCLA's campus, and her home commute. Her approach to the elevated world of Thomas Szasz (1974, *The Myth of Mental Illness*) was literally a process of getting from here to there, traveling into the world of the sacred to the profane while commuting to and from and within the labyrinth of the university:

We left Campbell Hall and headed southeast, me toward a sandwich, Lucia toward the buses that ran up and down Hilgard on UCLA's east boundary. . . . Lucia talked about . . . her growing familiarity with this sprawling campus. . . . I began to think about how many pieces had to fall into place each day in order for her to be a student: The baby couldn't wake up sick. . . . [T]he three buses she took from East L. A. had to be on time. . . . Only if all these pieces dropped in smooth alignment could her full attention shift to the complex and allusive prose of Thomas Szasz. (Rose 1989, p. 185)

What we have to learn about the space for rhetoric in everyday life will include the study of design and how designed spaces signify within culture and within the day-to-day experiences of people. We must look to designers such as Marty and Lucia to learn how sites and countersites reveal patterns of social identity and interaction. Through their spatial practice, we can find the extraordinary in the ordinary, in the humblest facts of everyday life.

Notes

1. I use the term rhetorician, and refer to specialists in rhetoric, composition, linguistics and literacy as "we," not to dilute differences in training or assignment but to rely on an efficient shorthand within my argument. This "we" is no more or less inclusive than the collection of authors in this volume who by implication write toward a "rhetoric of everyday life."

2. I foreground dialectical method in this chapter for the same reasons that Lefebvre foregrounds the method across his writings and that is to identify two concepts or practices that operate in tension. By placing history against material context, or social space against the practice of everyday life, we recognize the poles within the argument and create a new conceptual interaction, the result of the primary contradiction.

3. From 1934 to 1986 Henri Lefebvre wrote well over 50 books, many yet to be translated from French, on subjects ranging across Marxism, analytical philosophy, everyday life, and urban and spatial practice. Any summary of his work is reductive, but my purpose here is twofold: to include his voice and work in this volume and to gather those insights and properties across Lefebvre's writing on everyday life and public space that may be generative for specialists in language, literacy and rhetoric. I am indebted to other scholars of Lefebvre who provide their own summaries of his work: Mary McLeod (1997), Michel Trebitsch (1991), and David Harvey (1991). In "An Inquiry, and Some Discoveries," Chapter 1 in Everyday Life in the Modern World (1971, pp. 1–67), Lefebvre offers his own retrospective on the basic arguments in his *critique de la vie quotidienne*

4. Permission to reproduce this graphic was granted by the Project for Public Spaces, Inc., a nonprofit corporation specializing in the planning, design, and management of public spaces. This organization grew out of the work of William H. Whyte's Street Life Project. The objective of PPS is to create and improve public space by focusing on the behaviour, expressed needs, and collaborative envisioning of communities. For further information, see the organization's web site: www.pps.org.

5. I use lococentrism in the anthropological sense and not as a reference to Derrida's criticism of the phonocentric bias within Western philosophy that confuses voice with presence (Derrida, 1976). Rather, lococentrism in western culture is the bias within cultural analysis to privilege writing over other symbolic systems and other rituals and performances (Conquergood, 1995).

References

Ackerman, J. & Oates, S. (1996). Image, text, and power in workplace writing. In Duin, A. & Hansen, C. (Eds.), *Multidisciplinary Research in Workplace Writing: Challenging the Boundaries*. Mahway, NJ: Erlbaum Press.

Ackerman, J. (1995). Traveling in Disciplinary Cultures. Conference on College Composition and Communication. Washington, D.C., 28 March.

Anthem by Del Webb. (1999). Advertising Supplement to the *Arizona Republic*, March 28.

Bazerman, C. (1992). From cultural criticism to disciplinary participation: Living with powerful words. In A. Herrington & C. Moran (Eds.), *Writing, teaching, and learning in the disciplines* (pp. 61–68). New York: Modern Language Association.

Brandt, D. (1995). Accumulating literacy. *College English, 57*. Urbana: National Council of Teachers of English.

Brandt, D. (1990). *Literacy as involvement: The acts of writers, readers, and texts*. Carbondale: Southern Illinois University.

Burns, C. (1991). On site: Architectural preoccupation. In A. Kahn (Ed.), *Drawing/Building/Text*. New York: Princeton Architectural Press.

de Certeau, M. (1984). *The practice of everyday life* (S. Rendall, Trans.). Berkeley: California Press.

Clifford, J. (1997). *Routes*. Cambridge: Harvard University Press.

Conquergood, D. (1995). Beyond the text: Toward a performative cultural politics. Paper presented at "The Future of Performance Studies." Indiana State University.

Conway, H. & Roenisch, R. (1994). *Understanding architecture: An introduction to architecture and architectural history*. London: Routledge.

Cook, J. (2000). The observation man. *The New York Times Magazine*, 2 January, 23.

Cushman, E. (1996). Rhetorician as agent of social change. *College Composition and Communication, 47*, 7–28.

Cushman, E. (1998). *The struggle and the tools: Oral and literate strategies in an inner city community*. Albany: SUNY Press.

Derrida, J. (1976). *Of grammatology* (Gayatri Spivak, Trans.). Baltimore: Johns Hopkins Press.

Dias, P., Freedman, A., Medway, P., & Pare, A. (1999). *Worlds apart: Acting and writing in academic and workplace contexts*. Mahway, NJ: Erlbaum Press.

Dressman, M. (1997). *Literacy in the library: Negotiating the spaces between order and desire*. Westport: Bergin & Garvey.

Fairclough, N. (1998). *Discourse and social change*. Cambridge, UK: Polity.

Foucault, M. (1986). Of other spaces. (J. Kiskowiec, Trans.). *Diacritics, 16*, 22–27.

Garreau, J. (1991). *Edge city: Life on the new frontier*. New York: Anchor Books.

Halloran, M. (1993). Afterthoughts on rhetoric and public discourse. In V. Vitanza (Ed.), *Pre/Text: The first decade* (pp. 52–68). Pittsburgh: University of Pittsburgh Press.

Harris, S. & Berke, D. (1997). *Architecture of the everyday*. New York: Princeton Architectural Press.

Havelock, E. (1982). *The literate revolution in Greece and its cultural consequences*. Princeton, NJ: Princeton University Press.

Hayden, D. (1997). *The power of place: Urban landscapes as public history*. Cambridge: MIT Press.

Henderson, C. (1996). A revolution in the Woman's Sphere: Grete Lihotzky and the Frankfurt kitchen. *Architecture and feminism*. Cambridge: Architectural Press.

Hull, Glynda. (1997). Hearing other voices: A critical assessment of popular views on literacy and work. In Glynda Hull (Ed.), *Changing work, changing workers: Critical perspectives on language, literacy, and skills* (pp. 3–42). Albany: SUNY Press.

Jackson, J. B. (1994). *A sense of place, a sense of time*. Cambridge: Yale University Press.

Kaplan, C. (1998). *Questions of travel*. Durham: Duke University Press.

Lefebvre, H. (1971). *Everyday life in the modern world*. Trans. Sacha Rabinovitch. New York: Harper & Row.

Lefebvre, H. (1991a). *Critique of everyday life, Volume 1* (John Moore, Trans.). London: Verso. Originally published as *Critique de la vie quotidienne 1: Introduction*. Paris: Grasset, 1947.

Lefebvre, H. (1991b). *The production of space*. Trans. Donald Nicholson-Smith. Oxford, UK: Blackwell.

Lefebvre, H. (1996). *Writings on cities*. Eleanor Kofman & Elizabeth Lebas (Eds.). Oxford: Blackwell.

Lefebvre, H. (1997). The everyday and everydayness. In Stephen Harris & Deborah Berke (Eds.), *Architecture of the everyday*. Originally published *Quotidien et quotidennete*, in Claude Gregory (Ed.), *Encyclopedia Universalis, Vol. 13*. Paris: Encyclopedia Universalis, 1972.

Mariucci, A. (1999). Anthem offers its residents time famine solutions. *Anthem by Del Webb*. Advertising Supplement to the *Arizona Republic*, 28 March.

Medway, P. (1993). Virtual and material buildings: Construction and constructivism in architecture and writing. *Written Communication, 13*, 473–514.

Myers, G. (1996). Out of the laboratory and down to the bay: Writing is science and technology studies. *Written Communication, 13*, 5–43.

Oates, S. (1999). English 101: The discourse of denial and resistance. *Literacy as an everyday practice: Case studies of students and literacy instruction in high school, community college, and university writing classes*. Dissertation. University of Utah. Salt Lake City.

Pascucci, E. (1997). Intimate (tele)visions. In Steven Harris & Deborah Berke (Eds.), *Architecture of the everyday*. New York: Princeton Architectural Press.

Rose, M. (1989). *Lives on the boundary*. New York: Free Press.

Soja, E. (1989). *Postmodern geographies: The reassertion of space in critical social theory*. London: Verso.

Szasz, T. (1974). *The myth of mental illness*. New York: Harper & Row.

Sullivan, P., & Porter, J. (1997). *Opening spaces: Writing technologies and critical research practices*. Greenwich: Ablex.

Trebitsch, M. (1991). Preface. In *Critique of everyday life, Volume 1*. Trans. John Moore. London: Verso.

Whyte, W. (1980). *Social life of small urban spaces*. Washington DC: Conservation Foundation.

Whyte, W. (2000, January 2). Cumulative sighting map. In J. Cook, The observation man. *New York Times Magazine*, 23.

Witte, S. (1992). Context, text, intertext: Toward a constructivist semiotic of writing. *Written Communication, 9*, 237–308.

Zukin, H. (1993). *Landscapes of power: From Detroit to Disney World*. Berkeley:University of California Press.

2

Rhetorics of Education
and Classrooms

5

Janet Emig, Frank Smith, and the New Discourse about Writing and Reading; or, How Writing and Reading Came to Be Cognitive Processes in 1971

Martin Nystrand

Introduction

Fundamentally, Bakhtin's dialogism is about revisionism. According to Bakhtin, there is "no final word." Voices and ideas are "refracted," never simply "received" as "transmitted." Individuals have only partial control over their identities, which can be "finalized" or "consummated" only through the perspectives of others. Examples of revisionism are indeed rife in Bakhtin studies today. Were he alive today, Bakhtin might well be surprised to learn that his association with Vološinov, Medvedev, and others as they discussed the Neo-Kantian ideas and precepts of their Marburg mentor, Professor Hermann Cohen, would eventually come to be widely known as the Bakhtin Circle. Arguably, the most celebrated instance of revisionism in Bakhtin studies is the frequent but almost certainly erroneous attribution of books written by Vološinov and Medvedev to Bakhtin himself.

Like any figure who gains influence, Bakhtin would have been surprised by these and other consequences of his valorization. But the transformation through which Bakhtin's identity became independent of him was clearly inevitable. As a process of social construction, influence so refracts and reifies the identity of its source that the source figure frequently finds the result, even if fortuitous, surprising, unrecognizable, at times wrong, even alienating.[1] We only begin to understand Bakhtin's influence by examining the sources of his ideas and the circumstances of his biography defining the "formative context" of his career. For the rest, we must focus on the acceptance of his ideas and their subsequent use by others in America and Europe, which defines the "receptive context" of his ideas.

In this paper, I use this framework of formative and receptive contexts to examine the sources and emerging influence of new ideas about writing and reading processes in North American during the 1970s and 1980s. A close look at the origins and consequences of these ideas clearly shows the extent to which the phenomenon of influence is itself a sociocultural and dialogic process of social change.

During the 1960s, Harvard University was the site of graduate studies for several young scholars who went on to shape ideas about writing, reading, and literacy in unmistakable ways: Courtney Cazden, a noted scholar of literacy and child language; Janet Emig, a pioneer in empirical research on the composing process and author of *The Composing Processes of Twelfth Graders*; John Mellon, author of the first empirical research on sentence combining; the late James Moffett, well-known author of *Teaching the Universe of Discourse*; Charles Read, the 'inventor' of invented spelling; and Frank Smith, noted reading expert and author of *Understanding Reading*. Moffett was a research associate in the Harvard Graduate School of Education; the rest were all doctoral students. All went on to do important work in their fields, and the direct and indirect impact of their work continues even today to be influential. This is remarkable, especially because at the time Harvard had no program or faculty in composition research. Frank Smith, who was a psychology student, took no coursework in either reading or education. Just what was it about Harvard and Cambridge, Massachusetts during the 1960s that fostered and cultivated new ideas about composition and research on writing, reading, and literacy? And how are we to evaluate the substantial influence this remarkable set of individuals came to exert on our collective thinking?

Using Bakhtin's (1986) dialogic framework of speech communication, I focus here on the impact of two of these scholars, Emig's influence on writing, and Smith's on reading, and attempt to show that while Harvard clearly played a fundamental role as a key *formative context* for the work that these individuals did, a full account of their influence also requires accounting for the *receptive contexts* beyond Harvard that valorized their ideas. Which is to say, it is important to examine which cultures supported their thought: the intellectual culture of the university and the culture of the world beyond the university. Understanding the eventual, unpredictable influence of these innovative scholars requires a close look at how, in Bakhtin's terms, their work was refracted and valorized, often in surprising ways, by teachers, by other researchers, by government officials, and by the general public—by the culture of their times. That is, by the unique sociocultural contexts, or chronotopes, of North America during the 1970s and 1980s.

Janet Emig and Frank Smith and the New Discourse about Writing and Reading Processes

In 1971, both Janet Emig and Frank Smith published books elaborating new cognitive views of writing and reading that became very influential among educators and researchers alike. Emig published *The Composing Processes of Twelfth Graders*, and Smith published *Understanding Reading*. Indeed, Emig was the first researcher to seriously study writing as a cognitive process. While others had written about writing as a process, Emig was the first scholar to conduct empirical research, and her effort was the first to draw sustained interest in the field.[2] In research reported in her seminal study, *The Composing Processes of Twelfth Graders* (1971), she asked eight twelfth graders to "compose aloud," uttering in her presence each thought and word that came to mind as they wrote. By recording and transcribing the resulting "think alouds," she attempted to capture the dynamics and thereby gain some insight into the nature of the composing processes of these students. As it turned out, the composing processes of her subjects were not very elaborate, a result due mainly, she concluded, to the superficial nature of school writing rather than to the composing process itself. Nonetheless, in a 1981 retrospective, she emphasized that writing is "predominantly learned rather than taught" and composing is recursive rather than linear" (Emig, 1981, p. 26).

In 1971 Frank Smith published his influential *Understanding Reading*. In this timely synthesis of psycholinguistic and cognitive psychology research applied to reading, Smith argued that comprehension is essentially information processing. Rather than extracting meaning from text,

Smith argued, readers do just the reverse: they bring meaning to texts as they form and test expectations while (and even before) reading.

Emig and Smith both sought to reform instruction, and each argued that effective reform required neither new curricula nor novel instructional techniques, but rather a fundamentally new conceptualization of the nature of literacy instruction, emphasizing learning rather than teaching. Their thinking was motivated first by their belief that effective writing and reading instruction had less to do with teaching techniques than was believed, and more to do with fundamental insights from psycholinguistics about the cognitive nature of language processes and learning. Their books sought to convey the pedagogical implications of these insights. Consequently, they sought to change the focus of teachers' attention from teaching methods to the cognitive processes of individual learners. Finally, they argued that learning to write and read, and, therefore, instruction in those areas, is best served when teachers emphasize less the specific products of writing and reading, such as prescribed text features in writing and the correct pronunciation of words in reading, and instead emphasize and foster the processes of engaged writing and reading.

The net effect of both works was nothing less than a redefinition of writing and reading and a new set of priorities and issues for those dedicated to their instruction. Emig showed that writing instruction (or what Fogarty [1959] had called "current traditional" rhetoric) had traditionally focused almost entirely on text features—errors in student texts compared to key features of exemplary texts. She stressed that any text is far more than just an example of description, narration, exposition, or persuasion, and she especially condemned formulaic, prescriptive approaches to writing, especially the one embodied by the five-paragraph theme: "One could say that the major kind of essay too many students have been taught to write in the American schools is algorithmic, or so mechanical that a computer could readily be programmed to produce it" (Emig, 1971, p. 52).

Smith's arguments about reading were similar. He moved the reader to the center stage of reading and instructional theory—boldly arguing that meaning is in the reader, not the text—and made a sharp distinction between instruction and learning. Schools, he said, too often teach reading as a matter of correctly pronouncing words rather than as a process of finding meaning. He argued against phonics instruction because "reading is not accomplished by decoding to sound—meaning must usually be grasped before the appropriate sounds can be produced" (1983, p. 195). When teachers put too much emphasis on fluent, word-perfect oral reading, he argued, they inhibit comprehension, which requires risk-taking and processing words in terms of overall meaning. Reading is an active cognitive process in which the readers interpret what they find in terms of what they already know.

The Formative Context for the New Discourse about Writing and Reading

It is tempting, of course, to conclude that the remarkable common ground of Smith's and Emig's works is due to the fact that they were both graduate students at Harvard during the 1960s, when they became caught up in the Cognitive Revolution then under way in Cambridge at both Harvard and the Massachusetts Institute of Technology (MIT). In their common emphasis on language as cognitive processes, both Smith and Emig did indeed bring such a perspective to education. MIT linguistics professor Noam Chomsky and Harvard psychology professors Jerome Bruner and George Miller were well known principals in the local, lively intellectual culture of the time, described by Smith as "the heady psycholinguistic atmosphere of Cambridge, Massachusetts, in the 1960s" (1971, p. x). Chomsky's (1959) cogent review of Skinner's *Verbal Behavior,* and his attack on the fallacies inherent in B. F. Skinner's behaviorism seemed to be on everyone's lips (and reading lists) in graduate studies at Harvard at the time. In her (1995) interview with me, Emig described it as "a very hot item—I found it stunning—utterly persuasive."

Yet to explain the similarities of Emig's and Smith's work wholly in terms of the prevailing zeitgeist in cognitive research simplifies a much more complicated and interesting story. At Harvard, Smith and Emig never crossed paths. Emig entered the Harvard Graduate School of Education in 1960 and left in 1965 to take a position at the University of Chicago. She wrote her dissertation only after leaving Harvard, and received her Ed.D. in 1969. Smith started his graduate studies in 1964, just one year before Emig left. A student in experimental psycholinguistics, he received his Ph.D. in 1967. Smith arrived in Cambridge just as Emig was leaving.

At Harvard, moreover, their experiences differed completely. They took different courses and worked with different faculty. Unlike Emig,

Smith was not involved with the Graduate School of Education; indeed, he took no courses in reading and did not become involved with reading or educational issues until *after* he left Harvard. While at Harvard, he served as Miller's research assistant at the Center for Cognitive Studies, an elite cutting-edge research center founded in 1959 by Miller and Bruner. There, Smith attended weekly colloquia presented by prominent scholars in psychology and linguistics, including Fodor, Katz, T. Bever, P. Kohler, and R. Brown. According to Smith in my (1995) interview with him, "What these things did for me was give me an opportunity to meet a lot of interesting people with very challenging ideas, and to get into an environment where ideas where brought up and debated and discussed and knocked around and sorted out." He internalized leading-edge issues of the day by writing the annual reports for the Center between 1964–67, as well as coediting with Miller *The Genesis of Language* (1966), an important set of conference papers on language and psychology still in print today.

Emig, by contrast, took no part in the activities of the Center for Cognitive Studies. Like Smith, however, she was drawn to Harvard by a charismatic member of Harvard's faculty who, denied tenure, left after Emig's first year of study. Emig could find almost no one to work with her; indeed, she had ten advisors in the nine years she was a Harvard student.[3] One advisor even belittled her interest in empirical research on student writing, comparing such investigations to studies of how "cripples skate" (Peter Neumeyer quoted in Nelms, 1995, p. 111). In fact, Emig's dissertation study languished during her years in Cambridge, and she conducted the study only after she became an assistant professor at the University of Chicago in 1965. She stayed at Chicago until 1969, when her tenure case foundered in a close decision that minimized the importance of her study, despite its acceptance as a research monograph by the National Council of Teachers of English (and subsequently published in 1971).

At the time, few might have predicted that within a few years Emig's work would become widely recognized as a pioneering work in English education. By all accounts, Emig's dissertation study began to have considerable influence among North American writing teachers and researchers by the mid-1970s. It established the composing process as a key concept in the new discourse about writing, and shifted pedagogical attention away from prescriptive characterizations concerning model texts to empirical descriptions of the real-time composing processes of ordinary student writers. Her use of think-aloud protocols foreshadowed the subsequent research of Flower and Hayes (1977, 1981), and gave the idea of cognitive process some currency and panache in departments of English. It clearly altered thinking about writing pedagogy.

Similarly, Smith's *Understanding Reading* quickly established him as a new breed of reading expert, interpreting the findings and principles of the then-new psycholinguistics for an educational context, emphasizing basic understandings rather than instructional methods. Now in its fifth edition, *Understanding Reading* continues to be a highly influential textbook and basic reference on reading processes.

How are we to understand the surprising, resounding influence of these two individuals who as graduate students in the 1960s must surely have seemed unlikely candidates to radically influence ideas about writing, reading, and literacy in North American schools? Few in the late 1960s—no doubt including Smith himself—would have thought an experimental psycholinguist schooled in language, mind, and perception, *but not in reading*—would articulate a seminal concept of reading as a cognitive process that would shape debate among reading researchers and educators in the 1970s and beyond. And few could have anticipated that a doctoral student scarcely able to find support for her new ideas about writing among the faculty of Harvard, and eventually denied tenure at the University of Chicago would subsequently become a key figure in the new discourse about writing as a cognitive process, a concept that influences research on writing and writing instruction to this day.

Harvard was not noted for its graduate programs in writing, reading, or literacy in the 1960s. There were no faculty members conducting studies of either writing or reading. How, then, are we to account for the preparation and vitality of its graduate students in these areas? Perhaps the most obvious source of ideas was the revolutions in linguistics and psychology. Without question, the 1960s Cambridge Cognitive Revolution—the new ideas about language and mind articulated in the pioneering work of Chomsky, Bruner, and Miller at both Harvard and MIT—helped propel the new research on reading and writing. In the early 1970s, the new discourse on reading and writing drew heavily on the new ideas about language and mind inspired by Noam Chomsky. Chomsky (1957) revolutionized linguistics by conceptualizing language as the rule-governed acts, which he called "performance," of an underlying, generative "competence," or mind. This competence, he argued, was genetic (innate), universal, and cognitive. From this perspective, to study language was to investigate the structure of mind, and in *Cartesian Linguistics* (1966) and *Language and Mind* (1968), Chomsky treated language as rule-governed, rational knowledge.

Chomsky's ideas were soon widely viewed as a new frontier of intellectual inquiry with profound implications for fields far beyond linguistics. In a 1970 volume on Chomsky in the Viking Modern Master Series, British linguist John Lyons wrote, "It is clear that an understanding of transformational grammar is essential for any philosopher, psychologist, or biologist who wishes to take account of man's capacity for language" (Lyons, 1970, p. 4). In *The Genesis of Language*, the published proceedings of a 1965 conference on language development sponsored by the Human Communication Program of the National Institute of Child Health and Human Development, the editors, Frank Smith and George Miller, noted, "participants in this conference felt themselves to be part of a much larger army of workers, contributing to the purification of ideas that rank among the great triumphs of the modern mind" (Smith and Miller, 1966, pp. 1–2). In short, they felt themselves part of a vigorous, cutting edge academic culture.

There seemed to be no limit to the power and promise of this new Cartesian view of language—"unprecedented in the whole history of the subject" (Lyons, 1970, p. 1), and it inspired collaborative work in particular between linguists and psychologists, led by Miller and Bruner, that quickly established a new discipline called psycholinguistics. Chomsky had insisted that linguistics was appropriately suited to investigating linguistic universals, that is, the abstract rules of competence underlying actual performance; the task of devising "a performance model" based on generative competence he reserved for others, especially in psycholinguistics.[4] Nowhere were such efforts undertaken more assiduously than at Miller and Bruner's Center for Cognitive Studies, where many scholars in psychology, linguistics, and other disciplines examined implications of the new theory of language and mind in the world. As Smith put it in his (1995) interview with me:

This whole area was a, was a region of order that suddenly appeared in the turbulence of language studies and behaviorism and all the rest. And to a lot of people, it made sense. And they grabbed on it. And I'm sure that's what happened to people in the [Graduate] School of Ed and to all of the other people who got involved, and it certainly did with me. . . . I mean, there were suddenly all kinds of pegs that you could hang ideas on. And so it wasn't that people went in accepting them blindly, but these were the debating points, the arguing points. It was very exciting replacing it now. And it just all happened to come together.

And so it is should not surprise us that Smith, with the other graduate students at Harvard at the time, sought to articulate the implications of the new ideas about language for understanding reading and writing, testing the scope of a powerful new theory. With his mentor, Miller, Smith characterized their mission as "the construction of a performance model based on the generative competence of the language user" (Smith & Miller, 1966, p. 4). Smith's model of the reading process is to be understood as just such a model. This emphasis on the generative competence of the language use also accounts for Emig's concept of writing as language production rather than as rhetoric; indeed, her 1971 monograph presents the writer's significant other as the teacher, not the reader or audience. The other Harvard dissertations on writing at the time also focused on problems of language production, such as Read's study of invented spelling and Mellon's study of transformational-generative sentence combining.

The cultural and formative context for work on language and literacy education in Cambridge during this time was highly interdisciplinary, involving several units at both Harvard and MIT. Though Chomsky was at MIT, he exerted a strong influence at Harvard. In my (1995) interview with him, Smith recalled that time:

So I went to this old house to meet George Miller, whom I hadn't met before, and I was very intimidated by him. But there was somebody also in the place, a young guy who I thought could have been a painter, who showed me around the place. A workman. And sort of leaning on the mantelpiece, and, I thought, listening to the curiosities of this conversation going on between George Miller and me because George and I sort of tried to get to know each other because our lives were going to get involved. And after about fifteen minutes, George introduced me, and he said, "Oh, by the way, this is Chomsky." (laughs) And I hadn't the faintest idea what to say to Noam Chomsky. I didn't speak his language at all. That was sort of the presence of Chomsky at that time, at the Cognitive Center. I mean, he was there in spirit all the time, but it was basically his students and his colleagues who were at the Center.

Harvard students commonly took courses with Chomsky and others at MIT. Emig, for example, studied psychology with Eric Lenneberg and linguistics at MIT with Edward Klema; she also heard some lectures by

Chomsky.[5] The new interdisciplinary research in psycholinguistics aptly reflected the high degree of collaboration characteristic of the discourse and research about language and mind in Cambridge at this time. It was the new frontier of research on language and mind.

The Receptive Context for the New Discourse about Writing and Reading

The intellectual culture of Harvard was an essential source for Emig's and Smith's new ideas about writing and reading, but it does not account for why they took root, developed as they did, and had the influence they did. We will recall that Emig's interest in writing was barely noted while she was at Harvard, and that Smith did no work on reading at all while he was there. Clearly, a full account of their success merely *begins* with the formative context of their graduate education. The rest concerns the receptive contexts in which the new ideas were used and valorized—the culture beyond Harvard.

The most obvious aspect of the cultural landscape in the United States during the late 1960s and early 1970s was the effect of social protests arising from the Civil Rights Movement and campus revolts against the War in Vietnam. Did the tumultuous political and social climate of the late 1960s affect the intellectual climate and thought about language in American universities? University campuses—both faculty and students— were so caught up in the Civil Rights Movement and in protests against the war that it is hard to imagine that any ideas of the day could have been somehow isolated from the torrents of political and cultural change. Yet there is no obvious and specific connection, and Noam Chomsky, the leading linguist of the day, has many times denied any link between his own ideas about language and his vigorous protests of the war. Nonetheless, several arguments can be made. First, Chomsky's validation of innate and universal qualities of mind provided compelling arguments supporting not only empirical investigations of human cognition, but also political appeals for a democratic ethos characteristic of both protest movements, challenging all assumptions about the inferiority of minority races and marginal groups. Moreover, his intellectual temperament challenging existing ideas and official accounts in both linguistics and national politics was completely consistent with vigorous protests and challenges to established authority of campus administration and to the established powers in Washington. Wayne O'Neil, head of Chomsky's linguistics department and his colleague at MIT, discussed Chomsky's broad influence in his (1996) interview with me:

[Consider all the] things that Chomsky brought to the world of linguistics, psychology, and lots of other fields. So then it's sort of maybe at that level that there's a connection, you know? Once you start questioning the verities, there's no reason to stop with the sort of scientific ones. Because there are things that exist that have no basis whatsoever of any kind. Well maybe [such speculation is] pseudoscience. Chomsky always says no, there's no connection. But then he'll retreat to that sort of higher ground. But uh, yeah, if you're a questioning person, you don't need limit your questions to any particular set of issues. I would say Chomsky as a model had a lot of influence on the political protests of the 1960s.

Indeed, in the late 1960s, radical challenge and critique touching both scholarly work and American society soon became the intellectual order of the day; it affected scholars in the social sciences and the humanities in particular, and students elsewhere—as far away as France and China.

If radical criticism shaped the discourse of the day both on and off campus, the Great Society initiatives of the Johnson administration promoted a more systematic intertwining of official politics and academic expertise. During the 1960s, there were unprecedented collaborations between the federal government and American universities. All in all, President Johnson commissioned 135 task forces to address critical problems of health, education, welfare, and the environment. In his Great Society address at the University of Michigan commencement in May 1964, President Johnson set the tone:

We are going to assemble the best thought and the broadest knowledge from all over the world. . . . I intend to establish working groups to prepare a series of White House conferences and meetings—on the cities, on natural beauty, on the quality of education, and on other emerging challenges. And from these meetings and from these studies, we will begin to set our course toward the Great Society. (Johnson, 1965a, p. 705)

He challenged his cabinet "to think in bold terms and to strike out in new directions" (7/2/65). His was to be

an activist Administration, not a caretaker of past gains. I want to get the advice of the best brains in the country on the problems and challenges confronting America, and I want their help in devising the best approach to meeting them. (Johnson, quoted in Graham, 1984, p. 56)

Membership in these groups was to be secret, and both Congress and the press were to be kept in the dark about meetings, activities, and recommendations until the administration sent its proposals for legislation up the Hill to Congress.

Most individuals on the task forces were academics, and the great majority of these were from Harvard and other Ivy League universities. Starting in 1966, the Secretary of Health, Education, and Welfare, Joseph Califano, annually visited American campuses to "harvest" the ideas and recommendations of the task forces. These he compiled for the President in series of "idea books," which became the raw material for the Great Society legislation.

If academics were a major source of ideas for federal programs, they were also beneficiaries, since their recommendations often resulted in substantial funding for ambitious new research programs and research centers, especially in education. The first "R&D" (research and development) centers in education were initiated in 1963 at the University of Wisconsin, the University of Oregon, Pittsburgh University, and Harvard. They were deliberately modeled after the academic research facilities of the Pentagon, such as Livermore Laboratories at the University of California at Berkeley, and R&D projects like the Manhattan Project, which had developed the atomic bomb.

An important American legacy from World War II was Americans' confidence in the power of know-how to solve major problems (Samuelson, 1995). This confidence had its roots in the Jeffersonian ideal that de Tocqueville observed to be "the indefinite perfectibility of man," and was subsequently enacted in many reform movements, including the Progressive Era of the early twentieth century. "Americans do not abide very quietly the evils of life," Hofstadter (1960) wrote. "We are forever restlessly pitting ourselves against them, demanding changes, improvements, remedies, but not often with sufficient sense of the limits that the human condition will in the end insistently impose on us" (p. 16).

By the end of the war, most Americans who had lived through both the Depression and the War believed that the US was capable of doing anything. All that was necessary was the political will to concentrate its expertise and resources on carefully targeted problems. Hence, the country that defeated Japan organized itself to land a man on the moon "before the decade is out." President John F. Kennedy's challenge was part of his state-of-the-union address in 1961. In his inaugural address (and several years before the Great Society programs), he proclaimed, "Man holds in his hands the power to abolish all forms of human poverty." World War II victory provided a ready metaphor for the fight against the nation's social ills as the Johnson administration launched its War on Poverty during the 1960s. Later administrations launched a War on Drugs (Samuelson, 1995). As Moynihan said, "[I]n the early 1960s in Washington we thought we could do anything" (in Dershimer, 1976, p. 69). There was an official culture of hubris.

This euphoric optimism fueled ambitious new federal efforts in education. The postwar baby boom increased demands on schools, and the resulting shortage of teachers was exacerbated by inflation. The states increasingly looked to the federal government for assistance. In addition, World War II had increased public awareness of widespread illiteracy, and this was regarded as a national defense problem (Graham, 1984, p. xviii); it became a crisis when the Soviet Union beat the United States into space with its successful launch of Sputnik in 1957. Congress passed the National Defense Education Act in 1958.

Related to this, the National Science Foundation funded a program of research to develop a new program of physics instruction for high schools known as PSSC (Physical Sciences Study Committee) Physics. Initial funding in 1957 was $445,000, an amount unprecedented for an education project. By 1959, funding had increased to $1.8 million. Jerrold Zacharias, an MIT physicist who had been a scientist at the Los Alamos Laboratory during the 1940s, directed the project. In 1960, he started Educational Services, Inc. (ESI) as an education research and development facility concerned with all phases of education reform. Zaccharias quickly became recognized as the "prototype of caliber" needed by new scholars in education (Dershimer, 1976, p. 60). Most important, in this new climate, he was *not* an "educationist," one of the professional educators who populated the teacher's colleges. More than most, Francis Keppel, dean of the Harvard Graduate School of Education, led the charge for change: "Education," he said, " is too important to be left solely to the educators" (Dershimer, 1976, p. 50).

Our principal faults from the past are these: The most common form of educational research has been and is still the small, easily-managed project which focuses on miniature, obscure and non-controversial issues, which are seldom taken seriously by administrators or teachers. Education research has been and is still short of the best minds needed for the best possible results. Without the best of researchers, we have yet to show an innovative, creative vigor matching our counterparts in medicine, science, agriculture and industry. (Keppel, 1964, 460)

For Keppel, the educationists represented the past; scientists and scholars like Zaccharias were to be the future of education.

Keppel did have long to wait. In 1962, he became U.S. Commissioner of Education in the Kennedy administration, taking readily to "the generation of a new momentum and mood, a new sense of dialogue and possibility" (Graham, 1984, p. 51). The major changes would come in the wake of the Kennedy assassination and especially the Democratic landslide of 1964, in which the Democrats gained control of the White House and both houses of the Congress. During the 1960s, federal aid to schools and colleges increased from $1.8 to $12 billion a year, and the number of federal education programs increased from 20 to 130. By the late 1960s, a new community college opened every week (Graham, 1984, p. 223). In 1965 alone, federal expenditures on education nearly doubled over the previous year, from 4.4% to 7.9% of total receipts; federal spending on elementary and secondary schools alone more than doubled from $896 million to more than $2 billion. The Office of Education "reached a pace that was reminiscent of military agencies during World War II" (Dershimer, 1976, p. 70).

According to President Johnson, a former school teacher in Texas, education was "central to the purposes of this Administration, and at the core of all of our hopes for a Great Society" (Johnson, 1965b, quoted in Dershimer, 1976, p. 69). By 1965, Keppel would say, "the educator is the captain in a nationwide crusade to improve the quality of life; goals that seemed unreachable have become practical and close at hand" (1965, p. 167). The country had won the War and built the Bomb and was well on its way to the moon. Surely it could fix education too. Indeed, in 1966, the William Friday task force recommended that the nation "undertake a massive 'moon shot' effort[6] in curriculum and instruction to avoid the "national calamity" that a quarter of our children pass through school without learning the 3 Rs" (from *Report of the 1966 Task Force on Education*, 30 June 1967. Task Force File, container 4, LBJ Library; quoted Graham, 1984, p. 173).

Ambitious new research and development (R&D) centers in education modeled after Argonne Laboratories and Brookhaven Laboratory, "the great national laboratories of the Atomic Energy Commission" (*Re-

port of the President's Task Force on Education, p. 34, quoted in Der-shimer, 1976, p. 65), were viewed as a key to the fix. $300,000 to $1 million a year was to be concentrated in long-term projects targeting significant and carefully defined educational problems;[7] each project, involving a team of empirical researchers and research assistants, was to start with ba-sic research and culminate in the development and implementation of new curricula, instructional methods, and materials.[8] The new education research was to be conducted according to the highest scientific stan-dards—"in its devotion to rigor, replicability, and presentation of data, as well as in its need for building a community of scholars to adjudicate dis-putes, relate the work to public needs and policies, and, of course, to gar-ner the funds needed to conduct the research" (Goslin, summarized by Kaestle, 1992, p. 67). In 1964, John Gardner chaired a presidential task force on education recommending "escalation of R&D labs like the Atomic Energy Commission" (Dershimer, 1976, p. 62). We believed, Ralph Tyler said, "that education research would make a difference, that if you brought knowledge to bear on social problems it would improve them" (quoted Dershimer 1976, p. 65). In 1965, the Elementary and Secondary Education Act expanded the programs of centers, and six more R&D cen-ters were approved for a total of ten. The R&D centers, devoted to basic research, were augmented by a number of regional educational laborato-ries (RELs) established to transform the basic research findings of the centers into useful classroom programs and materials.

In this climate, Frank Smith was the very model of the new modern education expert, and he was quickly hired by the new Ontario Institute for Studies in Education, colloquially known as OISE (and pronounced *OY-zee*), established in 1965 as an independent institute devoted entirely to basic research, field work in education, and graduate study. Like the new American education R&D centers on which it was modeled, its mis-sion stressed basic research; it had nothing to do with teacher education. The main purpose of OISE was to generate and disseminate basic re-search for organizing schools and shaping instruction according to the most up-to-date knowledge available. Smith's credentials as a psycholin-guist and his experience with Miller and Bruner were impressive enough for OISE to hire him as an associate professor with tenure even though he had no prior experience as an assistant professor.[9] What's more, he was hired with tenure prior even to his assignment to a particular department. In reviewing his credentials, the department of Curriculum and Instruc-

tion viewed him as a psychologist, but the psychology department dis-
agreed. He eventually joined Curriculum and Instruction where he was
assigned to teach courses in reading because of his expertise on word perception, the topic of his dissertation. Smith recalls,

Well, when I got to OISE, it was very odd. I had some status because I'd written
a book and my first appointment was—I was an associate prof. I'd never been an
assistant prof, and they put me into the curriculum department—it seemed the
obvious place to put someone who knew something about language, but I didn't
know anything about reading. But it was just assumed that anybody could teach a
course on reading. And so I was confronted by all these graduate students, very
experienced teachers, very bright and experienced teachers, and I was supposed
to teach them a course on the foundations of reading. And my colleague said to
me, "It's easy, you just go down to the library and find a book about reading, and
then you teach that to your students, you see." And I went down to the library, and
I found dozens of books on the topic of reading, but they were all on the topic of
teaching reading—they were all somebody's opinion about how to teach reading.
Somebody's recipe for teaching reading. There wasn't a book. I went back to
my students and said, "Look, there's not a book on reading we can use for this
course—we'll write the book." And I went through a series of seminars that were
basically the titles of the chapters and the visualized (inaudible) and things like
that. And basically I explored ideas with them and worked them out with them,
and the crux initially, it was mainly theoretical.

I thought you had to get away from this notion of how to teach reading before
you, until you got an idea of what reading was. And it was quite clear as soon as
you stopped to think about it—you know, what was so clear from all around you—
that reading was rooted in meaning. You couldn't talk about reading without talking about meaning. And all of these things that people call the mechanics of reading were byproducts. They weren't the foundations of reading. So it's almost
irrelevant consequences of becoming readers.

The result was *Understanding Reading*. First published in 1971, this book
was an expansion of his Foundations in Reading syllabus and significantly
reflects what he learned about the needs of his M.Ed. and Ph.D. students,
all experienced teachers. Smith's story clearly shows that it was only after
he began to teach graduate courses in reading that he began to be viewed
as a reading expert or even began to think of himself in that role. In short,
Smith never set out to become a reading expert; it was a role others created for him.

Emig's *The Composing Process of Twelfth Graders* was "kindly treated"

(Emig, 1995) by reviewers soon after it was published in 1971, but it was not until the mid-1970s that her monograph caught the attention of those in English education and, eventually, of those in the composition studies community. Indeed, Emig did not identify herself as part of the composition studies community until the mid-1980s when she found herself on committees within the Conference on College Composition and Communication (CCCC):

Nystrand: Um, so when you first went to Harvard, you went into the program . . .
Emig: Yes.
Nystrand: With an emphasis on writing?
Emig: No, I didn't know that then. It was just in English Ed.
Nystrand: Okay.
Emig: There were specialties. I mean—
Nystrand: You thought you were going to do a dissertation on writing and composing?
Emig: Hmmm. No. I didn't know. I thought I might.
Nystrand: I see. But by the time you graduated and got your degree that was certainly the case.
Emig: Yes, absolutely.
Nystrand: And you still thought of your field as English Ed?
Emig: Yes.
Nystrand: Even when you were at Rutgers?
Emig: It was English Ed at Rutgers.
Nystrand: Has that changed at all? Do you still think of your field as English Ed?
Emig: I think of my field as Composition Studies.
Nystrand: When did you begin to think of it as Comp Studies rather than English Ed?
Emig: When I got on committees . . . and I guess it was attendance at 4Cs [Conference on College Composition and Communication] meetings, and I realized my primary affiliation was—I didn't use the term—"composition studies." I don't know who first used it. I thought, "Ah, that identifies it." (from interview 6/23/95)

Just as Smith did not know that reading was his field until he was classified as such by OISE, Emig's own professional identity was determined by the institutional categories of a professional organization more than a decade after she had done the work that served as the basis of the categorization. The eventual discoveries of Smith and Emig by their respective fields reminds us of Bakhtin's materialist claims that meaning is always realized under "particular concrete circumstances" (1986, p. 83). Meaning, he writes, "does not inhere in the word itself. It originates at the point of contact between the word and actual reality, under the conditions of that real situation articulated by the individual utterance" (1986, p. 88). Smith became a reading scholar and Emig a writing scholar less through will and career plans than by cultural change that supported disciplinary shifts both inside and outside the academy, which conferred professional status upon them.

Influence as a Semiotic Problem

Though the works of Smith and Emig each bridged their respective formative and receptive contexts, there is a fundamental, telling difference in how this came about. Smith's foray into reading—one of the new frontiers of psycholinguistics—represents one path taken by the new science of mind as it grappled with problems in the world beyond the academy. His story, both intellectually and personally, is about moving out of the academy and into the world, into the problems of everyday culture. The movement in Emig's case is just the opposite: it is about bringing the world into the academy. Her intellectual legacy was making empirical descriptions of ordinary student writing legitimate as a research problem. Her personal story is that of a woman's struggle from the margins of academia to win respect as a female academic interested in both writing and instruction, or as Emig put it in my (1995) interview with her, "There's an intertwining among status as a woman, status of writing, and status of teaching—three classes of second-class citizenship going on simultaneously." These were difficult challenges.

Smith and Emig, then, represent two different dynamics at work in the emergence of the new discourse about writing and reading circa 1970. The first of these tested the scope of a powerful new theory in the world. Researchers began to uncover striking patterns in the developing speech of one- and two-year olds, which lead to findings that revealed grammatical rules for emerging language. Labov (1969, 1972) showed that nonstandard dialects like Black (African American) English Vernacular (BEV) were characterized by their own underlying grammars. And scholars like Read (1969, 1971), who studied the "invented" spellings of children who begin writing without instruction before school, documented a surprisingly common logic and structure in their idiosyncratic spellings, explaining why, for example, untutored preschool writers who had never met often wrote CHK for "truck" (because what sounds like "tr" to fluent adults sounds like "ch" to young children whose speech is still developing). Such studies, which found patterns and underlying structures in poorly understood and seemingly inchoate language phenomena, helped push the boundaries of the new conception of language into domains of experience never before explored by either linguistics or psychologists. The optimism bred by such successes supported ambitious efforts like OISE and other research-based applications of rational knowledge to problems of education, such as the National Institute of Education's (NIE's) R&D centers and regional labs. These included the Center for the Study of Reading, established in 1975 to bring new empirical insights into reading to bear on reading problems in the schools; and NIE's program of empirical writing research started by in 1979, and subsequently the Center for the Study of Writing at Berkeley and Carnegie Mellon University in 1985.

Emig and Smith figure as protagonists in my narrative because their work so clearly played a key role in these developments. Both Emig and Smith drew from then current concerns and intellectual traditions a set of more or less coherent ideas about language and mind. They transformed them into concepts and arguments that met a receptive audience in professional and instructional contexts, including departments of English and writing classrooms. Their subsequent impact on writing and reading research in North America illuminates the reciprocal relation between these two developments, showing how neo-Cartesian ideas about language helped shape ideas that became canonical in writing and reading research, and how the concerns of language learning and writing pedagogy motivated further development in this line of inquiry.

Thus, the emergence of the new discourse on writing and reading in North America in the 1970s, like any new discourse, is appropriately conceptualized as a semiotic problem. In dialogic terms, the problem is one of understanding the value and use of any given utterance, text, or voice by relating it (as a link in Bakhtin's chain of speech communication) to the voices and texts that precede and influence it, and to the voices and texts that follow and are influenced by it, which is to say, those that accept and find value in, or "valorize" it. In other words, tracing the influence of various actors and voices in the development of a field requires two complementary inquiries. Attention must be paid first to the formative contexts which influence the actors, and then to their receptive contexts in which their ideas are valued, used, and resonate. It is just such use and resonance, of course, that enable actors to become voices. Moreover, actors become disciplinary voices and elements of intellectual histories only if their work somehow bridges both formative and receptive contexts, and indeed, this is why Emig's *Composing Processes of Twelfth Graders* and Smith's *Understanding Reading* became key texts in the new pedagogical discourse about writing and reading. Disciplinary fields are fields of voices and texts. These voices struggle, echo, resonate, "refract," and sometimes "strive to ignore" each other, as Wertsch (1985, p. 65) puts it. Some, but not all, of the voices in the new discourse about writing and reading were conventional and institutional, including the instructional voices of teachers and students, as well as studies, dissertations, and published articles and books. The main formative voices came from graduate school, but some of the voices were cultural and political from sources much larger than the academy itself. Together these voices constitute the "textual space" in which disciplinary voices have meaning and gain influence (cf. Nystrand, 1982).

When texts like *The Composing Processes of Twelfth Graders* and *Understanding Reading* gain authority, the dominance of their meaning—defining writing and reading as cognitive processes—results from the distinctive way that voices from their formative and receptive contexts meet and interact. The authors are influential precisely because their texts uniquely mediate the two contexts. In other words, if ordinary meaning is the refraction of voices in discourse, then influence is meaning made dominant as it is consummated by the interaction of formative and receptive contexts. To understand the seminal influence of these two texts, then, requires that we situate them between the authors' sources and the subsequent uses of their ideas, including politics and culture, curricular reform, issues of professionalization, and the like. Our study shows how questions about the influence of Emig and Smith raise a key, Foucaultian question concerning discursive formation: What was it about historical circumstances and conditions in North America circa 1970 that promoted cognitive conceptions of writing and empirical methods of research and eventually fueled the new discourse about writing and reading? *Why these ideas then?*

Conclusion

Looking closely at the influence of Frank Smith and Janet Emig, we are easily struck by the unpredictable twists and turns of their careers. In

a very real sense, their graduate educations did not directly prepare them
for their eventual careers. Smith had no training as a reading researcher,
and Emig's interest in writing encountered obstacles at nearly every turn.
Not even their closest advisors could have predicted the nature and extent
of their eventual success. Their paths of influence begin to make sense
only when we expand our inquiry to include the contexts of their education and work, especially the latter. The receptive contexts are far harder
to grasp than the formative contexts; indeed, we have only to survey the
citations in their major publications to gain a reasonable understanding of
many if not most of the varied voices that influenced their thinking. Less
obvious are the effects of the receptive contexts in which their works were
used and achieved resonance. It is the receptive contexts that introduced
some of the most intricate twists and turns in their careers, and so they
complicate our efforts to understand their influence. Many key receptive
contexts simply didn't exist during their graduate work. (This explains why
Emig did not realize that her field was composition studies until long after her work had helped create the field!) In the early 1960s, who might
have predicted the rise of OISE and its creators' eagerness to hire and
tenure untested new faculty in psycholinguistics? Who might have fore-
seen the vigorous way in which the provincial government of Ontario and
the federal government in the United States would support basic research
as a way of improving teaching and learning? Who would have predicted
the literacy crisis of the 1970s and its impact on writing research? Who
even now fully understands how political and social forces that focused on
aspects of cultural difference turned academic interest away from prescribing model text features to empirically describing the processes of ordinary writers? In considering questions such as these, we begin to see
how empirical studies in writing in the 1970s provided a key forum for
mediating the new theory of mind as well as the complicated sociocultural contexts of the world.

Notes

    This chapter was presented as an introductory plenary paper at the International
Seminar "Bakhtinian Perspectives: Thinking Culture Dialogically" at the University of Science and Technology, Trondheim, Norway. Research for this paper was supported by a
major grant from the Spencer Foundation. This paper was prepared at The National Research Center on English Learning and Achievement, Wisconsin Center for Education
Research, School of Education, University of Wisconsin–Madison, which is supported in
part by a grant from the Office of Educational Research and Improvement (Grant No.

G-008690007-89). Any opinions, findings, and conclusions or recommendations expressed in this publication are those of the authors and do not necessarily reflect the views of the Spencer Foundation, OERI, or the U.S. Department of Education. Marjorie Jolles assisted ably with invaluable bibliographic help.

1. In my (1995) interview with him, Frank Smith put it this way: "What I produce is a book. And I don't regard a book as part of me, I regard a book as something outside of me. I mean, I think you have a bizarre kind of thrill to say, 'Well I produced that book.' Although I wasn't totally responsible for it, but also some people contributed, but nevertheless there's that book and it's my baby. It came from me. But it's independent of me. And I find that sort of other people know my books much better than I do. And claim them much better than I do, own them much more than I do."

2. Emig was by no means the first person to think about writing as a process. Town (1988), for example, found a "persistent awareness" of writing as a process in *English Journal* articles written from 1912–1960. In 1950, Drake outlined a four-stage pedagogical sequence featuring stages of writing, including drafting, revising, peer response, and more revising ("Developmental writing." *College Composition and Communication,* 3–6). In 1953, Mills published "Writing as Process" (*College English,* 19–26). And in 1964 Rohman and Wleke (1964) treated writing as a process when they sketched an approach to "prewriting" (*Pre-writing: The construction and application of models for concept formation in writing.* U.S. Office of Education Cooperative Research Project, No. 2174. East Lansing: Michigan State University). Emig's (1971) monograph differs from all these previous efforts, however, in two significant ways. First, every one of the previous cases lacked follow through. Moreover, by empirically investigating the composing process, Emig's focus differed fundamentally from those of her predecessors, who were more interested in teaching writing than in conducting basic research on the nature of writing. The issue here is not when someone first called attention to writing as a process but when someone began to focus on writing processes in a systematic, empirical way.

3. At the start of Emig's first year, the other Harvard Graduate School of Education faculty member in English education was fired for alcoholism and sexual harassment.

4. In *The Genesis of Language,* Smith and Miller wrote, "The construction of a performance model based on the generative competence of the language user is a further task for the theorist and one that linguists share with their colleagues in psychology" (p. 4).

5. Emig remembers reading a fellow student's notes of Jerome Bruner's lectures, though she was not a student in his course. She also learned about cognitive development from working with Roger Brown on an essay he submitted to the *Harvard Educational Review,* when she was coeditor of a special issue (see Nelms, 1995, p. 117).

6. Frank Smith was a witness to this approach to education. Before accepting a faculty position at the Ontario Institute for Studies in Education, Frank Smith briefly worked at the Southwest Regional Laboratory (SWRL) in Los Alamitos, California. Here, he described in his (1995) interview with me, "they were bringing these people in who were from NASA. They thought that NASA engineers could certainly help improve literacy—in fact, articles were published associating the drive for literacy with the space race. Essentially for education back in those days, people were referring to universal literacy as education's move. We were going to put kids into orbit would make them literate. And Rod Steiger, who was the executive secretary of the IRA in those days, published an article in an IRA journal saying that IRA and NASA had agreed to collaborate in teaching kids to read."

7. According to the Research and Development Center Program Act of 1963, the centers were "to concentrate human and financial resources on a particular problem area in education over an extended period of time in an attempt to make significant contribution

toward an understanding of, and an improvement of educational practice in, the problem area" (*Cooperative Research Programs: Application Instruction for Research Contracts*. U.S. Dept of aHEW, Office of Ed., Washington: U.S. Government Printing Office, 1963, p. 27.)

8. According to the request for proposals, "More specifically, the personnel of a center will:

1. Conduct basic and applied research studies, both of the laboratory and field type.
2. Conduct development activities designed to translate systematically research findings into educational materials or procedures, and field test the developed products.
3. Demonstrate and disseminate information about the new programs or procedures which emerge from the research and development efforts. These activities may include demonstrations in a natural, or operational setting, the preparation of films, tapes, displays, publications, and lectures, and the participation in symposia and conferences.
4. Provide nationwide leadership in the chosen area" (*Cooperative Research Programs: Application Instruction for Research Contracts*. U.S. Department of Health, Education, and Welfare, Office of Education, Washington: U.S. Government Printing Office, 1963, p. 27.)

9. Such institutional largesse seems odd indeed from our current perspective when publicly funded institutions are under nearly unprecedented pressure to scale down and cut back. The early 1960s were a time of great optimism about the possibilities of government as manifest, for example, by the Great Society programs, especially educational programs. These include *Sesame Street* and the Children's Television Workshop, Operation Head Start, and the efforts of the National Institute of Education, viewed as a key federal agency to improve education and learning, seeking especially to exploit insights and findings from basic research in the social sciences. The 1960s were also a period of rapid growth for the American Educational Research Association (AERA), which at that time separated from the National Education Association (NEA).

References

Chomsky, N. (1957). *Syntactic structures*. The Hague: Mouton.

Chomsky, N. (1959). Review of B. F. Skinner, Verbal *Behavior*. *Language, 35*, 26–57. (1966).

Chomksy. N. (1966). *Cartesian linguistics: A chapter in the history of rationalist thought*. New York: Harper & Row.

Chomsky, N. (1968). *Language and mind*. New York: Harcourt, Brace & World.

Davis, W. (1985). Reflections on the founding of OISE. *Orbit, 75*, 1–4.

Dershimer, R. (1976). *The federal government and educational r&d*. Lexington, MA: Lexington Books.

Emig, J. (1971). *The composing processes of twelfth graders*. Urbana: The National Council of Teachers of English.

Emig, J. (1981). Non-magical thinking: Presenting writing developmentally in schools. In C. Frederiksen & J. Dominic (Eds.), *Writing: process, development, and communication*. Hillsdale, NJ: Erlbaum.

Emig, J. (1995). Personal interview with author, June 23, 1995.

Flower, L., & Hayes, J. (1981). A cognitive process theory of writing. *College Composition and Communication, 32*, 365–387.

Fogarty, D. (1959). *Roots for a new rhetoric*. New York: Russell and Russell.

Gardner, H. (1985). *The mind's new science*. New York: Basic Books.

Graham, Hugh Davis. (1984). *The uncertain triumph: Federal education policy in the Kennedy and Johnson years*. Chapel Hill: University of North Carolina Press.

Hofstadter, R. (1960). *The age of reform from Bryan to FDR*. New York: Vintage Books.

Johnson, L. B. (1964). Memorandum, Moyers to Ackley et al., 6 July 1964, EX FG 600, container 361, WHCF, LBJ Library; quoted in Graham, 1984.

Johnson, L. B. (1965a). *Public papers of the President of the United States: Lyndon Johnson, 1963–64*. Vol. 1. Washington, DC: Government Printing Office.

Johnson, L. B. (1965b). Remarks to the White House Conference on Education, 7/21/65.

Kaestle, C. (1992, April). Everybody's been to fourth grade: An oral history of federal R&D in education (A report to the National Research Council, Committee on the Federal Role in Education Research). Research Report 92-1. Madison: Wisconsin Center for Education.

Keppel, F. (1964, February 17). Heaving before the subcommittee of the Committee on Appropriations, House of Representatives, 88th Congress, 2nd Session, Washington, D.C., p. 460.

Keppel, F. (1964, September 17). Research: Education's Neglected Hope. Memo to John Gardner. Container 412, OMB Records Division, National Archives.

Keppel, F. (1965) . The National Commitment to Education. *Phi Delta Kappan, 47*, p. 167.

Labov, W. (1970). The logic of non-standard English. In J. Alatis (Ed.), *Georgetown University Monograph Series on Languages and Linguistics 22* (pp. 1–44). Washington, D.C.: Georgetown University Press.

Lyons, J. (1970). *Noam Chomsky*. Harmondsworth, UK: Penguin Books.

Mellon, J. C. (1969). *Transformational sentence-combining: A method for enhancing the development of syntactic fluency in English composition* (NCTE Research Report No. 10). Champaign, IL: National Council of Teachers of English.

Moynihan, D. P. (1973). *Coping: On the practice of government*. New York: Random House.

O'Neil, Wayne (1986). Personal interview with author, April 8, 1996.

Read, C. (1969). Pre-school children's knowledge of English phonology. *Harvard Educational Review, 41*, 1–34.

Read, C. (1971). *Children's categorization of speech sounds in English*. Urbana: National Council of Teachers of English.

Sheils, M., Fuller, T., Kellogg, M., & Boyd, F. (1975, December 8). Why Johnny can't write. *Newsweek, 86*, 58–62.

Smith, F. (1971). *Understanding reading*. New York: Holt, Rinehart, and Winston.

Smith, F. (1982). *Writing and the writer*. New York : Holt, Rinehart, and Winston.

Smith, F. (1983). *Comprehension and learning*. New York: Holt, Rinehart, and Winston.

Smith, F., & Miller, G. (1966). *The genesis of language: A psycholinguistic approach. Proceedings of a conference on "language development in children."* Cambridge, MA: MIT Press.

6

The Stolen Lipstick
of Overheard Song
Composing Voices in Child Song,
Verse, and Written Text

Anne Haas Dyson

Introduction

Little girls smearing
the stolen lipstick
of overheard grown-up talk
into their conversation
unconscious of the beauty
of their movements
like milkweed in the wind
are beginning to drift
over by the drinking fountain
where they will skip rope . . . (from Koch, 1998, p. 74)

The little girls of Koch's poem slip on oversized but glamorous voices,
akin to stolen lipstick, before drifting over to the jump ropes. And if Koch's
girls are anything like those in this article, their borrowed voices come not
only from close-at-hand people but also from close-at-hand technology,
including television, videos, and that common traveling companion, the
radio. The mother of a child featured herein, 6-year-old Denise, told me
that once when the song "I'm Goin' Down ['Cuz You Ain't Around]"
(Blige, 1994)[1] came on the car radio, Denise started singing along in a per-
fect bluesy voice. "'What?!'" Her mother laughed, recalling her reaction.

"'She's only [then] 5. And she's singing "I'm Goin' Down"! What does she know about it?'"

Denise, like her close school friends, did not only slip on musical voices from the radio; she appropriated them from church and school, from movies and television, from parents and grandparents, and from neighborhood kids. Some songs, like "I'm Goin' Down," seemed akin to lipstick and high heels. Other songs were more like combat boots, tough and assertive, and yet others seemed sweet saddle shoes with Sesame Street ties, or shiny Mary Janes buckled for church. Then there were the songs like children gone barefoot, play songs learned from neighborhood kids.

My interest in the musical texts of Denise and her friends originated in a larger study designed to examine childhood literacy in the context of childhood cultures; central to these cultures are the popular media. The media themselves, as well as professional early childhood publications, reflect general societal concerns about the quality and quantity of media in young children's lives (for example, Levin, 1998). This project's concern, however, was ethnographic: to understand the nature of young school children's appropriations from textual practices outside the academic world as they learned the practices valued within the schools.

The project's site was an urban classroom and its case or focal study unit was a small group of self-designated friends, each 6 years old at the start of the school year. The children's unofficial (or child-governed) talk and play indexed their participation with family, friends, and community members in a media-saturated landscape. Thus, media material mattered because it was constitutive of children's identities and of their shared worlds with others they valued. Moreover, this material allowed children to assume varied stances and roles, to express varied emotions and moods through the genre material of raps, R&B, hymns, playground rhymes, and folk songs. Through their oral efforts, children composed their own coherent stanzas with semantic consistency and repetitive structures.

This replaying and transforming of media texts has been characterized as a central aspect of youth culture (Willis, 1990), but it is also central to child cultures, as folklorists have documented (for example, McDowell, 1995). Willis (1990, p. 21) uses the term "a grounded aesthetic" to characterize the symbolic processes through which young people engage emotionally, cognitively, and socially with readily available cultural art forms, particularly those provided by the commercial media. In these processes, people appropriate and transform symbols and symbolic practices, "selecting, reselecting, highlighting and recomposing,"(Willis, 1990, p. 21) to particularize media symbols within their own life spaces. The "aesthetic" in this sense is not about the distant and abstract thing of beauty, but about the processes of using one's senses—voice, body movements, visual images—for pleasure, expression, and social affiliation. And the aesthetic in this sense also describes the lively symbol-making of Denise and her friends.

The children's experiences replaying and transforming media texts were part of their entry into school literacy. The children's *oral* song composing was supported by their sense of the genre and the kind of voice they were appropriating; that sense allowed them to manipulate complex layers of symbols (syllables, words, phrases, even different vocal parts). The same sense was necessary for their written composing. Most depended initially on the straightforward "I went" and "I like" cadences learned in school. But their development as writers was marked by appropriation of diverse material from their travels in a complex cultural landscape, including the appropriation of songs themselves.

Here I elaborate on the project's conceptual and methodological tools. I also offer a vision of the children's cultural landscape constructed from their appropriations of available songs. I have concentrated on the unofficial world, documenting the social purposes undergirding the children's efforts. I venture as well into the official world, detailing what children did and did not appropriate from musical media, and, more broadly, illustrating how the children's sense of language rhythms and melodies influenced their literacy efforts, particularly their composing. Throughout I feature Denise and her close friends as my reference points.

Before beginning, let me offer some background information. I am a researcher of children's social lives and of their early literacy, and I am a writer. As such, I give particular attention to children's arrangement and manipulation of words and their sounds, and describe their melodies.

Unlike a children's folklorist, I am interested in how the communicative resources children display in peer-governed situations become relevant or at least visible in school-governed ones. I aim to contribute to research and practice regarding school literacy. The field has valued a remarkably narrow range of textual and conceptual knowledge and practice, particularly in light of advances in theories of childhood (Corsaro, 1997), development (Goodnow, Miller, & Kessel, 1995), and literacy itself, which is becoming a multi-modal affair (New London Group, 1996;

Street, 1995). If educators are to follow the educational axiom: 'Build on what children bring,' they must understand the communicative resources and strengths of today's children in today's times, which are clearly media-saturated times.

I acknowledge that readers might find it disconcerting to hear little children singing songs that they may deem inappropriate—a judgment they would share with the observed children's parents, their favorite radio deejay, and with me. On the other hand, many readers will hardly be surprised to read of little children doing what the little ones in their own lives do. However, I hope all find it useful to see the commonplace within a theoretical view of language use, and, more concretely, to see its place within the goals of schooling. It is my hope that those with skills and sensibilities different from my own will see beyond what may be my limitations.

Finally, I make no claim to be a media fan, although one of my most vivid childhood memories is of standing outside, in full view of the neighbors, swinging a hula hoop on my hips and singing a spirited rendition of "Itsy Bitsy, Teeny Weeny, Yellow Polka-Dot Bikini," which I learned from the radio.

Children's Compositional Genius

Young children's writing does not suggest, at least to me, anything akin to compositional genius. For most, writing is hard work. Some children, like Denise's friend, Wenona, find it easiest to lean repeatedly on a failsafe message during "free writing" time (Wenona's was "I like cats"). Often accompanying a child's early struggle with print, however, is lively, fluent, and frequently playful talk (Dyson, 1989). That playful peer talk may well reveal "an aesthetics of the ordinary" and a "genius of composition," as McDowell (1995, p. 62) comments.

Of course, any use of language is a kind of performance (Hymes, 1972), but that term typically suggests an "aesthetically marked and heightened mode of communication" that lifts it apart from other voices and puts it on display (Bauman, 1992, p. 41). Words so framed as performances are easily moved to new contexts for new performances, and such is the basic process undergirding folklore and everyday aesthetic activity (Bauman & Briggs, 1990; McDowell, 1995; Willis, 1990).

Traditionally, children's folklore has been portrayed only as preserving language rituals through child generations. But, McDowell (1995, p. 53) notes, "even the briefest exposure to children's folklore reveals the almost amoebic ability of children" to make ready use of any textual material for expressive and communicative purposes and for aesthetic performance (cf. Willis, 1990). Child cultures demonstrate an alertness to repetitive, rhythmic, and emotionally charged discourse, including that found in popular culture (McMahon & Sutton-Smith, 1995). This discourse is appealing as material for play, and thus children lift bits from the original, shift it to new contexts within, and transform it for performance.

In this article, I use children's textual appropriations and their ordinary aesthetics to construct a vision of the landscape of voices that provides potential communicative resources. Below I first discuss Bakhtin's theoretical description of such a landscape, and then turn to selected research demonstrating children's skill as voice borrowers and transformers.

A Landscape of Voices

Young children are surrounded by voices emanating from boxes and screens of varied sizes, as well as from the people with whom they share their lives. In a Bakhtinian view of this audible landscape, the voices become conceptually organized into genres indexing particular social scenes, and into social strata indexing societal categories (for example, class, gender, ethnicity, age, and profession). Although organized, the landscape is dynamic, not static, because individual speakers are not perceived as parts of a chorus of like voices, but rather, as entering into dialogues with many other speakers, both in the present and the past.

Present voices echo with the past because over time speakers have enacted particular social situations in similar ways; thus, their utterances acquire certain shared features and thereby the "flavor of a given genre," with characteristic forms, themes, and evaluative slants (1981, p. 289). New speakers must use words that sound appropriate or no one may attend and respond, but they must also give those expected words their own accent, infuse them with their own intention, otherwise the response may only confirm their own fear of anonymity. This relationship between self and social landscape, between individual emotions and genre types will be evident in the child singing and chanting. For example, as Denise's mom suggested, the observed children surely did not understand the complexities of adult relationships, but they did understand the evaluative tone of a rap, as opposed to a love song, and they chose appropriate genres for their "made-up songs."

In a complex society, identity in some social groups may depend in part on members' explicitly distancing themselves from certain genres, dialects, or registers, from certain kinds of voices. They may view those particular ways with words not as communicative resources, but *only* as "objects . . . as local color" (Bakhtin, 1981, p. 289), that is, as symbols of a social class, or of an age group, or a profession. A disdain for popular texts in particular has been used to mark socioeconomic class "distinction" (Bourdieu, 1984) among adults, and among children in school contexts (Buckingham, 1993; Dyson, 1997). Young children, though, initially are quite open "scavengers of form and theme" (Goldman, 1998, p. 143) and of voice, as explained below.

Voice Borrowers and Rhythm Makers

Children learn language through participating in the practices or activities of their everyday lives (Vygotsky, 1978; Rogoff, 1990; Wertsch, 1985, 1991). Moreover, these activities "come packed with values about what is natural, mature, morally right, or aesthetically pleasing" (Miller & Goodnow, 1995, p. 6). Thus, children's subjectivities (their perception of themselves and of their own possibilities for action) develop in tandem with their symbolic resources and cognitive capacities (Bruner, 1990).

In their daily activities, children across cultures attend to the music of words, their rhythm and melody, as well as to their implied sense. Indeed, very young children seem particularly attuned to language rhythms and melodies that are expressly and expressively directed to them; among those musical language patterns are staccato disapprovals, sweet, rolling approvals, and long, smooth "there-there's" (Fernald, 1992). Throughout early childhood, children remain drawn to voices that are aesthetically marked and affectively charged. Their attentiveness to, and appropriation of such voices is illustrated by research on family conversation and language development (for example, Dore, 1989; Nelson, 1996), storytelling (Miller & Mehler, 1994), literary response (for example, Miller, Hoogstra, Mintz, Fung, & Williams, 1993; Wolf & Heath, 1992), and dramatic play (for example, Garvey, 1990).

Moreover, songs and poetry have traditionally been part of childcare across cultures—children are comforted, lulled to sleep, and, conversely, livened up through verbal and kinetic routines involving, for example, little piggies or baker's men. In language play involving young children, phonology is more important than semantics, and this is true of young school age children's language play as well (Garvey, 1990; McDowell, 1995). In this, the everyday aesthetic activity of children is like the more formal and removed aesthetics of literary artists; for both, sound or form is not a handmaiden to sense but, rather, its forceful partner (Koch, 1998).

The everyday aesthetic is audible in many neighborhoods, day care centers, and playgrounds as children learn songs and rhymes from other children. They use those verses to regulate clapping, jump roping, and other games; to pass judgement on the deviant; and simply to enjoy themselves (Opie & Opie, 1959; Sullivan, 1995). These oral performances are notably more vulgar, more raucous, more focused on sexual and power themes than any songs adults deliberately teach children.

Through their early exposure to aesthetically marked language, children gain "an awareness of poetry and song as genres and . . . [of] rhyme and rhythm, stanzaic or episodic structure, and all the other technical details, inherent and unnamed, of oral performance" (Sullivan, 1995, p. 146). Since that knowledge is embedded in their everyday activity, it is not necessarily available for deliberate reflection and use. But helping children gain reflective control of such embedded knowledge is a basic aim of schooling (Nelson, 1996; Vygotsky, 1987). Although this study's descriptive information about the observed children's communicative resources cannot be generalized in their details, they can provide a kind of basis or template for observing, naming, and responding to the resources of other children constructing other versions of childhood.

After a brief explanation of my methodology, I will try to allow readers to walk around in the children's shoes, envisioning their cultural landscape, hearing what aspects of musical texts and knowledge they appropriated, discussing the social ends that energized them, and considering what musical appropriations they brought with them onto the officially regulated landscape of school.

A Local Child Culture and Its Music: Methodological Notes

The children's school was officially described as having the "greatest crosstown span" in this East San Francisco Bay district (that is, the greatest socioeconomic mix). Approximately half the school's children were African American, approximately a third were European American, and the rest were of varied Latino and Asian ancestries. The Appendix provides pseudonym and demographic information for the 20 first-grade children.

Denise's first-grade teacher was Rita, a British woman who had begun teaching in the London primary schools of the 1960s. Rita's curriculum included both open-ended activities (for example, writing workshop, where the children wrote and drew relatively freely, followed by class sharing), and more teacher-directed ones (for example, assigned tasks in study units, in which children wrote and drew as part of social studies and science learning).

Rita was herself a visual artist, but she was a music lover. She furnished her classroom with a CD player and wove a rich variety of music into the school day. The [Local] Symphony, Bobby McFerrin, Cat Stevens, Ella Fitzgerald, Wee Sing, Sweet Honey in the Rock, Jimmy Cliff, and Joshua Redman were some classroom companions lying side-by-side in Rita's CD collection. She used contemporary folk music to calm the children, jazz to get the work rhythm going, and varied genres, including gospel, to accompany study units. Rita also participated in the Arts in the Schools program, which included class visits to the local symphony orchestra and classroom visits (and performances!) by individual members.

Carol Tateishi, director of the Bay Area Writing Project, had recommended this classroom to me because of this official art-filled curriculum. However, during my very first visit, I stumbled from the official classroom sphere into the unofficial one; I overheard Denise and a small group of peers refer to themselves as "the brothers and sisters." The group, all African American, included Denise, her "best fake sister" Vanessa, Wenona, Marcel, Noah, and Lakeisha, who was less centrally involved in the project because she attended varied pullout programs for academic and emotional support.

The children's self-designation as "fake" siblings was linked to the use of the label "brothers and sisters" to refer to solidarity in the African American tradition, but it was much more literal. They engaged in elaborate narrative play, which they called "games." In these games, and in the imaginary world they constituted, the children were actual siblings. For example, in one kind of play, the children reported what happened or predicted what would happen "at home" when they had some dramatic encounter with each other and "their" mother. In another, the children went home with each other after school (although, as their parents confirmed, none of the children did this).

Most relevant for the project, much of the play was informed by the media. The children presented a unique opportunity to explore the cultural landscape of a contemporary childhood and its links to varied sources of texts. I had come upon a semiotic gold mine and, fortunately, the children, their teacher, and their parents all allowed me entry. And so, in the fall of 1996, I began to document (through written observations and audio taping) the children's official and unofficial participation in school.

I collected data over an 8-month period, approximately 4 to 6 hours per week. I focused on the daily language arts period, but I also observed throughout the day, including during the 15-minute morning recess. In addition, I collected approximately 460 written products from the focal children as well as all writing workshop entries from all non-focal children.

My own relationship with the children evolved over time. As a middle-aged white woman, I made no effort to become one of the gang. I told them I was "busy" writing in my notebook because I was "interested in children," and I wouldn't "tell on them." Denise, however, made some familial sense of me. She deemed me a "fake mama." As far as I could tell, a fake mama could sit and listen and, when asked, her children could explain their ways to her. "Speak to me when you—ever you need to again," Wenona said, after I'd asked about one of the children's games.

In the last two months of the project, the children developed a more active role in the playground data collection. The change was partly due simply to the passage of time and their familiarity with me and my note taking during recess. For example, if I had not been at school the previous day, Denise would report any playground incidents she deemed worthy of my recording. "I got something for you to write down," she would say, before telling me of a boy/girl chase game, for example.

Some of the relational change, however, was due to a technological change. I typically recorded children, inside the classroom and out, using a lapel microphone attached to a book bag. However, I decided to use a more powerful, and more noticeable, unidirectional microphone on the noisy playground in order to record their singing and radio station play. I explained to the curious children why I was using that big microphone, and they spontaneously re-performed all their songs for me. I felt like a postmodern Iona Opie.

Media leads from the children were all verified, and original media sources documented, primarily through the efforts of the project research assistant, Soyoung Lee, who was herself helped by many kind souls at local video and music stores. In the second year of the project, I discussed my findings with the children's parents, and also with the DJ and producer of the children's regular morning radio show. The children's knowledge of music came from varied sources, not simply from the morning show; however, the personnel of that local show were clearly referenced in the data, and they graciously responded to Soyoung's and my request for a media insider response.

In each of the following sections, a brief explanation of analysis procedures precedes my findings about the children's musical appropriations. I begin with the children's cultural landscape, then move to the social purposes energizing their appropriations from musical texts, the nature of those appropriations, and, finally, the way in which such appropriations figured (or did not figure) into early composing. Throughout I highlight the case of Denise, an ardent music fan.

A Musical Mapping of the Cultural Landscape

Like all children, Denise and her friends are unique individuals. They are also children of the United States and of African American heritage; they are urban children with much contact with adolescents and young adults; and they are participants in varied institutions where music is part of the ties that bind and the threads that weave through generations. Thus, their appropriations from music texts, and their accompanying talk allowed insight into the children's perceptions of the voices surrounding them and of the locations of those voices in time and space.

To gain that insight, I studied my field notes for all episodes of child references to the media. With the subset involving music, I paid attention to if and how the children named musical genres, the source of their experiences with those genres in some named time and space, and their expectations of the genres' consumers. The world thus named included their personal histories as "preschoolers," their anticipated futures as "teenagers," and their shared presents as kids.

Present Childhoods

"It's two more books that we can read with, you know, the voices," Vanessa commented, after she and Denise had sung a text from their basal reader, gospel-style, "like you're in church."

In related ways, the children constructed their own present childhood from available cultural materials. Those materials, taken from others' voices, situated them in their lives as participants in churches, families, neighborhoods, and, most immediately, in schools. Indeed, the most evident child-initiated appropriation of school material involved songs. Generally, the children appropriated such songs during official events thematically related to the original ones introducing the songs. One child would begin a song, and the singing itself recruited other children, folding them into the ongoing rhythm. Such recruiting was audible and visible, as when, for example, Marcel began a rendition of "Mother Earth" (Rose, 1990) to accompany his assigned construction of an Earth Day Crown.

Although less common, children's appropriations could situate them beyond the school walls and evoke their roles as church members. Not only had Denise and Vanessa "read" certain texts with singing "church" voices, occasionally they joined together for a "hymn," as in the following:

Vanessa and Denise are sitting side-by-side writing their observations of a silk worm. Vanessa starts singing:

Vanessa: One, two, three—The devil's after me
      four, five, six—
Denise & Vanessa: He's always throwing sticks
      seven, eight, nine—He misses every time
      Hallelujah, Hallelujah, Hallelujah
      Amen

Denise in particular wanted to get church teachings right, and music may have informed her knowledge, or so Vanessa thought in the following data excerpt:

Denise: Adam was the first person that got made, and he ate the apple.
Vanessa: And what apple was that? Shoot.
Denise: I don't know, but I don't think he was supposed to, and he was the first man on earth, that got made.
Vanessa: He ate a apple, so what? Why wasn't he supposed to eat the apple?
Denise: I, *don't, know.*
Vanessa: And who told you that somebody—oh that little ol' hymn.

In addition to church and school, the children's singing also located them as members of families. Some appropriated songs were from movies the family had seen. For example, one day, Lakeisha commented to Wenona, "Last night my mama had me singing 'I Believe I Can Fly' [Kelly, 1996, from the movie, *Space Jam* (Falk, Reitman, & Ross, 1997)]. She *love* that movie. She *love* that song."

Other songs, though, reportedly were learned from parents and grand-parents and, in that sense, were a kind of folk song. These were older, rhythmically riveting R&B songs. The children primarily knew the hook or repetitive refrain, and typically a child's comment triggered a semantic connection to that hook. For example, when the first graders were looking through their kindergarten portfolios, Noah repeatedly commented that "I done that real good." Denise then broke into lines from a James Brown (1965) classic "I Got You / I Feel Good." Denise, Vanessa and Noah dis-agreed about the placement of "so goods" and "so nices," but all compro-mised and sang, "I feel good. I feel nice. I knew that I would." On another day, Denise was extremely excited about her upcoming family move and the possibility that in this new place she could have a cat; she gave a little shudder and then sang the hook from "I'm So Excited [And I Just Can't Hide It]" (Pointer Sisters, 1983).

The songs children learned in school, in church, and in their homes generally belonged, at least initially, to adults—their teachers, parents, grandparents, and other older relatives. But the songs children appropri-ated most frequently as part of their present lives as children came from other children. Denise and Vanessa knew many such "songs," which they also referred to as "games" or "play"; they reported learning these songs from neighborhood kids, which Denise's mother confirmed. Unlike the previous songs, and the ones to come, these songs were almost exclusively playground fare.

The literature on such songs has tended to homogenize children's racial and ethnic cultures, emphasizing the raucous and irreverent nature of children's oral cultures (for discussion, see Sutton-Smith, Mechling, Johnson, & McMahon, 1995). Still, the children's repertoire included verses, especially jump rope songs, which have been particularly (but not exclusively) associated with the play of African American girls (Beresin, 1995; Gilmore, 1985). Indeed, verses heard on the children's Bay Area playground were included in Bessie Jones's collection, based on her own childhood in a black farming community at the turn of the twentieth cen-tury, and dating back at least to her grandparents' childhood (Jones & Hawes, 1972). For example, in the midst of the children's "Down by the Bank" came lines (in italics below) from Jones' "Green Sally Up" (p. 25):

This is a clapping song, where partners alternately clap their own and their part-ner's hands and, in the very end of the song, try to tag the other's hand "out":

Denise & Van: Down by the bank
      said a hanky pank
      said a bull frog jumped from bank to bank
      said E-I-O-U
      Feeling with the ding dong
      See that house on top of the hill
      That's where me and my boyfriend live
      Smell that chicken
      Smell that rice
      Come on baby let's shoot, some, dice
Denise: You're out!
Vanessa: Man! why you have to get me out!

Another song, "Rockin' Robin," echoed with past popular culture (Jackson, 1972; Day, 1958), as well as with old play songs. After the familiar verse about Rockin' Robin rockin' in "the treetops all day long / Huffin' and a puffin' and a singin'," came one that echoed Jones' "Sandy Ree" (p. 133) about tough farm life, and yet another incorporating the contemporary Batman:

Mama in the kitchen / Burning rice
Daddy on the corner / Shooting that dice
Brother in jail / Raising H——
Sister at the corner / Selling fruit cocktail

Batman and Robin / Flying in the air
Batman lost / His underwear
Robin said / I'll buy you a pair
But you don't know / What size I wear

Such songs were fast driving, syncopated, and made for performance. Thus, it is not surprising that out on the playground the children slipped easily from generations-old rhymes to the drama of very now songs.[2]

Children's (Audio)Visions of Past and Future

After Noah and Marcel sing the hook from "Gangsters Make the World Go Round" (Westside Connection, 1996), Marcel initiates a round of the theme song from *Barney* (Leach, 1993), a children's television show. "Ew!" is Noah's response. In turn, Marcel declares his hatred of Barney. Noah, however, believes that they both used to love Barney. He asks, "Member in kindergarten? You watch Barney?"

And when Marcel denies this, Noah asks, "How about in preschool? How'd you like Barney?"

The children's appropriated songs both situated them in and helped them construct their personal histories. These songs of remembered pasts and anticipated futures were popular songs rooted in media experiences, and unlike the playground songs, these could be intoned anywhere. The children's past songs were associated with kindergarten and preschool and also with home. Vanessa, for example, claimed that her grandmother still made her watch Barney.

The future was different, though. It was more gender-specific in consumption, more race-specific in cited artists, and quite unconnected to school. That future was associated with "teen-age-ers," as Denise and Vanessa explain below.

Denise and Vanessa are doing a rap as they finish up their pictures for their assigned essays on space. When I ask, they explain that they learn raps from the radio and from Soul Train (a television show). But then they enter into a playful frame, slipping on a way cool voice:

Denise: See, we like rap-ping, and like, singing songs . . . See, we in a club, kind of like.

Vanessa: See, if you know how to do a bounce, you can get in. But if you don't . . . you can't get in. 'Cause see, it's called, The Bouncy Club. . . . All we play is Brandy, TLC, um, a whole lot of stuff. . . . Teenagers.

Denise: *Teen-age-ers.*

Vanessa: It don't be no rock and roll.

For the children, then, popular music seemed akin to dress up—to that stolen lipstick in Koch's poem. Children reported learning youth songs primarily from radios, radios that provided the backdrop to morning routines and school commutes, radios in community center offices and public parks, and radios in the company of adolescents—cool people whom children admired. These appropriated songs reverberated with adult voices beyond the original singers; their parents were concerned about the content of certain "teenager" songs. When Denise drew herself as a singer in high heels and a slinky gown, Vanessa said,

I'm not putting high heels on me cause that's too fast, Denise. That's too *fast.* We're only 6 and 7. And that is too fast (with definiteness). 'Cause, Denise, I'm sorry if I'm breaking your heart . . .

The children's parents were indeed concerned about "too fast" music, with its "negative images" and vulgar language, to quote Noah's father. Similar sentiments were expressed by Noah and Wenona in the context of brother and sister play about what "Mama" said about the CD player:

Wenona has just said she listened to Noah's CD player at home.

Noah: You can't listen to it, cause I'm bigger than you.
Wenona: I'm gonna look at your CD player.
Noah: CD player! It got—it got bad words on it.
Wenona: So?
Noah: You can't listen to it cause I'm bigger than you.
Wenona: No you're not.
Noah: Yes I am (starts singing the commercial jingle for a chicken product, perhaps to change or at least stop the topic).

Although there is a widely discussed political dimension in hip-hop music in particular (e.g., Potter, 1995), this dimension did not seem evident in the children's music appropriations. Still, the music did situate the children in an African American cultural sphere, as well as in a youthful one. The children referred to the names of 43 popular performers or performing groups, all African American (with the exception of Cookie Monster and Barney). Listen to Vanessa's response when I ask her about the group, Immature, and one member of the group with the nickname, "Batman":

Vanessa: Not the Batman that flies through the air.
  Not the Batman that lost his underwear [as in the children's playground rhyme]
  But Batman. He black and he fine.

Perhaps because of the transitory nature of most popular music and its relatively sophisticated content, as well as their monitored exposure, the children knew primarily the hooks and the choruses from raps and R & B songs. Beyond the strongly patterned, rhythmic, and highly repetitive parts, children sang words that made sense to them. In a verse of "I'm Going Down," Denise sang that the rain was "slowly driving me inside," rather than "insane." In a verse from "Best Friend" (Brandy, 1994), Vanessa sang that it didn't matter "whether I lose or if I win" in the "good games and the bad," not in the "good times and the bad ones," as in the original. Thus, their sensitivity to musical voices reflected the oft-reported child ability to attend to the sensible and ignore the nonsensical—unless, of course, that nonsense has a rhythmic coherence (Garvey, 1990; Golomb, 1992; Nelson, 1996).

Despite the word changes and the concentration on hooks and choruses, the children did understand the aesthetics of these songs, their
usual beats and melodic contours, their moods, and their usual consumers. The children played with these songs and their genres in their
own oral composing more so than any other kind of musical genre. In the
course of such "popular" play, they sometimes slipped off the high heels
and wiped off the lipstick and re-situated themselves in their present
childhoods:

Out on the playground, Denise has been reciting the refrain from "My Baby
Daddy" (B Rock and The Biz, 1997). From my point of view, the song is about jeal-
ousy; from Denise's, the song seems to be about family.

Denise: K-M-E-L [hip hop radio station] (whistles)
      Who that is? / My baby daddy (softer)
      Who that is? / My baby daddy
      Who that is? / My baby daddy
      That ain't your baby daddy [not in original]

Denise then improvises verses to the same beat.

Oh Anne is my mama / Oh Anne is my mama
Oh Anne is my mama / Just my play mama
Oh Johnny and Robert / Oh Johnny and Robert
Oh Johnny and Robert / They always play together
Oh Joseph and Vanessa / Oh Joseph and Vanessa
Oh Joseph and Vanessa / They both cousins.

In sum, the children's socio-ideological landscape was partly enacted
through musical voices. These voices provided children with whole utterances, utterance types or genres, and particular lyrics, and thus they became cultural stuff with which the children could construct their present
lives, remember their pasts, and anticipate their futures. In so doing, they
were at the very same time constructing themselves as members of varied
social institutions, and, more broadly, of particular social and cultural
spheres.

The Social Usefulness of Music Media

As is usually the case with analysis, my descriptions of willful children
using the media are based on my own willful study of pages of field notes
and accompanying transcripts. I studied the episodes in my data in which

children referred to the media, and by examining their content and inter-active patterns, I developed a coding system or vocabulary for describing the intertwined social functions the media served. Herein, I highlight music media.

First and foremost, the media provided a source of *pleasure* or stimulation, including during official work times. For example, as the children worked on a class assignment, Wenona suggested to Marcel that they sing the movie *Space Jam*'s title song because "it's boring just sitting here." A dominant quality of their pleasurable singing was its fluidity, its movement from one topic to the next, one kind of song to the next. Moreover, appropriated songs were intermixed with their own playful creations.

Noah, who tended to be intense when he drew and wrote, with little tangential talk, marked his completion of his Mother's Day journal entry with "Oh my. I'm done / I'm shun / I shake that little bunny./ I'm done / I'm shun / A little little bunny." He then joined Vanessa on the repetitive hook of a rap:" Somebody's sleeping in *my* bed, messing with *my* head" (Hill, 1996). Vanessa announced that she knew how to spell *apple*, and the children were off again:

Denise & Vanessa: A-P-P-L-E.
Denise: (rapping) I want to A-P-P/ About my Fam-i-ly.
        As I walk these streets / Something scar-ing me.
Noah: Yeah. Right here (points to the scary dog's face he has drawn in his journal).

The spelling A-P-P reminded Denise of the opening line of a TuPac rap (under the name of Makaveli, 1996), which actually begins with an "A-P-B on my thug family." In addition to that change, Denise mixed his line "Since the outlaws run these streets" with a related one from a Coolio rap (which Vanessa explicitly noted). In both raps, something was scaring somebody, and Noah playfully suggested that it was the big dog in his journal entry.

As is common in children's early symbol-making (Golomb, 1992), children's playfulness with and pleasure in their own voices was in productive tension with their desires to create more ordered products. Thus, a second function of musical media was to provide material for *personal expression and performance*. These deliberate efforts at coherent performances occurred primarily on the playground. They included both group performances, with backup and lead singers, and individual efforts for friends and me.

For example, one day Denise and Vanessa were concerned about a classmate's "spying" on them. During recess, Denise "made up" a "rap" about this situation. The driving beat and aggressive tone of her performance contrasted her typical interactive style, which was playful, and during conflict, intent on compromise. Denise's effort to maintain a pattern of syllable stresses and rhymes led to some lexical nonsense, which she soulfully admitted during her performance:

Denise: It's called, "Why You in My Bus'ness?" (sternly)
        (rapping) Why you in my bus'ness?
        Cause I *got* you / In my far-*is*-mus
        And I *had* you / In my char-*is*-mus / my *bus*'ness
        Why you gotta be / In the *bus*'ness?

        Can you get one of your home-y?
        And you know you spy on me
        I'm gonna get your home-y
        Cause I know / How much / You spy on me
        (In an R & B style) That is true: oo
        That is true: oo / Yeah
        It is, true: oo oo

And after rapping again about her business, she sings:

I don't know these words I'm saying
So please forgive me for my words

Sometimes the singing was not primarily for expressive or performance purposes. Rather, the resources of popular media provided *a context for play*, and that social goal organized the talk around the singing, rather than the singing itself. In the transcript below recorded on the playground, Denise is being a radio deejay *and* a star. The play contains varied genres heard on her regular radio station, including teasing (sometimes insulting) exchanges with on-air personalities and spontaneous raps, as well as song introductions:

Denise: OK, K-M-E-L, 1-0-6. Everybody turn on their radio, right now. 1-0-6. Listen to this. Stay tuned. Somebody's gonna sing, "Who Can Love You Like Me? [Nobody]" This is Denise Ray.
        You remind me of eating. Yeah, right. The song is beginning.
        (Denise then sings a brief rendition of "Nobody" [Sweat, 1996]).

On another day, Denise interviewed herself:

Denise: (assuming a polite, interested tone) Denise. Tell us why do you like to sing—and your friends?
Denise: (rapping) We want to be a star / In the store
     We want to be on stage / For our cage.

Being a star allowed girls in particular to imagine a fantastic future for themselves (cf. Walkerdine, 1997). Beyond the pleasure of singing, a future as a star promised glamour, money, and the admiration of fans, both male and female. To quote Denise, the girls will say "'Go girl, it's your birthday' (Luke, 1994) and the boys will say 'I love you baby.'" Even having a relative who was a star might lead to a charmed life, or so thought Vanessa. Her remarks were themselves quite musical, with their repetitive but intensifying structure and vivid images:

Denise: If Aaliyah the singer was my cousin . . . I'll bring her to school one day.
Vanessa: But that's not your cousin.
Denise: I said *if*.
Vanessa: You would be rich, Denise. You would be—
     Candy full a your pocket.
     Can't even eat it all, in your pocket.
     OH Rolled up in your shirt and all up mixed up in—
Denise: And what if they didn't give me none of their money?
Vanessa: PHEW! Then I would be calling the police. "Shoot! My cousin won't give me some money! She rich. Think I'm stupid!"

(Of course Denise, like Vanessa, wanted to be "a lot of things" when she grew up, among them, a nurse, an artist, and a helicopter pilot.)

By providing a means for the children to act jointly, the media also served both *social affiliation and differentiation*. As already noted, just by their singing the children situated themselves in a cultural landscape of varied social strata and spheres. Those social boundaries were constructed and made visible locally in the patterns of singing classmates. Songs taught in school, like "Mother Earth" and "I Got Shoes" (Sweet Honey in the Rock, 1994) recruited almost all children. Others, like songs learned from the hip hop radio station, recruited only African American children, with the exception of Tommy (whose older brother had a hip hop CD collection). Even a widely popular song like the Grammy-winning "I Believe I Can Fly" (Kelly, 1996) from *Space Jam* was appropriated (or not) according to race and class in this classroom.

The children's talk suggested their awareness that musical and media preferences could serve as a social tool. For example, one day Denise decided to spend activity time planning a girls' club with Vanessa, April, and April's good friends, Nanette and Elizabeth both European American. (In the first grade, "clubs" were transitory affairs that mainly involved planning.) April, who was of Chinese and European descent, was considered by herself and others as "part African American" because her father was Chinese (a confusion that their teacher Rita eventually untangled). April had previously chosen on occasion to sit with Denise and her close friends. But Nanette and Elizabeth had not.

Denise took the lead in the group's planning, posing the decisions that needed to be made about the club. When she asked about the club's password, Vanessa suggested KMEL, a "word" only Denise knew. Moreover, as Denise continued to focus on the "club," Vanessa continued to use music to highlight her special relationship with Denise:

Denise is giving directions for making the pages of the club book. Ariel, Nanette, and Elizabeth are attending and responding to Denise with their own suggestions. Vanessa starts singing a "bouncy song," seemingly inspired by Mase (1997):

Vanessa: Look at those girls . . .
        OO— they look so fine
        Look at those girls
        OO— looking so fine

Denise is concentrating on the pages.

Vanessa: Come on, Denise. (to group) She's my best friend. She's hecka fun.
Denise: After you're done [with your page for the book], I'll sing with you.

And she did.

Sometimes the children explicitly commented on connections between social categories and musical taste, which they equated with singing. For example, the children made no gender distinctions about who could like, or sing, preschool songs, but they did make such distinctions for teenager songs, at least for boys, as I illustrate below:

The children are making Earth Day Crowns, decorated with nature scenes and sayings. There is a great deal of cutting and coloring, the sort of activities that lend themselves to spontaneous singing. Elizabeth, Denny, Cedric, Marcel, Wenona, and Noah are all sitting at the same table. Marcel begins singing the Mother Earth song and others join in. Then Marcel moves on to a different song, which he sings in a soulful style.

Marcel: "Baby, baby, baby, baby / I need you so much."
(I do not know what the song is. Wenona does though, and she joins in.)

Noah: (to Marcel) You like *girl* songs!
Marcel: No I don't.
Noah: Well, how come you singing 'em?
Noah, Marcel, and Cedric move on to a hip hop crowd pumper.

Noah, Marcel, and Cedric: "Put you hands in the air / Like you just don't care . . ."

Rita puts the Mother Earth tape on, and the children all sing along. She compliments the children on the time and thought they are putting into their crowns (which look very good to me too). She suggests they walk around the school later, wearing their crowns and singing Earth Day songs. "Cool!" says Marcel, quite pleased. He works a while, and then has another song selection:

Marcel: Let's sing the Barney song. (singing) "I love you / You love me / We're a happy family. . . ."

Noah joins in, to my surprise, since he has criticized Marcel for his enjoyment of the Barney song. This time Wenona offers the critique:

Wenona: Why are you singing a *pre-school* song?
Marcel: Whoops. (looking sheepish)

An additional way in which the media was socially useful was as a potential source of *displayed knowledge* and expertise. That displayed knowledge has been evident throughout this section. Children knew, and noticed who knew particular songs. They sometimes referred to the artists who sang certain songs, always accurately. Finally, the music media could provide resources for *participation in, negotiation with, and transformation of official school contexts*. It is this latter function that I will consider in the remainder of this paper.

Mining Musical Media for Resources

As has already been demonstrated, the children appropriated a wide range of material for use in their unofficial social lives, including their oral composing. An inductive analysis of children's talk *and* writing yielded the following categories of media appropriations:

1. *Conceptual content:*
   (a) *names* (e.g., singers, songs)
   (b) *themes* (primarily emotional, e.g., loving a person, rebuking an irritating one)
2. *Communicative forms:*
   (a) *entire textual forms* (e.g., as designated by the children, "interviews," "raps," "songs")
   (b) *discourse features of those forms* (e.g. voice arrangements, involving lead and back up singers; remix processes, in which one does not "make up" a song but uses "words [from] another song," in Denise's words; rhythmic and melodic styles, among them rap and gospel)
3. *Technological conventions:*
   (a) *symbols* (e.g., use of letters and numbers to designate radio stations)
   (b) *individual control of radio dial* (e.g., references of child deejay to audience need to "turn on their radio," and to "stay tuned")
4. *Voiced utterances*
   (a) particular *words spoken* by singers, deejays, fans, including actual or variants of
      (i) lines;
      (ii) verses;
      (iii) choruses
5. *Ideologies of race, gender, fame, love, power*
   (a) *values and beliefs* about material circumstance and social relations
      (i) implicit in products (e.g., drawings of female singers in slinky gowns and high heels, males in backwards baseball caps, t-shirts, and athletic shoes, and fans who say "You go girl");
      (ii) explicit in product (e.g., commentary on the nature of love, the consequences of money)

The general categories were similar across media sources. However, the particular kind of material appropriated did vary across sources, as did children's means for contextualizing media material in their official and unofficial school writing. For example, child writers embedded sports media materials most extensively in reports (e.g., of game results). This seems sensible, given the dominance of informational genres in both sports media and school contexts (Dyson, 1999). Both sports media and (even more so) popular movies provided conceptual material for experiential (e.g., "I saw . . .") or evaluative (e.g., "I like . . .") texts. Movies in particular provided narratively organized content (i.e., plots) that lent itself to a written retelling.

Children's recontextualizations of music media into written forms were less straightforward, as I illustrate below. In so doing, I feature Denise and her increasingly complex footwork as she and her friends traverse and cautiously observe interrelated social, ideological, and symbolic boundaries.

Denise: "If [the Music] Say 'Ba' You Say 'Boom'"

Six years and two months old when school began, Denise had gotten her first radio when she was 5; it was a birthday present from her father. As already demonstrated, Denise loved to sing; she was a player with musical sounds and words. She once tried to explain a music game she played to an uncomprehending Vanessa. "Do you ever make words out of music?" she asked her uncomprehending friend. "If [the music] say 'ba,' you say 'boom.' . . . If it say 'doo,' you go 'I.' Like if the teacher turn on some Nutcracker music, you make words out of it?"

Making written words out of music, so to speak, was not as common as appropriating from other media forms. Most children (15 of 20) appropriated material from films, for example; but only seven appropriated it from musical texts. Unlike watching movies or sports shows, singing was primarily an accompaniment to other activity. When it was given emphasis, it was primarily in the social context of unofficial play, of singing games and imaginary "star" turns. Such singing was not shared with *adults;* it was constitutive of the "mimicry and mockery" of *peer* culture (Sutton-Smith, 1995, p. 7).

Nonetheless, classroom free writing times were occasions when children could do just what the official curriculum promoted, that is, make functional use of print. Given that children were writing with their peers and that they had some control over their writing choices, their social agendas intersected with their official ones. It was then that unofficial material from peer culture was likely to appear (see also Dyson, 1993, 1997, 1999). And thus, for Denise the intersection of official and unofficial agendas eventually yielded texts with musical links, including making written words out of music, *and* making music out of written words.

Making Words Out of Music

Although Denise learned written language faster than most children in her class, like them she produced her first prose entries by appropriating brief forms from the class-generated "things to write about" list displayed on the white board. These forms (e.g., "I like ___" or "I went ___") served as framing devices within which she could insert the names of people or places. Most of her writing workshop entries in the fall of the year (from September through December) referred to Vanessa, and Vanessa's mentioned her. "I want [went] to Vanessa has [house] today," Denise wrote. "Vanessa wit [went] to my party" was another.

These texts were all fictional, since Denise and Vanessa's relationship was confined to school. Thus, from early on Denise's texts mediated her participation in overlapping official and unofficial contexts. Writing was a means to accomplish her first grade work, and also to participate in sisterly play. Sometimes the playful language so central to their relationship occurred in print too, as in this text from November:

Me and Vanessa was playegeg and
We fell down and we
sot [started] to laf and that is a
rum-tum-tum

In this self-initiated writing, Denise's content appropriations from the *official* world emphasized musical activities, as in the following text, also from November; the name "Mbuti Women" refers to an African people whose art and music were featured in a local art museum exhibit studied by the class:

The Two Little Grs

Once a pan. tam it was
a grl name is Vanessa and a grl
name is Denise and. They pley
and play then they hrd sahag [heard singing]
They loot and loot [looked and looked]
They did not see it bat
it was the MBT WAN ["Mbuti Women"]

Appropriations from the *unofficial* world of music occurred by midyear, when the children's writing generally began to reflect the influence of popular media genres and features. Utterances from hip hop songs and popular movies began appearing occasionally. For example, anticipating her upcoming move to Oakland, Denise wrote:

I am going to move
on Wednesday We
are famale I got all my
sisrs and me
sisrs and Jake [her brother] too

Those familiar lines about family and sisters were quite deliberately taken from Whoopi Goldberg's lines in the film *Sister Act II* (Steel, Rudin, & Duke, 1994; originally from a song by Sister Sledge, 1979).

Communicative forms from the media also began to appear as children moved from reliance on brief evaluative or experiential texts (e.g., "I like . . .," "I went . . ."). The appearance of those forms was one aspect of genre form expansion in the class, which also included children's efforts to organize their writing according to newly learned school rhythms. (For discussion, see Dyson, 1999.) Noah's texts, for example, came to read like *Little Bear* (Minarik, 1957) and other early reading texts, with their short, declarative sentences and brief dialogues. One day I observed him leaning against a desk, eyes focused somewhere in space, as he repeated over and over to himself by memory the complete text of such a book (Cowley, 1989): "'I like my home,' said the spider; 'I like my home,' said the bird. . . . 'I like my home,' said the space girl."

Among these newly observed forms were those from musical media. Denise, for example, expanded an evaluative text about a favorite movie, *Space Jam*, with an introductory phrase ("The song goes like this"). She did not actually write the song, however. With Vanessa's help, she *sang* it during oral sharing. Moreover, although Denise wrote her own R & B "songs" (more specifically, their lyrics), she never officially shared them, nor did any other child do so.[3]

Certainly special skills are required to record music. Beyond these skills, however, songs were socially, ideologically, and symbolically complex. In contrast to movies, which were more often family affairs and aspects of children's "present" childhoods, "teen–age–er" songs were part of their unofficial play, their glamorized futures, and their parents' voiced

concerns. Moreover, unofficial play with songs could involve the manipulation not only of sounds but also of voices in dialogues, joint chants, as
well as lead and back-up singing arrangements. This experience would
lend itself better to dialogues, plays, and choral readings than to the kinds
of textual forms associated with beginning writing.

Indeed, Denise and Vanessa engaged in their first song writing explicitly in the context of unofficial play, although they used official materials.
The girls took their writing books out for recess one day so that they could
write "a song . . . not a rap." Denise was to be YoYo and Vanessa, M. C.
Lyte, both female rappers who had recorded together. The girls, however,
did not write raps (beyond Denise's opening turn). They used phrases and
themes from R&B love songs, as illustrated by their playground performance of their product:

Denise: (rapping her text) "YoYo my name / Go go."
Vanessa: (singing her text) "Don't matter what I do / Say /
        I can't deny."
Denise: (singing) "Tell me what you want this to be / It can be anything that your
        heart desires." (based on lyrics from Ray J [1997], "Everything You
        Want")

This kind of writing was for unofficial ends and for play, even if it involved official tools and sometimes, official time. Indeed, Denise and
Vanessa explicitly played with the social and ideological boundaries between official and unofficial worlds. One day, Rita conducted an official
discussion about how the children knew they were loved. She said she was
"proud of them" because they didn't equate love with somebody buying
them things. As Zephenia commented (like the Beatles before him),
"Can't buy love." The children were then to work on their "Me" projects,
which included writing three wishes (not to involve money) and drawing
their portraits as grownups. But Denise and Vanessa had ambitions to be
singers—and part of the ideology of stardom is wealth.

In composing their official "Me" projects, the two girls played with Rita's
emphasis on the limits of money as a source of love and happiness—and
with whether or not the desire for money could be written on their papers:

Denise and Vanessa are sitting side by side. Denise is drawing herself as a glamorous Tina Turner singing "What's Love Got to Do with It" (1983), a song title
she writes. Denise jokes that she is going to make a $10,000 bill coming out of Tina

Turner's head (which she does *not* do). Vanessa then reads her completed three wishes to Denise:

Vanessa: Listen. (reading) "I wish that Denise will stay my friend. I wish the earth clean, and I wish my granny gets better."

Denise now abandons her drawing and starts to write her own three wishes. "I wish," she says to herself as she begins. Vanessa starts singing.

Vanessa: (singing) Got no money / All I got is you baby / Don't need nothing else / I got you baby . . .

Denise: (has just reread "I wish" and now says loudly) I MADE A LOT OF MONEY!

Vanessa: (singing) Ain't got no money / Ain't got no thing but you now / I got love."

Denise does not write that she wishes she had money. She returns to her portrait, adding the audience. Although she does not write the words, she comments:

Denise: And there's the audience saying, "I love you baby." Except the girls. They're saying, "Go girl. It's your birthday." (Vanessa joins in and recites with her) "Go girl. It's your birthday."

Denise and Vanessa's actions reflect the social and ideological boundaries *salient* to them, and also writing's potential to maintain or disrupt them. Neither they nor any class member, for example, commented on a more subtle connection between artistry and money that was evident to me. Money can't buy love, but it can buy violin and piano lessons, ballet dancing, and skiing trips—a connection evident in the experiential texts of a small group of middle class children who wrote about their very busy after school lives. On the other hand, Denise and Vanessa were quite aware of the ostentatious wealth of popular musicians (whose pockets Vanessa deemed "full"), just as they were aware that popular songs can make wealth problematic.[4] In the context of official concerns that they not equate love and money, the children monitored the acceptability of their desires and their texts.

As the school year progressed, the children generally began to engage in varied kinds of surreptitious writing. For example, they made private lists of "club" members, more exclusive than those Rita advocated (i.e., "Everybody Clubs"). Marcel's was named the "BC" club, after the radio station's BC [Breakfast Club]. This awareness of social boundaries and of writing's role in their construction was not considered a negative occurrence. Rather, it was a significant aspect of literacy development in school contexts, where official and unofficial agenda inevitably co-exist (Dyson, 1993).

At the same time, a basic premise of this article is that the enacted curricula would be enriched by building on communicative resources embedded in the children's appropriation from and play with the media. Included in these resources are the insights promoted by and constitutive of official boundaries (e.g., issues of textual appropriateness and of the thematic complexities and contradictions in texts of wealth, power, gender, and love). Before addressing curricular implications directly in the article's conclusion, another aspect of the children's musical appropriations to consider is their efforts to make music out of words, rather than words out of music.

Making Music Out of Words

From the perspective of an oral performance, a text can be considered as a sparsely written score that is to be rendered by human voices. In varied ways, Denise and her peers treated texts as scores, both other people's texts and their own. Denise and Vanessa could appropriate the discourse features of particular musical styles—"voices," in their words—when reading. In the following vignette, Denise and Vanessa appropriate from "church" music to perform a text during the morning reading period; they try to explain their performance and to encourage me to join in:

Vanessa and Denise sit together, each singing two pages of their chosen reader selection. That selection is a children's verse, "Lazy Mary Will You Get Up?" The children sing the text as if they were "in church," using quiet but vibrating voices that crescendo through each stanza (i.e., each page).

Denise: (singing) Laz-y Mary / will you get up / Will you get up? / Will you get up? Yes Mo-ther / I will get up / I will I will / I will get up. Yes Mother / I will get up / I will get up to-day-ay.

Vanessa "hates [the] da-ay" part (i.e., the part in which Denise rhythmically separated the syllable *day* into two syllables). When Denise's turn comes up again, she sings:

Denise: . . . today:
Vanessa: Whew. (with relief)

As they continue to sing, I notice that they are skipping some pages.

Anne: How come you keep skipping these pages?
Vanessa: No, no, because they don't count.
Denise: They not singing.
Vanessa: They not singing. They're talking.
Anne: How do you know this is singing?
Vanessa: Because it rhymes. (In my adult terms, the words do not "rhyme," but the phrases do rhythmically repeat.)

Denise tells me it's my turn, and I reply that I can't carry a tune. The girls respond as good teachers. First, Denise makes the task easier for me:

Denise: You can just try to say it like this, try to say it like this.

Denise sings with the same syncopated swing but slower. Vanessa interrupts and has another suggestion.

Vanessa: Or just try to sing it like this. Just try to sing it like a pretty—like a pretty one.

Vanessa then sings the song with a simple, on-the-beat rhythm. No vibrato. No swing. "Like in kindergarten," says Denise, teasing me.

This breaking up, elongating, and otherwise playing with sounds and this stylistic evocation of different moods seem essential aspects of literacy—the deliberate manipulation of language, and of literariness—the deliberate linking of form and emotion (Vygotsky, 1987). In fact, once Denise tried to make literary if not literal sense out of Wenona's text. During the winter months, Wenona began to match word and voice in a one-to-one correspondence. Sitting next to Denise, she wrote some words she "knew": *was, you, r* [are], *km* [coming] and separately on the bottom of her page, *to* ("in case I need it"). Wenona reread her text, and then Denise sang a bluesy variation, alternating *was* and *are:* "Was you coming too? Are you coming? Was you coming too?"

Most strikingly, Denise and Vanessa appropriated discourse features common to many kinds of musical or poetic texts—rhyme, repetitive phrases, and dramatic dialogue. Indeed, they chose to write poetry, the genre Koch refers to as a blending of song and statement, a "making music out of words" (1998, p. 21). Poetry was the *only* official school literature Denise ever appropriated for self-sponsored writing.

In the official curriculum, poems were treated as scores for performances from the beginning of the year. Rita read poetry to the class, and just as they did with group songs, the children spontaneously joined in and recited poems along with her. They also prepared a program in which they performed poems for the school and for their parents (in an event well-attended by all the children's families). Throughout the year, Rita featured Eloise Greenfield, a poet who renders child interests, including sports and music, in literary form. In her works, the themes of children's play with popular music—themes of love, money, and power—are rendered in children's present lives, not in their imagined futures. For example, her book *Honey I Love* (1978) includes a poem with the powerful, aggressive voice of "Harriet Tubman," who "didn't take no stuff," the playful voice of the child narrator telling "Honey [what] I Love," and that same narrator's firm voice as she recalls her father's message:

Love Don't Mean

Love don't mean all that kissing
Like on television
Love means Daddy
Saying keep your mama company
til I get back
And me doing it (not paginated)

(On one page of the poem's child-like illustrations, a couple kisses as they stand by a TV depicting another couple kissing. On the facing page, a couple and a child stand with their arms about each other, as a realistically rendered young girl reflects.)

Denise and Vanessa appropriated lines from these poems, just as they did from music. These poetic utterances, however, were more easily embedded in evaluative or experiential texts that could be officially shared, perhaps because they indexed children's "present" childhoods. For example, Vanessa appropriated bits from Greenfield's "Love Don't Mean" poem to write about Denise (corrected for ease of reading):

You might not know
But I am mad at Denise
But she is still my friend
I love her
The End
Love don't mean
All that nasty stuff
I went to bed singing
I love singing

Vanessa did not officially declare her love of her "boy toy" (referred to in both Denise and Vanessa's R&B songs).[5] She, like her female classmates generally, declared her love of a friend, someone a 6-year-old child could officially love without embarrassment.

Denise and Vanessa appropriated textual forms too. They wrote, "I like" poems inspired by Greenfield's "Honey, I love." The importance of the form and also of the rhythm and rhyme is evident in Denise's written love of peas—a food she really did not like at all, or so she told me:

I like apples / I like peas
I like bananas / On the trees
I like oranges / I like trees
And you all know / that I like peas
I'm not playing now / I like me.

One of Greenfield's books, *Nathaniel Talking* (1988), includes poems explicitly based on music forms, including rap and blues. In composing her hybrid texts, Greenfield articulated a child's emotions and reflections in distinctive musical rhythms constructed in a literary form—the picture book. In the context of the observed children's music making, however, "Nathaniel's Rap" is textually inconsistent. Its opening lines declare that "It's Nathaniel talking / and Nathaniel's me"; its repetitive hook reinforces that "I gotta rap." But Nathaniel's rap has no specific topic beyond that need, and the image of a child rapping until his "ear flaps flap" is sweet, not aggressive. Denise's own apparent appropriation from this "rap" was embedded in a less than sweet text, which she chose not to share:

On this day in late April, the children are to have come dressed as characters from favorite books. Most children are wearing t-shirts referencing favorite film characters; Denise is wearing her Pocahontas (Pentecost, 1995) t-shirt. Rita is wearing a baseball cap like Nathaniel, and she has just reread his "rap" to the class. Now she suggests that, during composing time, the children write about their characters. Denise begins to write what seems a dialogue. It is, she says to her table mates, "going to be funny":

Denise: (rereading, with a grin in her voice and on her face)
    Pocahontas is me. [Recall "Nathaniel's me."]
    Hey, you got a problem?
    Yes I do.
    Do you?

> Yes.
> Why?
> Because you—
> Pocahontas, don't go there now.
> Oh, Denise.
> Please, stop talking,
> Because your breath is humming.
> Your breath is kicking.

Anne: Who's talking to you in that?
Denise: Mm: Pocahontas . . . . That's a joke.
Vanessa: She capping on you.

I wonder if Denise is going to share this.

Denise: I get to take this one home! I get to take this one home!

And she puts "this one" in her cubby (her small, box-like space for her personal things).

Within the above event, a skillful 6-year-old composes with ease—a child who, in her own view and her mother's, learned to write in Rita's classroom. As an integral aspect of that school learning, Denise, like the other closely studied children, drew on a wide range of voices engaged in varied textual dialogues; moreover, she made at least some deliberate decisions about where those voices might best sound, as it were. What might be among her most sophisticated efforts in terms of textual length, elaborateness, and coherence, if not in terms of adult taste, might, in the end, best stay among friends.

With this event, I conclude the retracing of Denise's musical appropriations and textual maneuvering on official and unofficial landscapes. In the final section, I discuss the children's "scaveng[ing] of form and theme" (Goldman, 1998, p. 143), of voice. I comment on the children's musical travels, primarily by revoicing the views of interviewed parents and radio personnel. Then I consider, to use Tina Turner's words, "What's [Literacy] Got To Do With It?"

Summary and Conclusion: What's Literacy Got to Do with It?

"All God's children got shoes," goes an old spiritual that Rita played often. As a metaphor for voices, for communicative ways to get around, children do not have one perfectly fitting pair. As Denise and her peers illustrated, children slip into appealing shoes taken from diverse locations, and with experience and guidance, they become more skillful and more mindful of where they're going.

The children's discourse flexibility and sociocultural intelligence do not suggest simple or simplistic appropriations of children's unofficial material for official ends. They do, however, suggest the limits of the decidedly unpoetic, misleadingly linear, and, in my view, unsound theories of children's literacy dominating the current public and professional discourse in educational fields. Below, I situate a discussion of these limits within the comments of interviewed parents and radio personnel's concerning the children's singing itself.

"You Got to Grow with Your Children"

"Marcel is bouncing back and forth between some nursery rhyme and [the rap music] his brother listens to," reported his mother. For all children, those oversized radio voices—the ones big brothers, sisters, and cousins listened to—had particular appeal. Children's voices did echo richly with those of childhoods long past, but those were echoes of ritualized voices without individual authorship. In contrast, children tended to improvise around and with the voices of teenagers, and more directly, with stars whose names and songs were well known. Some of those voices seemed "too fast" for little children. The songs were akin to dress-up play, like the children's role playing of football players, hockey players, and cheerleaders (elaborated on in Dyson, 1999).

The interviewed parents recognized the pleasure children gained from music, and, moreover, the strength of children's musical memories and their eclectic tastes. The radio personnel I interviewed, neither of whom had children, seemed more startled by the data. On his show, Sway, a personable young man, African American and from the Bay Area, invited audience members to call in and improvise verse rhymes (sometimes caps [see Smitherman, 1996]) with him; he was "amazed" that the observed children could get into "the rhythm, the rhyme, the count." However, he and his producer stressed that their show was for teenagers and young adults, and that their target audience, like their station executives, expected the "risqué" to wake them up in the morning. If *they* had 6-year-olds, they said, their children "wouldn't be listening"; they would control the radio dial. As children grew older, though, they felt popular music could stimulate useful talk, if parents paid attention to what their kids paid attention to.

The children's parents felt that even now they were not in sole control of the dial. As Denise's mother said, "A lot of people are of the mind that if they don't hear it at home, it doesn't exist," but it does. No matter how selective parents are, "You can't control what your child hears; you can, however, "control how you talk to your child" about what they hear. Marcel's mother felt similarly. Like Denise's and Noah's parents, she tried to monitor what her children heard, but in the end, she could not "censor" their music. After all, "they are going to listen to it; they are going to hear it at a friend's house." But she did want her children to know her own feelings about music and lyrics:

If we're driving down the street and we hear something that I don't particularly find appropriate and then I hear them singing it . . . I'll ask them, "So what do you think that means? What does that word mean? Do you think that everybody thinks like that? What is your opinion? Because my opinion is blah blah blah, but yours doesn't have to agree with mine."

As Sway said in the radio interview, "you got to grow with your children," being aware of their interests, appreciative of their pleasures, straightforward about your own concerns, and insistent that they formulate and articulate their tastes and points of view. These responses seem to me key aspects of the project's implications for literacy instruction.

Discordant Notes and Skillful Remixes

The current California Reading/Language Arts Framework (California Department of Education, 1998) presents kindergartners learning letters and words, first graders writing "sentences," and second graders "paragraphs" (p. 31). First graders in particular should write brief narratives about their experiences. When teaching writing, instructors are to "sequence student writing activities so [students] first see good models, edit other writing, and then generate their own sentences or text" (1999, p. 61).

This linear presentation of written language learning and teaching constructs an imaginary world for adults anxious for control of the learning dial. But this cannot be. Children enter school as experienced participants in a range of social dialogues. They engage with school textual practices "in the context of their relationships with other texts" and against their cultural landscapes (Buckingham & Sefton-Green, 1994, p . 61).

Moreover, this landscape is not an open expanse of rhythms, melodies, and lyrics, but one crisscrossed with societal boundaries, as it was for the observed children.[6] In entering school, certain boundaries were highlighted and reconstituted, as teacher and children displayed their musical tastes—or not. As Denise illustrated, children could quite deliberately choose to use particular cultural material with particular audiences. Official writing time specifically involved such deliberation, in part because of its organizational nature. Sitting among friends, children could make writing choices that they then would not want to share with the class as a whole. Learning the deliberative process of writing itself—of choosing words—entailed making choices also of social relationships and ideological worlds (Dyson, 1997).

As a resource for this deliberative symbol making, popular culture is both powerful and controversial because it appeals directly to ideologies, to socially organized desires, dreams, and fears. The observed children were on their way from being "preschoolers" to the more gender-separated world of "teen-age-ers." In youth songs the children appropriated were ideologies of love, gender, wealth, and power. Denise in particular selected from these songs as she began to use official writing more extensively for unofficial ends.

Teachers have their own aesthetic tastes informed by musical histories, political alliances, and demographic categories (like age, gender, religion, region, and race) (Lewis, 1992). Teachers who share in children's tastes can bring in "a variety of music that touches the spirit of the child" (Secret & Miner, 1998, p. 86), as can those who continue to "grow with their children," in Sway's words. Teachers may share with parents (and young people themselves [Adewole-Jimenez, Adewole-Jimenez, Ucelli, & O'Neil, 1994]) concerns about images of women and of violence in strands of contemporary music. As Denise's mother said, adults cannot eliminate aspects of children's textual worlds they themselves may not understand or appreciate; but they can help children become reflective, able participants in an increasingly complex world.

To help children differentiate and expand their skills with textual forms, teachers, like parents, benefit from being aware of children's textual landscapes, straightforward about any concerns, and insistent that children reflect on their own and others' composing choices. Teachers' access is more limited, however, since their knowledge of children's unofficial landscape is filtered through school activities and outcomes. Listening to children's talk and singing provides evidence of their pleasure in strong rhythms, dramatic voices, and memorable language; it also reveals their eclectic tastes. However, such listening does not usually lead to the children's textual sources, especially not for people whose cultural landscapes are quite different. Similarly, young children's brief texts, encoded in inventive spellings and untamed letter forms, do not speak—or sing—for themselves.

Rather, talk between teacher and child about media preferences and habits is necessary if educators are to gain insight into their students' lives as participants in common culture. Such talk allows children to elaborate and explain their own products, and allows teachers to provide vocabulary and analytical talk for unexpected genres and helps them place those genres (including varied kinds of songs) in relationship to those emphasized in school (Dyson, 1993). Discussions with individuals or small groups about children's sharing decisions may also be valuable. Such discussions may allow teachers and children to display unexpected knowledge, skills, and concerns.

As evident in this paper, Rita incorporated a wide variety of culturally valued expressive forms in her curriculum. She did not bring in what the children referred to as teenager music, but she did feel that her role was to "open up their world to more things," not to devalue what they enjoyed. Most relevant to this paper, a variety of musical and poetic voices were incorporated into every aspect of the curriculum. Those official voices were appropriated by children for many uses, including pleasurable accompaniment to many of their activities, as well as personal expression in their writing. Moreover, it was those official voices that spoke to, or sung to, the childrens' emotions and to issues of love, gender, power, and wealth, just as popular music does.

Childhood Sounds and Researchers' Radio Dials

In matters of childhood and literacy, researchers, like many adults, have kept a relatively firm hold on the dial. They have listened to children primarily as voices filtered through teachers or parents. Over the last 20 years there have been influential theoretical shifts in perceptions of writing and culture. Street (1995), for example, stresses how literacy is transformed and adapted to communities' symbolic repertoires; he highlights not the impact of literacy itself, but the impact of people on literacy. But in such work children are absent, or they are seen only through the contexts of family socialization or school instruction. It is as though, to paraphrase Genishi (1997), children simply do as they are told.

The project reported herein has taken its direction, in part, from adulthood's disjunction from childhood, from the significance of semiotic rather than physical play spaces (Sutton-Smith, Mechlin, Johnson, & McMahon, 1995); and most particularly, from children's independent access to story, song, and other forms of cultural expression, particularly through the commercial media. Verbal play spaces—and the use of media texts as play material—have assumed increased importance as both time and space for physical play have decreased (e.g., due to less free time during "recess," more structured after-school programs, unsafe city streets).

Thus, most children enter school with a common background of textual material from the radio, videos, and television, rather than from adult storytellers or readers. These materials are made accessible by technology that is not under the control of adult teachers—or researchers, for that matter. Moreover, these materials are readily available to children with access to radio, television, movie videos, video games—and that encompasses most children in the United States.

Schools as institutions have key roles in guiding children's textual learning, but to understand that role and the nature of literacy development in these times, those charged with that responsibility must acknowledge these aforementioned qualities of many childhoods. In this chapter, I have featured a version of such childhoods, and, in particular, the version that is Denise's childhood, that of an aesthetically alert 6-year-old. She shares with many other children a readiness to slip into appealing voices to explore and construct her world. Children's adaptability, their openness to the playful and the dramatic, and their eagerness to imagine the future suggest the benefits of classroom communities richly infused with voices—and of researchers and teachers staying tuned to the sounds of children's worlds.

Appendix

Sex and Ethnicity of Rita's Children:

Sex	Ethnicity
Girls (7)	
April	Asian/European American
Denise	African American
Elizabeth	European American
Lakeisha	African American
Nanette	European American
Vanessa	African American
Wenona	African American
Boys (13)	
Cedric	African American
Denny	European American
Daniel	European American
Eddie	African American
Jamal	African American
John	African American
Marcel	African American
Noah	African American
Robert	African American
Rich	European American
Samuel	African/Asian American
Tommy	European American
Zephenia	African American

Notes

1. Children associated songs with singers, not with writers or producers. Thus, for clarity's sake, I also have linked songs to their associated artists; performing artists' names appear in parentheses following referenced songs. Those performing artists might be different than the ones readers, or even the children's own parents, associated with particular songs. For example, Denise's mother associated the song "I'm Goin' Down" with the group Rose Royce (1976), not with Mary J. Blige (1994).

2. There is a complex relationship between childhood rhymes and youth songs, especially rap. In Cooper's (1989) discussion of the broad sweep of contemporary music, he argues that adolescents are drawn to music that incorporates childhood rhymes and tales. Perhaps recontextualizing that material in new thematic contexts marks their own distinct passage from childhood, just as youth music seemed to mark the observed children's passage from "preschooler" status.

Rap music has particularly complex relationships to childhood verse. Davey D (1998) briefly chronicles rap's immediate roots in party emceeing in the West Bronx. In his account, deejays initially acknowledged party goers by name, and these acknowledgments evoked the crowd's own shouts of names and slogans. Deejays, to mark their distinctive skill, used rhymes in their acknowledgments and "began drawing upon outdated dozens and school yard rhymes" (p. 2).

Rapping is a verbal skill with roots in the oral traditions of African American culture. However, according to Rose (1989), rapping itself is a hybrid, part of literate as well as oral traditions. Unlike childhood's oral verse traditions, raps emphasize individual authorship of intricately constructed lyrics that are written and then performed. They combine material from many African American musical traditions, among them soul and gospel, far beyond children's rhymes.

3. For part of a writing workshop entry, Zephenia did write his own "Shabooya Roll Call," a verse used by hosts and call-in audience participants in the morning radio show. Sway said he designed the verse as a kind of cheerlead for kids. However "it went in the different direction," becoming more risqué; young children did not call in to the radio show. Sway gave me an example of a call-in verse, used after the Shabooya chant: "My name is Desiree / Hey hey Sway / You want to come over my house / Hey hey any day."

The observed children used the chant to identify themselves orally as a kind of game. Zephenia's *written* call was consistent with the children's use:

SHABOYA
SHA SHA BOYA ROLL CALL
MY NAME IS Z Zeph
I'M NOT OAN [Owen, another name]
DO YOU YA EAR [Hear er]
Get with me.

Although Zephenia shared his Shabooya Roll Call, which the children enjoyed, he did not share his whole text. The Shabooya Roll Call was the opening of what he labeled in print as a "remix." The written remix included "yo mama" jokes (see Smitherman, 1994), dollar signs, and lyrics from other raps, which were difficult to decipher. (Because Zephenia was not a focal student [that is, I had no special relationship with him], I did not ask him to read me a text he had not chosen to share.)

4. Karen, the executive producer of the Breakfast Club, felt that people are not aware of the financial and business aspects of the music business that are essential for commercial success. In her words, "There are a lot of people who are business [people] and entrepreneurs that, because of stereotypical viewpoints, you look at them and you don't think that they understand, that they have weight in the business world . . . [K]ids don't understand. They see them with the rings and money and the clothes and the gold around the neck, but they don't understand that, 'I put my money away too, I've got—I own this business here . . . my 401 [retirement plan] is already worked out.'"

5. "Boy toy" seemed to be used as a synonym for "boy friend" by Denise and Vanessa. In popular music, the term seems to be associated with the singer Madonna.

6. I am aware that white, male adolescents are major consumers of hip hop (for discussion, see Potter, 1995). However, as already discussed, in this particular class of very young children, from neighborhoods where class and race were interrelated, knowledge of hip hop and R & B music was not "common knowledge" among all class participants.

References

Adewole-Jimenez, A., & Adewole-Jimenez, D., Ucelli, J., & O'Neil, D. (1994). Women, men, rap, and respect: A dialogue. *Rethinking Schools, 8*, 14–15.

B Rock and the Biz. (1997). My baby daddy. On *My baby daddy* [CD]. New York: Bad Boy Entertainment.

Bakhtin, M. (1981). Discourse in the novel. In C. Emerson & M. Holquist (Eds.), *The dialogic imagination: Four essays by M. Bakhtin* (pp. 259-422). Austin: University of Texas Press.

Barney. (1993). Berstein, L. (Writer). I love you. On *Barney's favorites, Vol. 1* [CD]. Lyons Partnership.

Bauman, R. (1992). Performance. In R. Bauman (Ed.), *Folklore, cultural performances, and popular entertainments: A communications-centered handbook* (pp. 41–49). New York: Oxford University Press.

Bauman, R., & Briggs, C. C. (1990). Poetics and performance as critical perspectives on language and social life. *Anthropological Review, 19*, 59–88.

Blige, M. J. (1994). I'm goin' down. On *My life.* [CD]. London: Uptown Records.

Bourdieu, P. (1984). *Distinction: A social critique of the judgment of taste* (R. Nice, Trans.). Cambridge, MA: Harvard University Press. (Original work published 1979).

Brandy. (1994). Best friend. On *Brandy* [CD]. New York: Atlantic Records.

Bruner, J. (1990). *Acts of meaning.* Cambridge: Harvard University Press.

Buckingham, D. (1993). *Children talking television: The making of television literacy.* London: Falmer Press.

Buckingham, D., & Sefton-Green, J. (1994). *Cultural studies goes to school: Reading and teaching popular media.* London: Taylor & Francis.

California Department of Education (1998). *Reading/Language Arts Framework for California Public Schools.* Sacramento, CA: California Department of Education Press.

Cooper, B. L. (1989). Rhythm 'n' rhymes: Character and theme images from children's literature in contemporary recordings, 1950–1985. *Popular Music and Society, 13*, 53–71.

Corsaro, W. (1997). *The sociology of childhood.* Thousand Oaks, CA: Pine Forge Press.

Day, B. (1958). *Rock-in robin* [Record].

Davey D. (1998). The history of hip hop [On-line]. Available: http://daveyd.com/raptitle.html.

Dore, J. (1989). Monologue as reenvoicement of dialogue. In K. Nelson (Ed.), *Narratives from the crib* (pp. 231–262). Cambridge, MA: Harvard University Press.

Dyson, A. Haas. (1989). *Multiple worlds of child writers: Friends learning to write.* New York: Teachers College Press.

Dyson, A. Haas. (1993). *Social worlds of children learning to write in an urban primary school.* New York: Teachers College Press.

Dyson, A. Haas. (1997). *Writing superheroes: Contemporary childhood, popular culture, and classroom literacy.* New York: Teachers College Press.

Dyson, A. Haas. (1999). Coach Bombay's kids learn to write: Children's appropriation of media material for school literacy. *Research in the Teaching of English, 33*, 367–402.

Falk, D., Reitman, I., Ross, K. (Producers), & Cervone, T., Pytka, J., Smith, B. (Directors). (1996). *Space Jam* [film]. Burbank, CA: Warner Brothers.

Fernald, A. (1992). Human maternal vocalizations to infants as biological relevant signals: An evolutionary perspective. In J. Barkow, L. Cosmides, & J. Tooby (Eds.), *The adapted mind: Evolutionary psychology and the generation of culture.* New York: Oxford University Press.

Garvey, C. (1990). *Play* (enl. ed.). Cambridge, MA: Harvard University Press.

Genishi, C. (1997). *Representing children in educational research: Locating Asian-American children in and out of classrooms.* Paper presented at the annual convention of the American Educational Research Association, Chicago, IL.

Gillmore, P. (1985). "Gimme room": School resistance, attitude and access to literacy. *Journal of Education, 167*, 111–127.

Goldman, L. R. (1998). *Child's play: Myth, mimesis, and make-believe*. London: Routledge.

Golomb, C. (1992). *The child's creation of a pictorial world*. Berkeley, CA: University of California Press.

Goodnow, J., Miller, P. J., & Kessel, J. (Eds.). (1995). *Cultural practices as contexts for development*. San Francisco: Jossey-Bass.

Greenfield, E. (1978). *Honey I love*. New York: Harper & Row.

Greenfield, E. (1988). *Nathaniel talking*. New York: Black Butterfly Children's Books.

Hill, D. (1996). In my bed. On *Dru Hill* [CD]. New York: Island Records.

Jackson, M. (1972). Rockin' robin [record]. New York: Motown Record Company.

Kelly, R. (1996). I believe I can fly. On *Space jam* [CD]. New York: Atlanta Records.

Koch, K. (1998). *Making your own days: The pleasure of reading and writing poems*. New York: Scribner.

Leach, S. (1988). *Barney* [television program]. Texas: Lyons Group.

Levin, S. (1988). *Highbrow/Lowbrow: The emergence of cultural hierarchy in America*. Cambridge, MA: Harvard University Press.

Lewis, G. H. (1992). The dimensions of musical taste. In J. Lull (Ed.), *Popular music and communication* (pp. 134–151). Newbury Park: Sage.

Luke. (1994). It's your birthday. On *Freak for life* [CD]. Liberty City, FL: Luke Records Inc.

Makaveli. (1996). Hail Mary. On *The 7 day theory*. [CD]. Beverly Hills, CA: Death Row/Interscope Records.

Mase. (1997). Lookin' at me. On *Lookin' at me* [CD]. New York: Artista Records.

McDowell, J. (1995). The transmission of children's folklore. In B. Sutton-Smith, J. Mechling, T. W. Johnson, & F. R. McMahon (Eds.), *Children's folklore: A source book* (pp. 49–62). New York: Garland Publishing.

McMahon, F. R., & Sutton-Smith, B. (1995). The past in the present: Theoretical directions for children's folklore. In B. Sutton-Smith, J. Mechling, T. W. Johnson, & F. R. McMahon (Eds.), *Children's folklore: A source book* (pp. 293–308). New York: Garland Publishing.

Miller, P., & Goodnow, J. J. (1995). Cultural practices: Toward an integration of culture and development. In J. J. Goodnow, P. J. Miller, & F. Kessel (Eds.), *Cultural practices as contexts for development, No. 67, New Directions in Child Development*.(pp. 5–16). San Francisco: Jossey Bass.

Miller, P. J., & Hoogstra, L., Mintz, J., Fung, H., & Williams, K. (1993). Troubles in the garden and how they get resolved: A young child's transformation of his favorite story. In C. A. Nelson (Ed.), *Memory and affect in development: Minnesota symposium on child psychology* (vol. 26, pp. 87–114). Hillsdale, NJ: Erlbaum Press.

Miller, P., & Mehler, R. (1994). The power of personal storytelling in families and kindergartens. In A. H. Dyson & C. Genishi (Eds.), *The need for story: Cultural diversity in classroom and community* (pp. 38–56). Urbana, IL: National Council of Teachers of English.

Minarik, E. H. (1957). *Little bear*. New York: Harper & Row.

Nelson, K. (1996). *Language in cognitive development: The emergence of the mediated mind*. Cambridge: Cambridge University Press.

The New London Group. (1996). A pedagogy of multiliteracies: Designing social futures. *Harvard Educational Review, 61*, 60–92.

Opie, I., & Opie, P. (1959). *The lore and language of school children*. London: Oxford University Press.

Pentecost, J. (Producer), and Gabriel, M., & Goldberg, E. (Directors). (1995). *Pocahontas* [film]. Burbank, CA: Walt Disney Pictures.

Pointer Sisters. (1989). I'm so excited. On *Pointer sisters breakout* [CD]. New York: RCA Records.

Potter, R. A. (1995). *Spectacular vernaculars: Hip-hop and the politics of the postmodern*. Albany: State University of New York Press.

Quad City D.S. (1996). On *Space jam* [CD]. New York: Atlanta Records.

Ray, J. (1997). Everything you want. On *Everything you want* [CD]. New York: WE/Electra Entertainment.

Rogoff, B. (1990). *Apprenticeship in thinking: Cognitive development in social context*. New York: Oxford University Press.

Rose, B. (1990). Mother Earth. On *Sacred ground* [CD]. El Cerrito, CA: Kaleidoscope Records.

Rose, T. (1989). Orality and technology: Rap music and Afro-American cultural resistance. *Popular Music and Society, 13*, 35–44.

Rose Royce. (1976). I'm going down. On *Carwash* [LP].

Secret, C., & Miner, B. (1998). Embracing Ebonics and teaching Standard English: An interview with Oakland teacher Carrie Secret. In T. Perry & L. Delpit (Eds.), *The real Ebonics debate: Power, language, and the education of African American children* (pp. 79–88). Boston: Beacon Press.

Sister Sledge. (1979). We are family. On *We are family* [LP]. Los Angeles, CA: Rhino Records.

Smitherman, G. (1994). *Black talk: Words and phrases from the hood to the amen corner*. Boston: Houghton Mifflin.

Steel, D., & Rubin, S. (Producers), and Duke, B. (Director). (1994). *Sister act II* [film]. Burbank, CA: Touchstone Pictures.

Street, B. (1995). *Social literacies: Critical approaches to literacy in development, ethnography, and education*. London: Longman.

Sullivan, C. W. III. (1995). Songs, poems, and rhymes. In B. Sutton-Smith, J. Mechling, T. W. Johnson, & F. R. McMahon (Eds.), *Children's folklore: A source book* (pp. 145–160). New York: Garland Publishing.

Sutton-Smith, B. (1995). Introduction: What is children's folklore? In B. Sutton-Smith, J. Mechling, T. W. Johnson, & F. R. McMahon (Eds.), *Children's folklore: A source book* (pp. 3–9). New York: Garland Publishing.

Sutton-Smith, B., Mechling, J., Johnson, T. W., & McMahon, F. R. (Eds.). (1995). *Children's folklore: A source book*. New York: Garland Publishing.

Sway and the Breakfast Club. (1997). Shabooya roll call. On *Sway and the breakfast club*. [Radio]. San Francisco, CA; KMEL Radio Station.

Sweat, K. (1996). Nobody. On *Keith Sweat* [CD]. New York: Electra Entertainment Group.

Sweet Honey in the Rock. (1994). *I got shoes* [CD]. Redway, CA: Music for Little People.

Turner, T. (1983). What's love got to do with it. On *Private dancer* [CD]. Hollywood, CA: Capitol Records.

Vygotsky, L. S. (1978). *Mind in society*. Cambridge, MA: Harvard University Press.

Vygotsky, L. S. (1987). *L. S. Vygotsky, collected works: Volume 1, Problems of general psychology*. New York: Plenum Books.

Walkerdine, V. (1997). *Daddy's girl: Young girls and popular culture*. Boston, MA; Harvard University Press.

Wertsch. J. V. (1985). *Vygotsky and the social formation of mind*. Cambridge, MA: Harvard University Press.

Westside Connection. (1996). Gangsters make the world go round. On *Bow down*. [CD]. Los Angeles, CA: Priority Records.

Willis, P. (1990). *Common culture: Symbolic work at play in the everyday culture of the young*. Boulder, CO: Westview Press.

3
Rhetorics of Modern Institutions

7

On the Rhetorics of Mental Disability

Catherine Prendergast

Schizophrenia never had an easy access code.
                         Avital Ronell, The Telephone Book

When Barbara[1] said that she was aware of her mind as having been re-constructed by the discipline of psychiatry, I started listening.

At this point Barbara had not been on the inside of a lockdown ward for five years, hadn't been living in a halfway house for over four years, and was working, though not steadily. She was talking to me from her own (albeit heavily subsidized) apartment. At the time of our conversation, I was completing a dissertation in the field of composition and rhetoric. My specialization often involves tracking the effects of social formations—disciplines, institutions, texts—on the creation and management of knowledge. Her comment reminded me of McCarthy and Gerring's (1994) analysis of the revision of the American Psychiatric Association's (APA) *Diagnostic and Statistical Manual of Mental Disorders* (DSM). Their conclusion, which I have much admired, was that the resulting document is largely an artifact of the professionalization of psychiatry. To have an "insider" to the psychiatric system like Barbara validate the impact of disciplinary formations on the construction of her thoughts was perhaps part of the reason I perked up at her statement. In all honesty, however, I really started listening because to me, her statement made sense. Above all, I wanted Barbara to make sense.

Barbara and I have been close friends all my life. I would like to be able to say that mental illness has done nothing to shatter that closeness, but it has—perhaps in greatest part because of our inability to broker a shared understanding of it. Her comment offered me schizophrenia in a way I could understand it. In short, it was to my mind an index of sanity, and I had developed an ear for indexing where Barbara was concerned. I reasoned her condition had been steadily improving over the course of the seven years since her original diagnosis. She had passed, I had noted, into progressively less restrictive settings to receive care. But in the year after that phone call, Barbara was admitted to her county's psychiatric hospital four times in six months, and I have been forced to reconsider the value of one of our few shared insights—its utility, if not its validity. As I reflect on the trajectory of her life since her diagnosis, it seems that both our lives and our relationship have been shaped by multiple ideological currents (not simply disciplinary ones), as well as by biological forces. The nature of these seem to surpass anyone's understanding.

Just to be clear, at this point I believe, as does the National Alliance for the Mentally Ill (NAMI), that schizophrenia is as much a brain disorder as Alzheimer's disease or multiple sclerosis. This is apparently a belief that puts me on a collision course with many of my colleagues in rhetoric, English literature, and cultural studies. These are colleagues with whom I generally share—along with office space, copy machines and hours of conversation—a number of basic epistemological assumptions. I've noticed that if I mention mental illness in the company of many of these colleagues, I become suddenly unintelligible to them. As literary scholar of madness, Carol Neely observes, in the present theoretical climate "contradictions within the subject are inscribed by institutions, social formations, representations, and discursive practices" (1991, p. 786). She suggests that many of the most current theoretical orientations have had the effect of rendering insanity at once ubiquitous and irrelevant. For an academic like myself with generally poststructuralist leanings, to think of schizophrenia as a "disease" makes me sound at best, conservative, and at worst, theoretically unsound. I am, therefore, left wandering far from my usual terrain to find language with which I can address the dilemmas and gaps in understanding that mental illness presents. The growing literature on disability would seem a natural place to turn to find such language, yet it seems that disability studies, with its emphasis on the body and not the mind, creates fissures through which attention to the mentally disabled easily falls. One might ask if there are any discourses in which people with severe mental illness might comfortably reside. I proceed with that question in mind with hope of identifying the rhetorical slippages that have left many of mentally ill of the 1990s in as poor straits as those of the last century, despite the advent of anti-psychotics and the institution of formal rights. Specifically, I'm hoping to discover how it happened that in the 1990s, to be mentally ill is practically a crime.

A Short Disclaimer

This account will resemble a pastiche more than a teleological argument. This is not to enact stylistically my concept of schizophrenic thought patterns. As I will describe later, such mimicry is problematic because schizophrenics are, by virtue of having been diagnosed schizophrenic (or "SZ"), in a distinct and complex relationship to "audience"—a relationship that I do not share, by virtue of not sharing that diagnosis. This, then, is my own account, my own trek through case studies, textbooks, theoretical essays, films, manuals and memoirs: texts that treat the same subject from radically divergent perspectives and with widely variant rhetorical sensibilities. In the absence of a unifying grand narrative, I trace recurrent tropes and ironies that slide between the public discourse on insanity, the scholarly discourse, and my own personal experience with hope that charting this movement will produce a kind of coherence. As a result, I have many more questions than answers. Barbara, by the way, is quite capable of telling her own story. However, as I observe in the following pages, since the diagnosis of schizophrenia necessarily supplants one's position as rhetor, Barbara may tell her story, but no one can hear it.

Paperwork: Part 1

A poststructuralist perspective suggests that insanity is a discursive construct, expressed, reinforced and sometimes subverted by public discourse, the discourse of experts, and by institutional structures, which themselves can be viewed as discursive constructs.

Barbara has been perpetually in the midst of paperwork, holding on, against the deluge of uncompleted forms, to her refusal to be declared officially "disabled." It is a designation she doesn't particularly enjoy, but one that she is entitled to according to the provisions set forth in the Americans with Disabilities Act. Among other things, the designation of "disabled" is facilitated by a diagnosis in line with the *DSM-IV*. Like most of the mentally ill, Barbara's diagnosis has migrated among the categories of severe mental disorders outlined by the *DSM-IV*, and her numerous medications have changed along with each diagnosis.

I asked her recently, between her third and fourth trip to the hospital this year, what the "diagnosis de jour" (an internet chat term) was:

"They have me down as bipolar with psychotic features."
"What happened to the diagnosis of schizophrenia?"
"That was a leftover from that doctor years ago who decided I had sufficient thought disruptions to be diagnosed schizophrenic. I have no use for her so I can't remember her name."
"Oh. So it's bipolar with psychotic . . . with psychotic what?"
"Features."

I got stuck on that word "features" because images of cartoon characters with their tongues hanging out in zigzags or their eyes turned into gyroscopes started flying through my mind. I wondered silently just what "features" of Barbara were psychotic, and perhaps she wondered that too because we both laughed. Nonetheless, that I can so easily reconfigure Barbara as a cartoon character—two-dimensional and fragmented—is symptomatic of a certain perceptual problem that has arisen on my part. My problem could be a result of dealing with symptoms of the disease ("flattened affect," "pressured speech"), or with the disturbing "side-effects" of the drugs used to suppress symptoms of the disease; or perhaps as a consequence of the oft-noted depersonalizing effects of the psychiatric system. Under the weight of all these effects and affects, I search for ways in which I can think of Barbara without first re-categorizing her in my mind as a mass of misfiring molecules.

Rhetoricians have indicted the categories of disorders presented by the *DSM-IV* on the grounds that they contribute to such perceptual distortion. The APA's *ur*-text has been viewed by many as an illness-constructing document of incredible rhetorical power. For example, Berkenkotter and Ravotas (1997) suggest that as a result of the discursive tools of categorization provided by the *DSM-IV* nosology, "[i]n effect, the client becomes the sum of his or her symptoms" (p. 271). Theodore Sarbin, a denouncer of all versions of the *DSM*, charges that "schizophrenia, originally a metaphor created to help communicate about crazy behavior, is now regarded as a disease entity by most medical practitioners," completing what he calls the "metaphor-to-myth transformation" (1990, p. 313). McCarthy and Gerring (1994) point to the proliferation of disorders in the *DSM-IV*, and suggest, "[t]he *DSM* classification system adopts the biomedical assumption that there are clear boundaries between diseases and between the sick and the healthy" (p. 183). For McCarthy and Gerring, the *DSM* is the psychiatric profession's main vehicle for maintaining dominance over other mental health disciplines, firmly entrenching the biomedical model of mental disorder.

Though he whole-heartedly endorses the biomedical model and the very assumption of a clear boundary between sick and healthy in particular, NAMI's favored spokesperson/professional, E. Fuller Torrey, is no less critical of the *DSM-IV*, and no less willing to grant the document rhetorical force as fabricator of illness. However, Torrey's (1997) conclusion is the opposite of that of McCarthy and Gerring: he believes the proliferation of disorders that characterizes the current edition is problematic because it dissolves the boundaries between the sick and the healthy. Torrey argues that the document expands the definition of mental illness to include potentially everyone. He suggests that the present proliferation of disorders ("the Woody Allen Syndrome," he calls it) allows psychiatrists to devote their attention to "the wealthy and worried well"—those Torrey believes are in a different category of need altogether from the severely mentally ill. If everyone is sick, Torrey complains, then no one is, and funds originally earmarked for the most needy are spread thin to accommodate everyone (1997, p. 182). Torrey nevertheless does not assign the APA complete blame for what he sees as misdirected attention and funding. He suggests the Woody Allen Syndrome is connected to wider social and political trends, not simply to the actions of a particular discipline or organization. It would seem that for Torrey, as for Neely, mental illness is—discursively speaking—at once everywhere and nowhere.

Progress

One might argue that this is a good way to remove the stigma from the mentally ill, to place them in the context of the vast spectrum of mental health and hygiene and make them "not other." Ironically, other attempts to improve the lot of those with severe mental illness have relied on fostering a perception of the mentally ill as a distinct group. The concern for rights of the mentally ill in this century came after decades of appalling treatment: enforced lobotomies and sterilizations, the use of aversive conditioning, uncontrolled medical experimentation and scandalous conditions in asylums. All this led many to call attention to the need for reform. And wide-reaching reform has been a fairly recent phenomenon. In *Is There No Place on Earth for Me*, Susan Sheehan documents that "Creedmoor" State Hospital's 1952 annual report referred to lobotomy as "'further evidence of the desire here to keep up with the modern trend in the care of patients'" (quoted in Sheehan, 1983, p. 10). I am every day grateful—especially when Barbara is in the hospital—that psychosurgery is now discredited and illegal.

According to Sheehan (1983), sociologists' accounts of the horrible and over-crowded conditions in asylums were routinely attacked by New York State's Department of Mental Hygiene until the advent of anti-psychotics made the possibility of relieving some of the overcrowding a reality. Then, she suggests, "the department's very pronouncement agreed with its critics: State hospitals were hazardous to the health of mental patients" (p. 12). In the wake of mass de-institutionalization, the Dorothea Dix-style reform of asylum conditions gave way to a more integrationist approach in which the emphasis was placed on defending the rights of in-patients and, increasingly, outpatients. By the late seventies, "litigation to correct inhumane institutional conditions had turned to advocacy for the development of community-based services as a means to advance social justice for people with mental disabilities" (Levy & Rubenstein, 1996, p. 3). The rise of identity politics helped make possible the application of the rhetoric of rights to the mentally ill. The irony of this development is that while the presence of a diagnosis would be the very thing that would "identify" the mentally ill, the thrust of identity politics—to end discrimination—effectively recasts the mentally ill not as "ill," not as being in need of treatment, but as being in need of social empowerment and liberation, much like other historically excluded groups, such as Native Americans and African Americans.

"Liberation" in terms of the discourse surrounding mental illness, however, necessarily involves addressing the practice of involuntary commitment, a practice that allows holding people against their will under special legal circumstances. The legal standard for involuntary commitment is that a person be deemed "likely to cause serious injury to himself or others" (Levy & Rubenstein, 1996, p. 353). This phrase, and the word "likely" in particular, is vague enough that for someone to make that judgment is to create and recreate dramas of diagnosis and doubt. Almost always, it seems, the practice of involuntary commitment invokes scripts of oppression. Many of the mass-market images of involuntary commitment center around malevolent family members or government agents trying to control free-thinkers or snatch someone's assets (for example, the movies *Terminator 2* and *The Madness of King George*). Barbara has, at times, compared the managed care organization that handles her outpatient treatment to the Gestapo, forcing her against her will into "voluntary" commitment. As she puts it, the managed care representatives ask if you want to go to the hospital, when they really mean, "you're going to the hospital." Sociologist Erving Goffman's (1961) critique of mental asylums, published in the early 1960s, also employs the Gestapo analogy. He compares (with a weak qualifier regarding intentions) the "betrayal funnel" relatives help construct to facilitate "the pre-patient's progress from home to hospital" to the coaxing of concentration camp victims toward the gas chambers (p. 137).[2]

It's quite possible that Goffman's (1961) study was one of those reports Sheehan mentions that were routinely ignored until anti-psychotic drugs came to be regarded as the biochemical equivalent of physical restraints. Indeed, Foucault's (1965) *Madness and Civilization*—another blast at institutionalization—became popular around the same time. More to the point, however, is that neither Goffman's (1961) ethnomethodological account of the dynamics of commitment in the 1950s, nor Sheehan's (1983) journalistic account of her subject's experiences with institutionalization in the late 1970s, nor even Foucault's (1965) meditation on confinement throughout the ages is sufficient to represent the conditions under which the mentally ill are held involuntarily today. Now, in the 1990s, it is more and more the case that the mentally ill will progress from street to jail, or from homeless shelter to hospital, as Barbara initially did. For most, however, there aren't many hospitals left to progress to, as mental institutions have become a thing of the past. In 1955, the year Goffman conducted his study, there were 559,000 patients in state mental institutions (an all time high). As of 1995, there were 69,000 (Butterfield, 1998). Where are the rest?

Too Vast

This book does not discuss rights in the criminal process. Although these rights are important, the subject is simply too vast to be included in this small volume.

R. Levy and L. Rubenstein (1996), The Rights of People with Mental Disabilities: An ACLU Handbook *(p. 13).*

The [Los Angeles County] jail, by default, is the nation's largest mental institution. On an average day, it holds 1,500 to 1,700 inmates who are severely mentally ill, most of them detained on minor charges, essentially for being public nuisances. . . . On any day, almost 200,000 people behind bars—more than 1 in 10 of the total—are known to suffer from schizophrenia, manic depression or major depression, the three most severe mental illnesses.

F. Butterfield (1998), New York Times (p. A1)

A 1998 investigation by the Federal Justice Department of the Los Angeles County Jail revealed that the severely mentally ill comprise a significant proportion of the number of people in prison. According to the investigation, the mentally ill upon admission "would be issued yellow jumpsuits, which made them easy targets for guards or other inmates. They might be locked 23 hours a day in dirty isolation cells. And any medication they had would be confiscated until a jail psychiatrist saw them— which could take weeks" (Butterfield, 1998, p. A1). Record keeping was so inconsistent that many of the inmates had either received no treatment, were misdiagnosed, or were receiving the wrong medication. Understandably, many others who had been admitted before were loath to "identify" themselves as mentally ill, knowing the treatment they would receive, and so received no medication at all. The federal investigation led to improved conditions in the LA jail, primarily through the transfer of the mentally ill to another facility. In effect, a mental hospital was created within the prison system, but inmates are seldom there long enough to receive adequate care or to plan for follow-up care after their release. After years of working toward integration into the wider community, it seems that the mentally ill are being segregated again, even within the institutionalized community of the prison system.

LA might be the worst-case scenario of a nationwide problem. Following a period of de-institutionalization in which states slashed their budgets by closing mental hospitals, but began building prisons, jails have become one of the only "asylums" open to the mentally ill around the clock. Managed-care policies and the legal gymnastics that must be performed to prove that someone is "likely" to injure him or herself make hospital admissions difficult. It's much easier to arrest someone, particularly if that barrier of injury is crossed. Torrey (1997) and others have argued convincingly that arrest is much more "likely" to happen the longer someone remains untreated. The de-institutionalization of the mentally ill has, therefore, resulted in trans-institutionalization. Through legal and economic policy, mental illness has become increasingly criminalized, and the mentally ill increasingly housed, if housed at all, in jails instead of in state hospitals. In LA, a startling 70% of the severely mentally ill have been arrested at some point (Butterfield, 1998).

In a sense, this trans-institutionalization should have been predictable. The penitentiary is quickly becoming the repository for other historically excluded groups whose rights have been formally recognized (Native American, African American, for example). As for Barbara, to my knowledge she has not spent much time in jail, but has always been referred to the hospital. This I attribute at least in part to her being white, young, pretty and not particularly aggressive. Even at her worst she looks "likely" to have insurance. These attributes have not saved her, however, from spending quite a few nights on the street or in homeless shelters, the other fast-growing repository for the mentally ill.

There are such things as "mercy busts," arrests officers make to subvert the bureaucratic machinery and shelter people like Barbara from the perils of homelessness. The usual perils the homeless face are, in fact, multiplied for the mentally ill who are at greater risk of injury, and death (and particularly in the case of women, rape). One survey of 529 homeless people revealed that the pre-hospitalized participants were three times more likely to eat out of garbage cans and much more likely to use garbage cans as a primary food source (Torrey, 1997, p. 19). I actually haven't asked Barbara if she ate out of garbage cans during the six months she was homeless in New York City. The details she revealed to me about that period are sketchy on actual events, or perhaps what I would call events. She recalled voices guiding her this way and that into certain peril or into protected spaces. She recalled her first thought in the morning often being to wonder whether she had been raped. I asked her once what she was doing during all that time, and she explained that she was making "connections": she would find things, like a bullet hole in a pane of glass, and then ride the subways around until she found another bullet hole in a pane of glass.

For Barbara, this constituted her work. Though she was aware she was in danger, she does not to this day think of her time on the streets with as much regret as she thinks of her time in the hospital. She was at one point writing a spy thriller based on her experiences on the streets: Government investigator turns to a mental patient with mystical insight for help on a case.

Insight

It sounds nice. . . . Who could be against insight? Who could be against motherhood? But clinically, it has zero effectiveness.
         Mark Vonnegut, author of The Eden Express, *a biographical account*
                of his descent into madness (Quoted in Wyden, 1998, p. 84).

She's a fine mind, but no insight.

                                           one of Barbara's doctors

Historically, the severely mentally ill have been granted either no insight or insight of an enhanced and often creative or spiritual nature. Having "no insight" or "impaired insight" in clinical terms means that a patient does not recognize him or herself as having a disease. Schizophrenics, who generally have religious inclinations of some kind, have a very different definition of insight. To many schizophrenics, impaired insight is what you get from taking anti-psychotic drugs.

In accounts written by relatives of schizophrenics, there seems to be an awareness that any impaired insight the mentally ill might have is at least matched by our own incomplete understanding of mental illness or of the experience of madness. The title of Robin Hemley's (1998) memoir of his schizophrenic sister, *Nola: A Memoir of Faith, Art, and Madness*, seems to place all forms of insight on the same level. "She was a good person. She was a holy person. She was deluded. She was pompous, self-important. I am reminded that whatever I say condemns her, romanticizes her, lies about her, idolizes her, but never, never recreates her in all her complexity" Hemley writes. His portrait of his sister retains the complexity that the word "and" in his title suggests (p. 121). Author Susan Neville observes of her mother's speech, "When there are recognizable words but no one else can make sense of them, they call it 'word salad.' No one ever thinks to call it music" (1994, p. 214). I include this last statement because I'm not sure that I agree with it. It seems to me that after "word salad," "music" is the next inevitable descriptor. Thinking of popular movie portrayals of the mentally ill, I notice that there isn't much gray area between *Psycho* and *Shine*.[3] I sense from reading Foucault (1965) that the position of mad poet is to be regarded as preferable to the position of mental patient. I would argue, however, that these polarized positions effectively place the mentally ill and schizophrenics in particular in a rhetorical black hole: whether it's music or word salad, one never has to think about "it" at all.

Paperwork: Part 2

Patients' own writings were included in the record only at the discretion of clinicians. This was done in order to exemplify psychopathology. Sometimes poetry was included as evidence of patients' creativity but writing which merely displayed rational thinking or logical planning was not actively sought by clinicians to be included.

> *Robert Barrett (1988), "Clinical Writing and the*
> *Documentary Construction of Schizophrenia"(p. 267).*

Barrett's observation suggests that clinicians use something like the word salad/music filter to sort patients' writings, and suggests that the psychiatric gaze functions as a kind of "terministic screen" (Burke, 1990, p. 1035). It is blind to any kind of writing that might be evidence of complexity, of sanity intermingled with insanity. Berkenkotter and Ravotas (1997), too, note in their study that case records as a genre tend to screen out complexity. They compare client accounts of states of being with therapists' written translations of the initial accounts to demonstrate how emic (deeply contextual) descriptions are translated into the language of *Diagnostic and Statistical Manual of Mental Disorders*, largely for purposes of establishing credibility and billability. "The resulting written account supports a billable diagnosis, thereby fulfilling its institutional purpose. It fails, however, to serve another important purpose to many therapists, which is helping the therapist to guide the therapy process by providing a record of the client's perspective of his or her lifeworld" (p. 256). They repeatedly note the loss of "richness" in the translation of "the client's *rich* lifeworld account" (p. 269), "the client's *richly descriptive* narrative" (p. 271, italics added). In doing so, they echo Barrett's earlier lament over the loss of "nuance" in clinician's writing: "They attempted to record what they saw as the essential meaning of the conversation but in doing so, *much of the radiant meaning, ambiguity and nuance was eliminated*" (1990, p. 272, italics added).

I can see how these rhetorical analyses are attempting to demonstrate the dehumanizing effect of the *DSM-IV* and the biomedical model, as well as the bureaucratization of therapy. What seems missing in these rhetorical analyses, however, is some sense of the significance of the loss of the descriptive account, besides the loss of descriptiveness in and of itself. Without such analysis it seems that the real failing of the biomedical model is that it turns clinicians into unimaginative literary critics, translating poetry into psychopathology. Except to note that there is loss in translation, the rhetorical analyses cited above don't engage with "it," the sense of what the patient is saying or writing, any more than the clinical analysis does. The lack of analysis of "it"—that which is lost—and what "it" might possibly mean only reassigns the mentally ill to the rhetorical black hole. Furthermore, it avoids approaching what to me is the most complex rhetorical quandary of all: how or when does one recognize schizophrenics as rhetorically enabled subjects?

This is not an easy question. Over the course of time I've known her, Barbara's "rich lifeworld" accounts have involved CIA drug-testing at parties she's been to, visions of Jimi Hendrix visiting ward B3, and detailed descriptions of thoughts projected into her head by outsiders, including myself. They consist of a number of things I don't believe in, though more significantly, things her doctors don't believe in. Initially, while talking to her about these subjects I felt the privilege of suspending my disbelief long enough to consider that, well, she might be right. She might be a canary in the mines, more sensitive to the vagaries and possibilities of the technological, political and spiritual present than I am. At the very least she has an experience of certainty I can't even approach.[4] The writing teacher in me would be drawn to this wealth of uncommon, raw description, although I would think of her stories as underdeveloped ideas and rough "first drafts": I would await clarification that never arrived. Then I read in manuals like *Surviving Schizophrenia* (1988), *Conquering Schizophrenia* (1998), and the disarmingly entitled *Understanding Schizophrenia* (1994) that one of the most characteristic marks of SZs is that they claim that thoughts are being projected into their heads. Schizophrenics by the score testify to being followed by the CIA. Noting the similarity between Barbara's accounts and the accounts of others, I found myself feeling a little schnuckered, as though I'd been taken in by a plagiarist. Lately I've come to think of that initial pedantic reaction as wishful thinking on my part. It's hard to think of anyone you care about as a textbook case, especially when the revelation comes so literally.

All this has led me to wonder about the therapeutic value of rich, descriptive and ambiguous narratives; too often that value is assumed. I think it's worth noting that the assumption that rich, descriptive, nuanced and ambiguous narratives have therapeutic value harkens back to Freud, who had no patience with the severely mentally ill and no interest in treating them. He made a distinction between neurotics and psychotics and devoted his attention to the former, barely regarding the latter as human. Furthermore, when American Freudians, who didn't acknowledge Freud's self-imposed limitations, still dominated the psychiatric profession, record-keeping and diagnostic features took on a more narrative and nuanced, but nonetheless dehumanizing and invasive character. Goffman (1961) observed: "Current psychiatric doctrine defines mental disorder as something that can have its roots in the patient's earliest years, show its signs throughout the course of his [*sic*] life, and invade almost every sector of his current activity" (p. 155). Thus, Goffman notes, clinicians are justified in invading every sector of the patient's past. Nothing is without relevance. From Goffman's reported data we find this record of a patient, which is quite rich and descriptive, though obviously not representative of the patient's perspective:

Armed with a rather neat appearance and natty little Hitlerian mustache, this 45 year old man who has spent the last five or more years of his life in the hospital is making a very successful hospital adjustment living within the role of a rather gay liver and jim-dandy type of fellow who is not only quite superior to his fellow patients in intellectual respects but who is also quite a man with women. His speech is sprayed with many multi-syllabled words which he generally uses in good context, but if he talks long enough on any subject it soon becomes apparent that he is so completely lost in this verbal diarrhea as to make what he says almost completely worthless. (quoted in Goffman, 1961, pp. 157–158)[5]

This passage stands in stark contrast to the case records produced after the rise of APA that Barrett (1990), and Berkenkotter and Ravotas (1997) studied. It is short on nominalization and devoid of jargon. Nevertheless, in its reluctance to report the "sense" of what this man was saying, it stubbornly refuses to allow him into the world of rhetoric, and thus implies that he shouldn't be allowed into the world at all. This patient may have had a narrative of his own, but neither Goffman nor the clinician could render it.

A Multiple-Choice Test

Barbara once thought it might be interesting to write down every instance in literature where a narrator invoked the phrase, "I heard a voice inside," and then present this list to her psychiatric evaluators.

If I transcribed here a passage of poststructuralist texts like Deleuze and Guattari's (1987) *A Thousand Plateaus* or Avitar Ronell's (1989) *The Telephone Book*—both of which were written to enact rhetorically the experience of schizophrenic thought—and a passage from a letter Barbara wrote to me from the hospital, you might be hard pressed to distinguish them. If you saw the first two in their published form, and Barbara's letter as it reached me—on a crooked rectangle of unlined paper, written in green cramped pencil scribbles that looked as if she had written it in a moving vehicle—your task would be a lot easier. Of course what stops me from actually conducting this test is that I have noticed that anything a person with a severe mental disorder on their record writes is that much more liable to be appropriated and translated in any number of medical and legal contexts. I would love to cite here the many passages from Barbara's writing: the logical ones, the incoherent ones, the poetic ones. Unfortunately, given this possibility of selective appropriation, she and I both thought it best that I didn't.

Suffice it to say that there is a moment at which something or someone is granted what might be called "rhetoricity"[6]—a moment that has little to do with syntax, grammar or vocabulary. Nowhere has this moment been more clearly dramatized than in Ted Kacyzinski's pre-trial hearings during which teams of psychiatrists examined Kacyzinski in order to determine whether or not he could be considered a rhetorically enabled subject capable of defending himself—a status for which he was willing to risk the death penalty. Were his words to be presented in defense of his actions, or as evidence that his condition rendered any defense of his actions irrelevant? The latter interpretation was eventually chosen to avoid a trial that almost certainly would have ended badly for him (Finnegan, 1998, p. 61). And so he was put in a bizarre situation—your rhetoric or your life. Paradoxically, his own journal was offered as evidence that his testimony should be inadmissible.

To be disabled mentally is to be disabled rhetorically, a truth Barbara knows as well as any. Her definition of disability she has phrased at times as "a life denied significance." In the field of rhetoric, her statement might be translated into "a life denied signification." Given the present configuration of discourses on mental illness, the writing of schizophrenics can only be seen as a-rhetorical, simply as data: the test, the record of symptoms, Exhibit A. At best, it is seen as music, as poetry, as some personal expression that has no bearing outside of itself, no transactional currency. In this respect, it shares much with the writing of first-year composition students (see Miller, 1991). That the mentally ill are treated as devoid of rhet-oric would seem to me to be an obvious point: If people think you're crazy, they don't listen to you. But I wonder about the implications of that phe-nomenon as I confront them in everyday life, as friend, as researcher, as scholar of rhetoric, to the extent that I have ceased to cherish theories—like post-structuralism—that used to provide the bedrock assumptions of my professional work. Specifically, if, as anthropologist Renato Rosaldo (1989) offers, we have much to learn from the way the oppressed analyze their own condition, the question of how one listens to the mentally ill in an age in which they have been oppressed by the effective criminalization of their condition becomes vital. Does some kind of (al)chemical trans-formation need to take place before the mentally ill can be heard? And who must be transformed?

Illogical Fear

> As a public relations dilemma, schizophrenia was ever a disaster. 'Illogical fear,' as Senator Domenici had put it, was only one of the barriers giving the illness a reputation as dreaded as leprosy. Other obstacles were resig-nation that engendered hopelessness; and a near-total ignorance—a NAMI poll found that fifty-five percent of the American public denied that mental illness existed. Denial was rooted in intense repugnance.
> *Peter Wyden (1998),* Conquering Schizophrenia *(p. 200).*

As Wyden (1998) points out, the mentally ill are the most reviled of the disabled: Schizophrenia has no poster child. There is no Special Olympics for institutionalized patients. Nobody runs telethons to raise money for "the cure." Despite all the lip service paid to integrating the severely men-tally ill into society (of which I think the newest label, "consumer," is the most revealing of greater cultural values) the repugnance Wyden speaks of is palpable, and his analogy to leprosy apt. Tellingly, when Goffman (1961) described the five categories of total institutions, he divided the physically disabled, those he classified incapable of caring for themselves and harmless, from the mentally ill, those he classified incapable of taking care of themselves and a threat to the community. The other groups Goff-man included under this heading were TB patients and lepers. Schizo-phrenia, it seems, is contagious.

Barbara senses this. She has said that she feels like there's a red light that goes off every time her brain gets too close to someone else's brain.

Back when she lived in a halfway house the very small child next door with whom she had had no previous interaction came up to her and said "I hate you," a child's translation of "My Mommy told me not to talk to you." The founding and maintenance of the kind of community enterprises like halfway houses that are so essential to the treatment plans of many outpatients is difficult in the face of frequent hostility from the community.

Of course this kind of repugnance is meted out to the physically disabled as well. The late anthropologist Robert Murphy, who suffered from ever-deepening quadriplegia, noted that the physically disabled are reviled by the able-bodied because the able-bodied feel themselves at threat: "The disabled serve as constant, visible reminders to the able-bodied that the society they live in is shot through with inequity and suffering, that they live in a counterfeit paradise, that they too are vulnerable. We represent a fearsome possibility" (1987, p. 117). But while it is the visible aspect of the physically disabled that poses a threat, for the mentally disabled the threat is in speech. As historian of perceptions of schizophrenia S. P. Fullinwider (1982) has observed, "Certain sorts of people—those the profession learned to call schizophrenics—place an almost unbearable perceptual strain on the psychiatrist. As the doctor confronts the patient he feels his world break apart. He begins to lose perceptual control over his environment" (p. 4).

Perhaps this illogical fear is what accounts for the present banishing of the severely mentally ill to steam grates, dumpsters, jail cells and isolation tanks. Perhaps in our most closeted imaginations we fear schizophrenics as the most able rhetors of them all. Although cultural constructions of mental disability have varied widely in the last two hundred years, passed through several crises of categorization and rigorous rhetorical shifts, this banishment, this inability to treat sufferers with humanity—or often to treat them at all—has sadly remained a cultural constant. At this point, the criminalization of the mentally ill has effectively negated many of the gains toward more humane treatment that have been made over the last fifty years. Whether they are interpreted theoretically as acts of faith, art, or madness, the reality today is that the acts of many of the mentally ill are perceived as criminal, and the actors treated accordingly. I wonder about the utility of a rhetoric of rights without a corresponding rhetoric of public responsibility. I wonder how a rhetoric that renders mental illness irrelevant can contribute to healing. I wonder if there will ever be a rhetoric of mental disability that the mentally disabled themselves will have the greatest part in crafting.

Postscript

As of the spring of 2000, four years after she and I had the conversation about the effect of the discipline of psychology on her brain, Barbara was pursuing a doctoral degree in recombinant DNA technology at a prominent research university. She credits her recent successes to three things: a stable support network of friends, the therapeutic effects of returning to school, and two new drugs, Olanzapine and Venlafaxine, which make it possible for her to study.

Notes

This chapter originally appeared in J. C. Wilson and C. Lewiecki-Wilson (Eds.) (2001). *Embodied rhetorics: Disability in language and culture.* Carbondale: Southern Illinois University Press.

I would like to acknowledge the helpful comments of Cynthia Lewiecki-Wilson and James Wilson who patiently read and thoroughly responded to several previous versions of this essay. I thank as well Gale Walden and David Eng for their thoughtful comments. Most especially I would like to thank Barbara for her continuous engagement and support.

1. All efforts have been made to conceal Barbara's identity, including the use of a pseudonym.

2. Ironically enough, given the Gestapo analogy, the hospital Goffman studied was, at the time he was studying it, shielding from trial one of this country's most renowned anti-Semites, Ezra Pound, by exaggerating his condition (Torrey, 1984).

3. The award-winning documentary *Jupiter's Wife* is a rare exception, providing a more realistic portrayal of mental illness in which the narrator's desire to either believe or discount everything his schizophrenic subject says is itself presented and examined. The film was not a popular success, however.

4. I am indebted to my colleague Lori Newcomb for the phrase "experience of certainty" which she used to describe Joan of Arc's zealousness.

5. In the library book I took this excerpt from, a previous reader had written next to the last line, "sounds like a professor."

6. I am indebted to Martin Nystrand for suggesting the term "rhetoricity" to articulate this moment.

References

American Psychological Association. (1994). *Diagnostic and statistical manual of mental disorders*. (4th ed.). Washington DC: American Psychological Association.

Barrett, R. J. (1988). Clinical writing and the documentary construction of schizophrenia. *Culture, Medicine and Psychiatry, 12,* 265–299.

Berkenkotter, C. & Ravotas, D. (1997). Genre as tool in the transmission of practice over time and across professional boundaries. *Mind, Culture and Activity, 4,* 256–274.

Butterfield, F. (1998, March 5). Prisons replace hospitals for the nation's mentally ill. *The New York Times*, p. A1.

Burke, K. (1990). Language as symbolic action. In P. Bizzell & B. Herzberg (Eds.), *The rhetorical tradition: Readings from classical times to the present* (pp. 1031–1041). Boston: St. Martin's. (Original work published in 1966).

Deleuze, G. & Guattari, F. (1987). *A thousand plateaus: Capitalism and schizophrenia*. (B. Massumi, Trans.). Minneapolis: University of Minnesota Press.

Finnegan, W. (1988, March 16). Defending the Unabomber. *New Yorker*, 52–63.

Foucault, M. (1965). *Madness and civilization: A history of insanity in the age of reason*. (R. Howard, Trans.). New York: Vintage Books.

Fullinwider, S. P. (1982). *Technicians of the finite: The rise and decline of the schizophrenic in American thought 1840–1960*. Westport, CT: Greenwood Press.

Goffman, E. (1961). *Asylums: Essays on the social situation of mental patients and other inmates*. Chicago: Aldine.

Hemley, R. (1998). *Nola: A memoir of faith, art and madness.* Saint Paul, MN: Graywolf.

Keefe, R. & Harvey, P. D. (1994). *Understanding schizophrenia: A guide to the new research on causes and treatment*. New York: Free Press.

Levy, R. M. & Rubenstein, L. S. (1996). *The rights of people with mental disabilities*. Carbondale: Southern Illinois UP.

McCarthy, L. P. & Gerring, J. P. (1994). Revising psychiatry's charter document Diagnostic and Statistical Manual of Mental Disorders-IV. *Written Communication, 11,* 147–192.

Miller, S. (1991). *Textual carnivals: The politics of composition*. Carbondale: Southern Illinois UP.

Murphy, R. (1987). *The body silent*. New York: Henry, Holt.

Neely, C. T. (1991). Recent work in Renaissance studies: Pyschology. Did madness have a Renaissance? *Renaissance Quarterly, 44,* 776–791.

Neville, S. (1994). *Indiana winter*. Bloomington: Indiana UP.

Ronell, A. (1989). *The telephone book: Technology, schizophrenia, electric speech*. Lincoln: University of Nebraska Press.

Rosaldo, R. (1989). *Culture and truth: The remaking of social analysis*. Boston: Beacon Press.

Sarbin, T. R. (1990). Metaphors of unwanted conduct. In D. Leary, (Ed.), *Metaphors in the history of psychology* (pp. 300–330). New York: Cambridge University Press.

Sheehan, S. (1983). *Is there no place on earth for me?* New York: Vintage.

Torrey, E. F. (1997). *Out of the shadows: Confronting America's mental illness crises*. New York: John Wiley.

Torrey, E. F. (1984). *The roots of treason: Ezra Pound and the secret of St. Elizabeths*. New York: McGraw Hill.

Torrey, E. F. (1988). *Surviving schizophrenia: A family manual*. New York: Harper & Row.

Vonnegut, M. (1975). *The eden express*. New York: Praeger.

Wyden, P. (1998). *Conquering schizophrenia: A father, his son and a medical breakthrough*. New York: Alfred A. Knopf.

8

Subjects of the Inner City
Writing the People of Cabrini-Green

David Fleming

Introduction

Among the more difficult problems associated with the practice and theory of public discourse is determining exactly who, in any given case, the public is, who belongs to the community of argument, who is accorded the right to speak, listen, read, write, and deliberate in it. Although the ideal often espoused is one of maximum inclusiveness—Dewey (1927/1991) defined the public as "all those who are affected by the indirect consequences of transactions" (pp. 15–16), and Dahl (1979) argued that, in a "full" procedural democracy, the *demos* should include all adult members (p. 129)—and although it is commonly held that the only truly valid political decisions are those reached through "unrestrained and universal discourse" (Habermas, 1970, p. 372), the public is always, in practice, exclusive to one degree or another. The United States is no exception to this: we may claim an egalitarian theory of political identity, but history shows that citizenship here has often been assigned on the basis of ascribed characteristics like race, gender, religion, and national origin (Smith, 1997).

The problem of determining the public is doubly vexing, however, because the determination is itself typically a matter of public discourse. In other words, we often decide whom we will treat as equal partners in talk through talk itself, excluding people from deliberation by representing them as deserving that exclusion. What is so troubling about this, of course, is that those excluded from the public are also excluded from the deliberations that exclude them. After a century and a half, the U.S.

Supreme Court's 1857 decision in the Dred Scott case remains disturbing, at least in part, because of the unilateral character of its exclusion: white men deciding who black people are and whether or not they should be classed as "citizens."

> The question is simply this: Can a Negro, whose ancestors were imported into this country, and sold as slaves, become a member of the political community formed and brought into existence by the Constitution of the United States, and as such become entitled to all the rights, and privileges, and immunities, guarantied by that instrument to the citizen? . . .
>   The words "people of the United States" and "citizens" are synonymous terms, and mean the same thing. . . . The question before us is, whether the class of persons described in the plea in abatement [people of African ancestry] compose a portion of this people, and are constituent members of this sovereignty? We think they are not, and that they are not included, and were not intended to be included, under the word "citizens" in the Constitution. (quoted in Finkelman, 1997, pp. 57–58)

Although a war was fought in part to make such things harder to argue, the question about who belongs in the public sphere remains a contentious one.

The city is an especially problematic public because it contains, almost by definition (see, e.g., Wirth, 1938), a more diverse population than one typically finds in communities of kinship, leisure, or work. At the same time, the very concentration of that population makes its diversity hard to avoid. In the city, in other words, human beings very different from one another share space, their proximity forcing them to manage their differences somehow. Although in theory this combination of diversity and density is celebrated (e.g., Jacobs, 1961; Mumford, 1961), in practice, it is usually managed through fragmentation:

> Every American metropolitan area is now divided into districts that are so different from each other they seem to be different worlds. Residential neighborhoods are African American, Asian, Latino, or white, and upper-middle-class, middle-class, or poor. . . . Traveling through this mosaic of neighborhoods, metropolitan residents move from feeling at home to feeling like a tourist to feeling so out of place that they are afraid for their own security. . . . Everyone knows which parts of the metropolitan area are nice and which are dangerous. We all know where we don't belong. (Frug, 1999, p. 3)

The city, then, is not just a spatial category. It is also a social scene, a place where people are constantly seeking out and avoiding physical contact with one another. A rhetorical view of that process, which I adopt here, emphasizes the role of language in building the city, in making some people our neighbors and others not.

In what follows, I examine the discourses surrounding plans to build a mixed-income neighborhood in inner city Chicago. The idea of the economically integrated "urban village" has taken center stage recently in efforts to rebuild the American inner city and the public housing complexes that comprise so much of it. Chicago is an important test site for such an effort; it has sponsored for more than a half-century now the hyper-concentration of very poor black families in federally subsidized projects on the South, Near West, and Near North sides of downtown. The very names of these projects—Robert Taylor, Henry Horner, Cabrini-Green—have become synonymous with urban African American poverty and its seemingly intractable problems. As part of a $1.5 billion, 5-year urban revitalization plan, Chicago's public housing authority has recently proposed to demolish all 51 of its most distressed high-rise buildings, occupied by more than 14,000 poor black families, and replace them with mixed-income townhouse communities.

My focus here will be the Halstead North project, a $60 million private development on a seven acre, city-owned parcel of land adjacent to the Cabrini-Green housing project on Chicago's Near North Side. Emerging at Halstead North is a community that will ultimately house 280 families, 30% of whom will be former residents of Cabrini-Green. The question I pursue here is this: How are the people of Cabrini-Green represented in the discourses surrounding this development? What names are they given? What names do they give themselves? Data for this analysis come from more than two hundred written documents concerning Halstead North and similar developments, including business plans, government reports and regulations, non-governmental position papers, legal documents, articles from the mass media, and scholarly and historical materials.

My analysis of these data leads me to several conclusions. First, there is enormous variation in how public housing residents are represented in discourses about them. Second, this variation can be seen as rhetorical in nature: although references to and descriptions of public housing residents almost always pretend to be neutral, what they actually do is characterize individuals in highly partisan ways, emphasizing some of their characteristics and de-emphasizing others, defining by reduction, omission, and juxtaposition. Third, this variation is not random but can be tied to the interests of participants in the debate. Fourth, these representations have effects, certain ones being "picked up" and disseminated across time and space, developing into argumentative topoi that exert considerable influence on public belief and action. Finally, many of these representations function, whether intentionally or not, to disempower public housing residents, depriving them of the rhetorical and political agency they need to participate fully in their own—and in their city's—self-determination.

I describe below four categories of representation. The first three, pertaining to income, race, and behavior, involve representations of public housing residents advanced by others. The fourth includes residents' representations of themselves.

The Meaning of Class

Economic class is the key linguistic marker of individuals living in public housing. In fact, in order even to be eligible for federally-funded public housing in this country, a person must by law be "poor," i.e., have an income below 80% of area median income. According to the U.S. Housing Act of 1937 (as amended) (1998):

dwelling units . . . shall be rented only to families who are low-income families at the time of initial occupancy . . . the term low-income families means those families whose incomes do not exceed 80 per centum of the median income for the area. (42 U.S.C. § 1437a(a)(1) & (b)(2))

What does it mean to build a community exclusively for the poor, to identify the inhabitants of that community solely by their economic class, to refer to them only as "low-income" people? In what follows, I describe how economic labeling works in U.S. housing policy and suggest what some of its rhetorical implications might be.

The restriction of public housing in the United States to the poor was a decision that can be located quite precisely. In the debates leading up to the passage of the U.S. Housing Act of 1937, the National Association of Home Builders, the U.S. Savings and Loan League, and (especially) the National Association of Real Estate Boards waged a relentless and ultimately successful campaign to ensure that government-owned housing in this country would be unavailable to the middle class and would, therefore, compete as little as possible with the private real estate market (Bowly, 1978; Hays, 1995; Meyerson & Banfield, 1955; Mitchell, 1985; Schill, 1993). The legislative means for effecting this restriction was to impose income ceilings on tenancy. According to the 1937 Act, "[N]o family shall be accepted as a tenant in any such project whose aggregate income exceeds five times the rental [including utilities] of the quarters to be furnished such family" (as quoted in Fisher, 1959/1985, p. 241). In other words, from the beginning the federal government supported, rather than checked the economic segregation of the U.S. population. It did so through a language that, even today, equates "public" housing with poverty: "The term 'public housing' means low-income housing" (U.S. Housing Act of 1937 [as amended], 42 U.S.C. § 1437a(b)(1), 1998).

Three classes of the poor are eligible to live in the "projects": "extremely low-income" families, those whose income is 0–30% of area median income; "very low-income" families, those at 30–50% of area median income; and "low-income" families, those whose income is 50–80% of the area median.[1] Let me briefly describe each of these classes.

The "extremely" poor is a group that was legally defined only in 1999 (see "Changes to Admission," 1999, p. 23471). The U.S. Department of Housing and Urban Development (hereafter, HUD) (1999a) has elsewhere referred to members of this category as "struggling families." Most current residents of public housing are in this group, the median income nationwide being $6,939, or 21% of area median income (HUD, 1998a). (The figures listed by the Chicago Housing Authority [2000] for its projects are lower: the majority of residents at Cabrini-Green, for example, earn less than 13% of area median income.)

The next group, families at 30–50% of area median income, appears to be gradually disappearing from policy discussions, squeezed out by those with greater needs, on one side, and the "working" poor, on the other. This latter group, families with incomes between 50–80% of area median and often called simply "low-income" residents by the federal government, is thought to have largely abandoned public housing during the last 40 years. This was the result of the deteriorating condition of U.S. inner cities from the 1950s on, which prompted first white then black middle-class flight; as well as the 1969 Brooke Amendments, which fixed rent for public housing at 30% of family income with no adjustment as income increased; and the Reagan-era restriction of public housing to those with incomes below 50% of area median (later repealed). The government is currently trying to lure this third group back to the projects. Through "deconcentration" it hopes to raise the average income in public housing projects by increasing the number of residents in the 50–80% group, thereby alleviating some of the negative effects of putting so many "extremely" poor families in one place (see HUD, 1996a, 1998c, 1999c, 2000). The 1998 Housing Act, for example, now requires that only 40% of new units be targeted to families below 30% of area median income (Sard & Lubell, 1998, "Eligibility and Targeting Requirements"; see also Lubell & Sard, 1998); and public housing authorities can now "skip" over "extremely poor" applicants in favor of "working" families (those making 50–80% of area median income) (General HUD Program Requirements, 24 C.F.R. § 5.415, 1999).

The problem with deconcentration, of course, is that since the current residents of public housing are almost uniformly "extremely poor," the only way to create mixed-income communities on project sites is to displace these residents and bring in new ones. Thus, when the Chicago Housing Authority (hereafter, CHA) recently proposed to limit the proportion of "extremely poor" tenants to 50% of project totals, critics wondered how this could be done given that 98% of current residents are in that group (Oldweiler & Rogal, 2000, "Half and Half"). Residents at ABLA Homes have even sued the CHA, claiming that redevelopment plans there would reserve more than 70% of new units for families above 50% of area median income ($28,700), even though the average income of current residents is only $5,833 (National Center on Poverty Law, 1999, paragraph 11). But deconcentration forges ahead: both the 1995 consent decree in *Henry Horner Mothers Guild v. Chicago Housing Authority* and the 1998 consent decree in *Cabrini-Green Local Advisory Council v. Chicago Housing Authority* reserve a substantial proportion of new housing units for the "working" poor, usually defined as those making 50–80% of area median income.

An even more dramatic form of deconcentration, however, is occurring on non-CHA, city-owned property adjacent to the projects, where developers are not restricted to low-income tenants. Here, public housing residents are being mixed in with two higher income groups: families at 80–120% of area median income and those above 120% of area median income. The first group corresponds to the "middle class" of American social ideology—in *Henry Horner Mothers Guild v. Chicago Housing Au-*

thority (1995), families above 80% a.m.i. are referred to as "middle-income" families (p. 46). The second group includes all those who can afford "private" housing rented or sold at the "market" rate.

North Halstead is one such development. As part of the City of Chicago's 1996 Near North Redevelopment Initiative, which seeks to revitalize the whole area around Cabrini-Green as a "mixed-income community" (City of Chicago Department of Housing, 1998, p. 1), the site must include public housing families. But the mix of residents will not be the one-half "very poor" (0–50% area median) / one-half "poor" (50–80%) that the CHA now envisions for its properties. Rather, former Cabrini-Green families will make up only 30% (or 82 units) of the North Halstead development, the "affordable" group (families making 80–120% of area median) taking up 20% (54 units), and "market-rate" families (those above 120% of area median income) occupying the remaining 50% (135 units) (see City of Chicago Department of Housing, 1998).

The request for proposals to purchase and develop the seven acre site, which the city issued in January, 1998, says very little about people; the three categories described above (public housing, affordable, and market-rate) serve rather as adjectives for physical structures (e.g., "[P]roposals must show that the following mix of housing units will be developed: 30% public housing eligible (CHA) units; 20% "affordable" units; 50% market-rate units" [City of Chicago Department of Housing, 1998, p. 1]). And most of the document concerns legal, financial, and design objectives, the latter drawn largely from the "New Urbanism," a set of architectural and planning principles that HUD has been promoting lately as an alternative to the "tower-in-a-park" concept behind so many Chicago public housing projects (HUD, 1996b). The New Urbanism is about building compact, pedestrian-scale, mixed-use, townhouse and low-rise urban communities, using the traditional city block with an active street life and ample public space (see Congress for the New Urbanism, 1999).

The proposal that eventually won the right to develop the site, however, pays less attention to design principles than it does to social, and even discursive issues. The Holsten Real Estate Development Corporation (hereafter, Holsten) makes it very clear that its biggest challenge at Halstead North is in attracting, mixing, and managing people from very different social and economic backgrounds. So, for example, the proposal emphasizes repeatedly its commitment to working closely with Cabrini-Green residents in planning, building, and maintaining the development

(Holsten, 1998a). The proposal includes a letter of support from the Cabrini-Green Local Advisory Council; and, in Holsten (1998b), the firm summarizes contacts with eleven more neighborhood groups. As for the goals of the redevelopment, they include "building a bridge" with current Cabrini-Green residents, working with them on their priorities and maximizing community hires and participation ("Development Team Approach, p. 1; see also "Management Plan," p. 1). Holsten claims that the success of the development will hinge on "respect for all persons in all walks of life. This is especially essential for a mixed-income development to avoid a class system and two tiers of expectations" ("Development Team Qualification," p. 1).

In addition, the firm's design for the neighborhood has "persons of all income levels living next door to other persons of all income levels" ("Development Team Approach," p. 1), satisfying the city's requirement that "[e]ach economic category of units . . . be dispersed evenly throughout the Halstead North parcel with no visible distinctions from the outside" (City of Chicago Department of Housing, 1998, p. 5). Holsten's design concept, meanwhile, includes numerous common areas, parks, and meeting rooms to serve as "public" space in the development. And the firm pays prominent attention to the role of "naturally occurring" and "staged" interactions among residents as a way to break down mistrust and isolation (for example, residents are required to attend monthly "storytelling" meetings) ("Management Plan," pp. 1–2). I will have more to say about the Holsten plan below.

What we have seen so far, then, is that regardless of whether the goal is to segregate or integrate individuals from different backgrounds, and regardless of whether the neighborhood in question is a federally-subsidized public housing project or a public-private partnership, building a city is about managing classes of individuals defined in socioeconomic terms. Language plays a key role in such a process, since both public and private entities need to identify people by their income before they can dictate which groups and how many people in each will inhabit the community in question. What might the effects of this kind of language be? First, and perhaps most obviously, to refer to a person by his or her income (e.g., "Ms. Jones is 'extremely poor'") is to give only a partial description of that person, taking one part of her character and making that the basis of her public identity. We might see such usage as an example of synecdoche, the rhetorical figure defined by George Puttenham this way: "by part we are enforced to understand the whole, by the whole part, by many things one thing, by one many" (quoted in Lanham, 1996, p. 868). One problem with such a figure, of course, is that there are always other parts that could be used to characterize the whole. Ms. Jones may be "poor," but she is also "black" and "a parent," each label motivating a different kind of argument about her. We can go even further and criticize the whole enterprise of linguistic categorization, this taking of a person— an individual with a history and dreams, virtues and vices, a complex, ir- reducible whole—and turning her into a social type. As we will see below, in representing themselves, public housing residents consistently ask to be seen and treated not as poor, or as black, or as any other social type, but as human beings.

Second, housing policies that define individuals exclusively by their economic class inevitably stigmatize those who end up in the lower classes. To be "poor" is to be a member of not just any group, but of a historically disparaged one. Schorr (1986), for one, calls policies that provide benefits and services only to the poor "exceptionalist" (p. 7) because they deal with individuals defined as exceptions, people who earn *below* a certain level, who have *failed* a means test, who have *less* than the norm (pp. 28–29). Such policies construct aid recipients, he writes, as "shamefully different and needy" (pp. 28–29). It is, unfortunately, a relatively easy step to go from disparaging a class of individuals to isolating them in one part of the city, consigning them to live "in a mean and . . . angry world, closed off from the rest of the citizenry" (p. 32).

Third, basing social policy on class distinctions contributes to the in- creasing fragmentation of our society. In identifying some people as "poor" and consigning them to certain neighborhoods, we not only de- mean them, we hurt the society as a whole, making all of us more selfish, distrustful, and isolated from one another. We create a society where the majority are private citizens, and the minority are clients of the govern- ment, provided with just enough food, housing, and health care to make sure they don't become too desperate. From this perspective, "public" housing was never about building a "public" city; it was about protecting the private interests of the majority and consigning the rest to a ghetto. Writing of the post-1949 housing debate and its obsession with class and race, Meyerson & Banfield (1955) argued that "[i]n almost no city was a public housing program developed as part of a long-range plan for all types of housing or as part of a . . . comprehensive plan for the growth and development of the community" (p. 25). To enact such a plan, we would have to "mainstream" our social programs, meeting the needs of "those who may be poor without asking them to perceive themselves as poor" (Schorr, 1986, p. 7). In Europe, most programs already operate this way. For example, two to three times the U.S. percentage live in public housing there, in developments which thus contain a much broader socioeconomic mix of residents than do the means-tested projects of the United States (Nivola, p. 22).

It would seem that the Halstead North development is moving in that direction, towards a more diverse public sphere that includes rather than isolates the poor. But notice that its residents are still defined primarily in economic terms, and it is unclear whether they will ever be able to transcend such a construction. For one thing, despite the avowed intention here to make housing units "indistinguishable" from one another, the conspicuous discrepancies in wealth that the development seeks to erase, or at least hide, will surely "come through" somehow and manifest themselves in visible ways. The Holsten proposal notes, for example, that, just among its renters, the range of incomes will go from $6,000 to $60,000 a year, a tenfold difference. Other developments in the area are dealing with the same problem. Notice, for example, the stark contrast painted by McRoberts (1998b) in an article about mixed-income housing on the Near North Side:

This isn't the very poor moving next to working poor or even middle-class neighbors. In recent weeks, more than a dozen Cabrini residents, half of whom are unemployed and paying as little as $3 a month in rent, have moved above and below people who plunked down as much as $185,000 to buy condos. (paragraph 5)

And in another piece (1998a), she asks whether Cabrini-Green residents can succeed living alongside owners of $350,000 townhomes (paragraph 1). Kamin (1997b) describes in similarly stark language how $397,000 townhouses are going up next to the "notorious" Cabrini-Green high-rises (p. 63). What are the social implications of identifying people by their economic class, putting them together with people from radically different classes, and then asking them all to simply forget about class? Holsten admits that its first contact with prospective tenants will be to divide them into income groups ("Management Plan," p. 4); and although Cabrini-Green families are assured that "community standards" will not favor one group over another and that non-discriminatory language will be sought to refer to the different income groups, there are subtle indications that behavioral expectations at Halstead North will be linked to class: "Holsten has learned from its mixed income developments some keys to success within this environment. Principally, management must meet the standards of the highest income group while having strong on-site management and troubleshooting skills" ("Development Team Qualification," p. 1). My point here is that community-building is hard to achieve when the only language we have for talking about our neighbors is one based on economic class.

Fourth, the use of relative income as a way to identify public housing families deflects attention away from the *material* reality of poverty. The ratio of a person's income to area median income tells us how that person stands economically in relation to his or her community; but it obscures the fact that someone making, say, 30% of area median income will not be able to afford adequate, nutritious food, since such an income corresponds roughly to the government's "poverty" threshold, defined as three times the cost of an "economy food plan."[2] Being "poor" from this point of view is not about having less income than others but about being unable to feed one's family.

The focus on median income also deflects attention away from the cost of housing, since a single mother with two children living at the poverty line in Chicago (that is, at about 30% area median income) would pay almost 50% of her income for "fair market" housing in the area ($737 per month for a two-bedroom apartment [HUD, 1999b]), a "severe" rent burden (HUD 1998b, "Appendix B"; see also Daskal, 1998; Dolbeare, 1999). Even someone at 50% of U.S. median family income ($23,900) would still pay approximately 30% of his or her income for housing at the fair market rate, the "affordable" threshold for HUD (although by European standards this is still a high rent level [Meehan, 1985, p. 296]). And all this assumes, of course, that families can find housing at the fair market rate, something that is apparently increasingly difficult to do (Daskal, 1998; HUD, 1998b, 1999a).

Median income figures also say nothing about work since, in 1999 someone could be employed full-time at the minimum wage and still make below 30% of area median income in 54 of the nation's 55 largest metropolitan areas (Lubell & Sard, 1998, "What Effect"; see also Daskal, 1998). Thus, calling only those in the 50–80% group the "working" poor is misleading.

Finally, references to relative income also divert attention away from
the *powerlessness* of the poor. In the discourses surrounding the Cabrini-
Green redevelopment, the rich are consistently described as risk-takers
and choice-makers, autonomous agents with power to determine how
they will inhabit the city. The poor, meanwhile, are seen as people without
choices, recipients of help, stuck where they are at others' mercy. As
McRoberts (1998b) argues, mixed-income developments are

> an extraordinary opportunity for the former Cabrini families and, so far, a good
> deal for the homeowners, who knew they'd have poor neighbors but couldn't pass
> up the financial opportunity of homes made cheaper by the city assembling the
> land. (paragraph 7; note the rhetorically-charged "but")

Later in the same article, one of the homebuyers says of her $500,000
home in a mixed-income development: "We thought this was a lot of
house for the money" (paragraph 8), while the former Cabrini-Green residents in the piece see living in the development as a way to keep their
children from being killed. Holsten also sees those in the "market" group
as people who are "taking a chance" on the inner city ("Management
Plan," p. 3). They are described as young and affluent, mostly single individuals and childless couples in their thirties who are looking for good
financial deals. They will want bedrooms that can be used first as home
offices ("Proposed Use and Concept Description," p. 2), while the poor
need all the bedrooms they can get just for their children. Holsten's whole
design approach, in fact, is geared towards the deliberative agency of the
rich: the firm wants the development to be beautiful, exciting, architec-
turally diverse, and long-lasting because "[m]arket households have choices
other than to live in a mixed-income environment" ("Proposed Use and
Concept Description," p. 1). And in an interview with the *Chicago Sun-
Times*, Peter Holsten argues that mixed-income housing can only work in
certain places: "Otherwise, you never get the people who can choose to
live wherever they want" (Roeder, 1999, paragraph 3).

Money also emboldens in these discourses: Developers are "brave,"
"saviors," "conquerors" (Breitbart & Pader, 1995); the middle-class residents of Chicago's Parc Place are the "vanguard" of an economically integrated community, and former CHA executive director Vince Lane's plans
for the project are "audacious . . . brave and important" (McCormick,
1991, paragraph 2). The CHA's efforts at transformation, meanwhile, are
"sweeping" (Garza, 1999b, paragraph 2) and "bold" (Garza & McRoberts,

1999, paragraph 3); Mayor Daley is a "powerful" official out to "transform" Cabrini-Green (Kamin, 1997a, p. 87); and Peter Holsten is described as a "developer-idealist" in one paper (Roeder, 1999, paragraph 4) and "earnest," "boyish," "shrewd," "firm," and "eager" in another (Pallasch, 1998).

The middle-class, meanwhile, may not have the power and mobility of the rich, but it has in these discourses a great deal of moral authority. Mixed-income developments are often, in fact, justified on the grounds that contact with middle-class role models improves the character of the poor (Schill, 1997, p. 149), the middle-class possessing standards of behavior that the poor need to emulate in order to lift themselves out of poverty (Sarkissian, 1976, *passim*). The most eloquent recent advocate of this view has been Wilson (1987), who argues that when middle- and working-class black families fled the ghettos in the 1970s and 80s, the urban poor were left without "mainstream role models that help keep alive the perception that education is meaningful, that steady employment is a viable alternative to welfare, and that family stability is the norm, not the exception" (p. 56). In an interview with the *Christian Science Monitor*, the former CHA head Joseph Shuldiner described public housing residents as lost without working people (Walker, 1997, paragraph 9). Unfortunately, evidence from the few studies that have actually tested the theory that living in proximity to the middle class helps the poor has been mixed (see, e.g., Bennett, 1998; Schill, 1997; Schwartz & Tajbakhsh, 1997): Status differentials in economically-integrated communities often persist, even grow.

So what happens when we define the people of Cabrini-Green as "poor"? We reduce and stigmatize them; we contribute to the social fragmentation of our communities; we obscure both the causes and the effects of poverty; and we accord to some more power and worth than others. Changing our language will not change all that; but if we want to build more just and equitable cities, we will need to talk about and to one another in more just and equitable ways.

The Elision of Race

In their obsession with income, federal policies and regulations virtually ignore other possible descriptors of public housing residents. Let's look, for example, at how race figures, or doesn't figure in discussions about public housing in Chicago. If the residents of the Cabrini-Green housing project are, by law, poor, they are also, in fact, overwhelmingly

African American. According to the CHA (2000), 99% of Cabrini-Green residents are black; for ABLA, Henry Horner, and Robert Taylor, the figures are 97%, 100%, and 99.9% respectively. And because these projects are themselves so large (6,335 residents at Cabrini-Green, 6,087 at ABLA, 2,500 at Henry Horner, and 11,040 at Robert Taylor) and are concentrated in particular areas of Chicago (especially the South and Near West sides) where they dominate their neighborhoods, the social environment of most Chicago public housing residents is extremely racially homogeneous. Just as it is for the country as a whole, although housing patterns are also clearly tied to class, the most prevalent form of residential segregation is by race, especially segregation between blacks and whites (Darden, 1998, p. 523). This segregation is, in fact, largely independent of income. As Darden claims,

> For other minority groups, socioeconomic mobility leads to significantly reduced levels of residential segregation and ultimately to greater assimilation. For blacks, socioeconomic mobility is no guarantee of freedom of spatial mobility—that is, freedom to move into the residential area of one's choice subject only to ability to pay. . . . Census data have shown that, given the same occupation, education, and income, most blacks and whites still do not live in the same neighborhoods. (p. 524)

Yet as I will argue below, race is largely elided from discourses about public housing in this country. How could this be? Perhaps the elision stems from the continuing disinclination of white Americans to talk openly about race and to see racism around them; note, for example, George Will's (2000) recent assertion that "race relations have never been better, and arguably would be better still if there were less obsessing about them" (p. 2B). Perhaps silence concerning race can be traced to Wilson's (1978) thesis about the "declining significance of race" in urban poverty. The "new" poverty, Wilson (1996) writes in his most recent book, is primarily a function of joblessness. Discrimination matters, he admits, especially historic discrimination, but it is not sufficient to explain the current lack of social organization in inner-city neighborhoods, most of which were just as segregated in the past, but had much higher levels of employment. ABLA tenant leader Deverra Beverly appears to endorse this theory: "When I was growing up, every parent who lived here was employed . . . We knew that No. 1, there should be jobs . . . this was the problem in public housing" (quoted in McRoberts, 1998c, paragraph 25).

Finally, many still hold onto the belief that residential racial segregation in this country is largely voluntary in origin, despite the fact that,
when asked, blacks consistently say that they would prefer to live in integrated neighborhoods (Massey & Denton, 1993, pp. 88ff). As tenant
leader Michele Townsend says, "I have talked with a lot of residents from
different developments and they would like to see public housing deseg-
regated. . . . [T]he way public housing is isolated does a disservice to the
residents" (quoted in Jewish Council on Urban Affairs, 1999, p. 2).

Regardless of its origin, the inability to "see" racial segregation at work
in the inner city is a crucial failure. In *American Apartheid*, Massey &
Denton (1993) write in response to Wilson's (1978) thesis:

It seemed to us amazing that people were even debating whether race was declining in importance when levels of residential segregation were so high and so
structured along racial lines, and we did not understand how the volumes of material written on the underclass could gloss over the persisting reality of racial segregation as if it were irrelevant to the creation and maintenance of urban poverty.
Our research indicates that racial residential segregation is the principal structural feature of American society responsible for the perpetuation of urban
poverty and represents a primary cause of racial inequality in the United States.
(p. viii)

The disappearance of the word "segregation" from social and economic
policy debates in this country is a mistake, Massey & Denton continue, because, *pace* Wilson, the problem of the urban underclass is first and foremost a racial one:

No group in the history of the United States has ever experienced the sustained
high level of residential segregation that has been imposed on blacks in large
American cities for the past fifty years. This extreme racial isolation did not just
happen; it was manufactured by whites through a series of self-conscious actions
and purposeful institutional arrangements that continue today. Not only is the
depth of black segregation unprecedented and utterly unique compared with that
of other groups, but it shows little signs of change with the passage of time or improvements in socioeconomic status. (p. 2)

Just as public housing in this country was not "naturally" restricted to poor
people, the United States has not always been marked by racially segregated residence patterns. In fact, over the course of the twentieth century,
our cities, and especially the large northern ones, were made that way.

Blacks were kept in the ghettos and out of white neighborhoods by horrendous physical violence, intimidation by neighborhood "improvement associations," legally binding restrictive covenants, unfair bank lending patterns, "racial steering" by realtors, and government building programs (Massey & Denton, 1993, pp. 33ff).

Nowhere is residential racial segregation in the United States more pronounced than in Chicago, which in 1980 was the most segregated city in the country, with a 91% index of black-white dissimilarity (meaning that 91% of Chicago blacks would have to move to achieve an integrated residential configuration in the metropolitan area) and a 90% index of black isolation (meaning that 90% of blacks live only among other blacks) (Massey & Denton, 1993, p. 71). But segregation in Chicago involves more than just the uneven distribution and racial isolation of blacks; black neighborhoods there are also tightly clustered (that is, they form a large contiguous enclave), concentrated within a small area (blacks live in smaller neighborhoods than whites), and centralized around the urban core (a place associated with high levels of crime, social disorder, and economic marginality). According to Massey & Denton, a high score on at least four of these dimensions indicates the presence of "hypersegregation" (p. 74); in such cities—and Chicago is at or near the top of the list on all five counts—blacks live in true ghettos:

> Typical inhabitants of one of these ghettos are not only unlikely to come into contact with whites within the particular neighborhood where they live; even if they traveled to the adjacent neighborhood they would still be unlikely to see a white face; and if they went to the next neighborhood beyond that, no whites would be there either. People growing up in such an environment have little direct experience with the culture, norms, and behaviors of the rest of American society and few social contacts with members of other racial groups. Ironically, within a large, diverse, and highly mobile post-industrial society such as the United States, blacks living in the heart of the ghetto are among the most isolated people on earth. (p. 77)

This isolation was dramatically depicted by a 1985 Philadelphia study in which blacks there were shown to have remarkably racially homogeneous friendship networks, something directly related, the researchers argued, to their residential concentration (Massey & Denton, p. 161). The same can be said of Chicago: White people are conspicuously absent, for example, in the two best-known popular accounts of public housing in

Chicago: Alex Kotlowitz's (1991) *There Are No Children Here* (about life in the Henry Horner Homes) and Nicholas Lemann's (1992) *The Promised Land* (in part, about a family in the Robert Taylor Homes). "A white person in the project," says Lemann of the late 1980s, "was an extremely rare sight, except on television. 'People didn't talk about white people,' Robert Haynes [a resident of Robert Taylor] says. 'You couldn't *conceive* of what they'd do except put you in jail. . . . White people weren't an issue'" (pp. 266–267). Further evidence for racial isolation in the inner city is provided by a 1991 ethnographic study of Chicago's poorest neighborhoods, which found that blacks there have extremely narrow geographic horizons, many informants from the South Side never having been to the Loop (Chicago's downtown shopping district), a large number never having left the immediate confines of their neighborhood, and a significant percentage leaving the neighborhood for the first time only as adults (Massey & Denton, 1993, p. 161). The social, economic, and psychological results of such residential isolation are devastating. As Darden (1998) puts it, "Segregated housing leads to segregation in other areas of life—schooling, religion, recreation, and employment, for example. Housing segregation is related to inequality and subordination; it limits the options for social mobility by consigning the segregated group to inferior life chances" (p. 523).

Once blacks were "ghetto-ized," and public housing "pauper-ized," it was perhaps inevitable that the two would combine, so that urban public housing in the United States has become largely a program for poor blacks. In Chicago, the connection between public housing and race is firmly entrenched; white neighborhood groups and realtors there worked hard, especially around the time of the 1949 Housing Act, to keep public housing sites confined to the black ghettos (see Hirsch, 1983; Meyerson & Banfield, 1955). According to Hirsch (1983), white hostility, with government sanction and support, is the direct cause of the segregation, isolation, and persistent powerlessness of Chicago blacks.

If all of this is true, it suggests that our first descriptor of inner city residents, economic class, is an artifact of another, race; and that the city we should be building in Chicago is not one that mixes economic classes but one that integrates races. The only place, however, where race is openly acknowledged as a factor in the problems of and proposed solutions for public housing is in the federal courts. The earliest and still one of the only examples of court-mandated residential integration in this country is the

Gautreaux decision involving public housing in Chicago (see Peroff et al., 1979, *passim*; Polikoff, 1978, pp. 147–159). In February 1969, ruling on a class-action lawsuit brought by CHA residents with the help of the American Civil Liberties Union, U.S. District Court Judge Richard Austin ruled that the CHA had violated the constitutional rights of the plaintiffs in its racially discriminatory housing policies, both in site selection (99.9% of units were in areas with more than 50% blacks) and in tenant assignment (in the few projects located in white neighborhoods, 0% of residents were blacks; in CHA projects as a whole, 90% were black). In July of that year, Austin divided the city into Limited (black) and General (white) Public Housing Areas (LPHA and GPHA), ruling that the first 700 units of new public housing in Chicago had to be built in the GPHA, that future projects were to be limited to 120 persons and could comprise no more than 15% of the total residential units in a single census tract, and that no families with children could be housed above the third floor of a government-subsidized building. For the next 20 years, the CHA virtually ceased to act: there was no new construction, and maintenance and security declined precipitously. Having been told in court that its policies were based on and perpetuated racial segregation in the city, but with little political support for integrating neighborhoods in the metropolitan area, Chicago's public housing bureaucracy ground to a halt, not to revive again until the late 1980s when Austin assigned a receiver (the Habitat Corporation) to build "scattered-site" public housing in the GPHA, and the U.S. Department of Housing and Urban Development threatened to take over the agency unless it got back to work.

Thirty years after *Gautreaux*, the courts are still the only place where race is made explicit in the debate about public housing in Chicago, although even there the focus often quickly turns to income groups. In 1996, after Mayor Daley announced the Near North Redevelopment Initiative, Cabrini-Green residents sued both the city and the CHA, alleging that the plan would displace Cabrini-Green residents and reduce affordable housing in the area, resulting in a discriminatory impact upon African Americans, women, and children (see *Cabrini-Green Local Advisory Council v. Chicago Housing Authority and City of Chicago*, 1998, paragraph 2). In a similar case, ABLA tenants in 1999 filed a class action lawsuit against the CHA and HUD, alleging that redevelopment plans there would "greatly reduce very low-income housing in the area, violate the federal housing and relocation rights of tenants, and have a disproportionate impact on African Americans, women, and children" (National Center on Poverty Law, 1999, paragraph 1). The suit claimed that more than 1,500 families, virtually all of them African American, female-headed households with children, would be displaced under the plan.

Although residents themselves are no doubt acutely aware of the racial fields on which public housing projects sit, there is, as Lemann (1992) notes, little overt organizing on racial grounds these days. In general, the debate about public housing in Chicago usually dissolves race into class. This goes back some time; in 1950, for example, George Stech, then president of the United Home Owners of the 23rd Ward, later president of the Southwest Neighborhood Council, said in an interview:

You know, a lot of people say it's the colored we don't want, but the kind of whites who live in public housing are just as bad. It's not the colored alone. It's the whole class of people who live like that. I talked to a colored woman who spoke against the site at Lake Park and 43rd. She called me to ask if we could give her any help. I asked her what her reasons were for being against public housing, and she said, "We're high-class niggers, Mr. Stech, and we don't want any low-class niggers living next to us." (quoted in Meyerson & Banfield, 1955, pp. 110–111)

The tendency persists, though in a less blatant form. The city's request for proposals for an economically-integrated neighborhood at the North Halstead site never mentions race at all (City of Chicago Department of Housing, 1998); the winning proposal ignores it as well (Holsten, 1998a). McRoberts (1998b) argues that the tension in the new developments is first and foremost about class, not race. When a group of Northwest residents recently protested the building of public housing in their midst, for example, they insisted that their motivation wasn't racial: "The only color they were concerned about," wrote journalists covering the story, "was 'green,'" though others admitted that this was simply "code for not wanting black public housing residents as neighbors" (Martin & McRoberts, 1998, paragraph 37). The focus on economic rather than racial issues may be occurring, according to Kamin (1995), simply because "class is tepid stuff compared to race" (p. 8). Finally, some individuals deny race and class as motivating factors in housing patterns. According to an article in the *Chicago Sun-Times*, "people just want to live in a community that shares the values of neighborliness and consideration for others" (Rumbler, 1998, paragraph 7).

So, the historical fact of the matter is that the residents of Chicago's public housing projects are overwhelmingly black, a major reason for their poverty is racism, and any solution to the problems of the inner city must deal with that fact. Yet the programs themselves discursively sidestep race in their obsession with income, seeing the solution to the problem of public housing in exclusively economic terms. We need to learn to put race back into our sentences about the city.

Finally, if the residents of Chicago's public housing projects are, by law, poor and, in fact, black, they are also predominantly female and young. According to Breitbart and Pader (1995, paragraph 13), 84% of HUD families nationwide are headed by women; in some places, the figure is as high as 95%. Because of this, the discourse on public housing in this country is always implicitly about black women, their struggle for a better life for themselves and their children, and the erasure of that struggle in most accounts of inner city redevelopment. Note, for example, the way Rosenbaum (1994) responds to worries that dispersal programs leave the inner cities without leaders:

Some have criticized the Gautreaux program for removing the most qualified people from the central city. This would be a serious problem if true. The central cities certainly need good black leaders. Yet the people who are selected for the Gautreaux program are not able to exert strong leadership in their communities. They are mostly single mothers on AFDC struggling to survive and keep their children safe. When we see their ability to go out and get jobs in the suburbs, this is a new behavior for many of them, and one they were not able to do in the housing projects. (p. 24)

In fact, women—most of them "single mothers on AFDC"—have played a vital role in the Local Advisory Councils and Resident Management Corporations of Chicago's public housing projects, many of them becoming quite prominent locally, for example, Mamie Bone, Cora Moore, Carol Steele, Deverra Beverly, and Ferrell Freeman. (Kamin [1997b] refers to them as the "queen bees" [p. 65]).

Similarly, little has been done to address the fact that the largest single group of residents in Chicago's public housing projects are children. Bowly (1978) claims that of Robert Taylor's original 27,000 residents, 20,000 were children (p. 128). The CHA (2000), meanwhile, says that 70% of current Taylor residents are under the age of 21; for Cabrini-Green, the figure given is 62%. At ABLA, 58% are under age of 18; and at Horner, 55% are under 18. Kamin (1995) claims that nearly half of public housing residents nationwide are under the age of 15 (p. 11). For the sake of comparison, the 1990 census for the United States as a whole gives the proportion of the population under age 15 as 22.9%, with 31.8% under 21 (U.S. Census Bureau, 2000a); thus, Chicago public housing projects appear to have on average twice the proportion of children as the general population. What would happen if we began in earnest to call these projects what they very nearly are, "cities of children"?

The Rule of Scene

If federal and local governments and the developers they work with have been obsessed with income, and if the courts have made race prominent, others (most notably the mass media) have represented Chicago's public housing residents almost exclusively through behavior. This is not irrelevant in federal policy—see for example, "Admission to, and occupancy of, public housing," 24 C.F.R. § 960.204 (1999), which precludes admission to housing projects of applicants "whose habits and practices reasonably may be expected to have a detrimental effect on the residents or the project environment" ((a)(2)(ii)). Nor has it been absent in the courts; the Horner consent decree, for example, gives extraordinary power to a "Tenant Selection Committee" to admit or refuse residents based on "the behavior of the applicant and household members at prior residences," including housekeeping practices, treatment of neighbors, general conduct in and around the residence, school attendance patterns, employment record, etc. (*Henry Horner Mothers Guild v. Chicago Housing Authority*, 1995, "Exhibit C"). As we saw above, however, the dominant language in legal and business discourses surrounding the projects has been economic. In mass media discussions of public housing, by contrast, income and race are present, but they are overshadowed by teenage pregnancy, single parenthood, welfare dependency, unemployment, school failure, drug and alcohol abuse, gang membership, and crime. As Lemann (1992) puts it, referring to the fact that the Robert Taylor Homes are in the poorest census tract in the country: "In the context of the rest of the world, the social disorder in the project is even worse than the poverty: plenty of places outside the United States have lower per capita incomes, but very few can match it in such measures as infant mortality, birth weight, life expectancy, crime, and family structure" (p. 296). In the minds of outsiders, public housing is first and foremost a refuge for the "socially disorganized" (Mayer, 1997, paragraph 2).

The topos at work here is a relatively simple one. If our first two

categories operated through an argumentative connection (or "liaison," as
Perelman [1982, p. 49] called it) between public housing and the poverty
or race of its inhabitants, this one works by linking the condition of the
projects to the character of the people who live there: container known
by thing contained or vice versa. All such arguments function, as Burke
(1945/1969) claimed in his discussion of the "scene-agent ratio" (p. 7), by
positing or implying a metonymic relation between person and place
("metonymy" is a rhetorical figure in which the subject is replaced with
an attribute or related image, cause for effect, container for contained
[Davis, 1998]).There are two variants of this topos. In the first, environment is an explanation, even an excuse, for behavior. The *locus classicus*
of this argument is Jacob Riis's *How the Other Half Lives*, his influential
1890 photographic essay about life in the tenement slums of New York
City. Riis begins his book by quoting the testimony of a New York prison
official before an 1865 state legislative committee investigating the crime
wave that occurred in the city during the great riot of 1863. According to
the official, crime is caused by environment:

By far the largest part—eighty per cent at least—of crimes against property and
against the person are perpetrated by individuals who have either lost connection
with home life, or never had any, or whose *homes had ceased to be sufficiently separate, decent, and desirable to afford what are regarded as ordinary wholesome
influences of home and family. . . .* The younger criminals seem to come almost
exclusively from the worst tenement house districts, that is, when traced back to
the very places where they had their homes in the city here. (emphasis in original,
p. 60)

Riis himself sees more than crime emanating from such places:

[I]n the tenements all the influences make for evil; because they are the hot-beds
of the epidemics that carry death to rich and poor alike; the nurseries of pau-
perism and crime that fill our jails and police courts; that throw off a scum of
forty thousand human wrecks to the island asylums and workhouses year by year;
that turned out in the last eight years around half million beggars to prey upon
our charities; that maintain a standing army of ten thousand tramps with all that
that implies; because, above all, they touch the family life with deadly moral con-
tagion. (p. 60)

At the time Riis was writing this, others were arguing that the problems of
poverty were caused by the poor themselves, one report claiming that

40% of their distress was due to drunkenness. Riis refutes this argument, tracing the causes of alcoholism back to the conditions of "human life and habitation" and recommending as a solution that every man be provided "a clean and comfortable home" (p. 61).

As we will see below, environmental theories of poverty are often implicit in proposals to demolish public housing projects and either build "healthier" neighborhoods in their place or disperse the residents into the suburbs. Though Lemann (1992) below will blame the state of the projects on the gangs, he closes his book, *The Promised Land*, with a withering condemnation of the places themselves:

The one government program that can fairly be accused of having gone wrong in a way that deeply harmed the Haynes family is public housing. . . . Living in public housing doesn't absolutely doom people. . . . But the atmosphere of these federally funded projects—the rampant crime, the drugs, the sense of absolute apartness from the rest of American society, the emphasis on an exaggerated and misguided version of masculinity that glorifies gang membership and sexual conquest—clearly helped to cause the troubles of most of Ruby's children. (p. 346)

Included in this category would also be the "culture of poverty" argument that has dominated discussions of the American ghetto for nearly 40 years now. Traub (2000) has recently reiterated this theory, summarizing Kenneth Clark's influential 1965 book on the "pathology" of the ghetto, which had described the emotional and psychological damage inflicted on inner-city residents not by poverty per se but by the values and behaviors of a culture beset by violence, alcohol and drug abuse, and family breakdown. Traub marshalls recent evidence to suggest that earlier studies had actually underestimated the negative effect of the ghetto on child development:

Clark did not reckon with the cognitive harm done to children who grow up in a world without books or even stimulating games, whose natural curiosity is regularly squashed, who are isolated from the world beyond their neighborhood. A study carried out in the early '80s at the University of Kansas reached the almost unfathomable conclusion that 3-year-olds in families with professional parents used more extensive vocabularies in daily interactions than did mothers on welfare—not to mention the children of those mothers. Here is a gap far greater than even the gulf in income that separates the middle class from the poor; it is scarcely surprising that [James] Coleman [sociologist who conducted a large survey in the mid-1960s on differences among public schools] found that the effects of home and community blotted out almost all those of school. (paragraph 28)

In a study of the 17-point difference between black and white scores on the Peabody Picture Vocabulary Test, Traub continues, researchers have found recently that equalizing such factors as parental income and years of schooling only accounts for about three of those points. Between half and two-thirds of the gap, however, can be erased by addressing such social factors as "middle-class parenting practices": reading to one's children, taking them on trips, using reason rather than flat edict, etc. (paragraph 31).

Clearly, research such as this allows for the influence of poverty and racial discrimination on development, but the focus is on the "conscious values and unconscious behaviors" (Traub, paragraph 27) that not only result from the economic and racial isolation of inner-city residents but also perpetuate it. Traub writes that we need to be more truthful with ourselves about the powerlessness of schooling to "erase" the influence of home environment on children; the only real solution to the problem of inner-city poverty, he says, is to change the "ecology" of the children who currently grow up there: "[Y]ou cannot disentangle the objective conditions of a place like East New York from the habits and values of the people who live there. The most effective solution—and the most unlikely one of all—is to move families out of the ghetto environment altogether" (paragraph 45).

In a somewhat different and less benign view of the relationship of environment and character, the former is not the cause of the latter but rather its effect. A degraded environment, in other words, is less an explanation than a sign of the degraded people who live there. As one resident put it: "The problem is not the housing, it's the people in the housing" (quoted in Brackett, 1997). Especially troublesome, of course, are the gangbangers:

For thousands and thousands of . . . black kids in Chicago, gang life was an interlude taking up all of the adolescence of the projects, which lasted from age eleven or twelve to sixteen or seventeen—years devoted to fighting, petty thievery, selling drugs, skipping school, and otherwise making life miserable for their neighbors and completely unpromising for themselves. The gangs were the main visible force responsible for the Robert Taylor Homes' changing from the oasis of decent housing for the black poor that they were intended to be, and that their initial occupants like Ruby and Luther Haynes expected them to be, into a hellhole whose residents were terrorized by constant violence. (Lemann, 1992, pp. 227–228)

From this perspective, Chicago's projects are "hellish"—both the *Chicago Tribune* editorial against the Cabrini-Green consent degree ("On Cabrini," 1998) and Kamin's (1997b) piece on Cabrini-Green for *Architectural Record* (p. 62) use the alliterative phrase "hellish high-rises" to describe public housing—because the people who live there are hellish:

It is as if the gates of Hell . . . opened and these people were let out. I had to ask again, where did these people come from? And, lo, I was told they came from the projects, the CHA. And as they tear down more projects, we can expect more of these people to be relocated in our neighborhoods. (an unnamed resident, quoted in McRoberts & Pallasch, 1998, paragraph 4)

Given this attitude, we should not be surprised when people advocate literally blowing up these buildings to eliminate the problems inside.

Still, it's never quite clear how the connection between environment and behavior works. As Kotlowitz (1991) says of his main character:

But though the isolation and the physical ruin of the area's stores and homes had discouraged LaJoe, it was her family that had most let her down. Not that she could separate the two. Sometimes she blamed her children's problems on the neighborhood; at other times, she attributed the neighborhood's decline to the change in people, to the influx of drugs and violence. (p. 13)

And even if with Riis we blame residents' problems on their environment, many of those problems seem to persist even after residents move to new environments. One former Henry Horner resident, now living in a scattered-site townhouse near the project and dealing again with drug-dealing and violence, said: "I didn't expect to be just moving across the street with the same stuff going on. But you still have the same people with the same mentality. . . . The buildings have changed, but the people haven't" (quoted in Garza, 1999a). An especially disturbing image of public housing residents depicts them as carrying bugs with them wherever they go. An article in *Newsweek*, for example, described CHA officials spraying public housing residents' belongings for roaches before letting them move into a middle-class neighborhood (McCormick, 1992).In a meeting with prospective residents of the Near North's Orchard Park, a CHA official told families preparing to leave the projects, "The expectation is that you're going to be loud, you're going to be raw, you're going to be bringing roaches" (quoted in McRoberts, 1998b).

Since the early 1980s there has been a steady increase in the behavioral demands placed on the recipients of public assistance. The CHA's 1999 *Transformation Plan*, for example, calls specifically for "strong and consistent lease enforcement efforts by professional property managers" to insure that projects are attractive to families with a broad range of incomes (p. 17). It's the absence of such standards that is often seen as the cause of the projects' decline (see, e.g., Lemann, 1992, pp. 107, 228). Unsurprisingly, the image of "screening" pervades many of the discourses on the new housing developments; according to articles in the *Chicago Tribune*, tenants approved for mixed-income developments must make it through criminal background checks, housekeeping inspections, and questions about their children's behavior (McRoberts, 1998b; McRoberts & Pallasch, 1998). Holsten's success with mixed-income developments has been attributed to its strict management of public housing tenants: only a third get through the firm's screening procedure (Pallasch, 1998).

Rhetorical Empowerment

What of the residents' representations of themselves? When we turn to these, we find, unsurprisingly, a refusal to be reduced to a single characteristic (such as income), a refusal to be dissolved into their background (a "dissociation" of the argumentative liaison of character and environment [Pereleman & Olbrechts-Tyteca, 1969, pp. 411ff]), and a refusal to be represented by people who do not know them. When given an opportunity to be something other than the object of a dehumanizing gaze, public housing residents become the subjects of their own sentences, the verbs of which are not criminal actions, but rather remembering, choosing, acting, arguing, and dreaming. Such positive interpretations are not unheard of in discussions of public housing—see for example Porter's (1995) claim that inner-city residents live in desirable, centralized locations and are potentially valuable customers, employees, and entrepreneurs, etc.—but they are rare.

There are at least three strategies of self-representation employed by Chicago public housing residents in the written documents reviewed here. First, like the posters from the 1968 Memphis garbage strike telling others, "I am a man," public housing residents sometimes simply remind outsiders that they are human beings. Barbara Moore, president of a tenant board at Robert Taylor, says, in an interview published by the Jewish Center for Urban Affairs (1999):

Public housing residents are considered the lowest scum on earth. At the mere mention of Robert Taylor people get scared and hold their purses. It is wrong to stereotype, not everyone is on drugs, not every girl is pregnant or prostituting. Not all guys are carrying guns or stealing. We have college graduates come from this area also. People should not prejudge us, there is good and bad everywhere. . . . We want to be thought of as human beings. We are not the worst of people. We are people. (p. 2)

Similarly, Cabrini-Green residents refuse outsiders' characterizations of them "as gangbangers, welfare-dependent, . . . drug abusers, hopeless people, uneducated, and not caring about their homes" and assert that their neighborhood "is a lot more like the average Chicago neighborhood than you might think" (Cabrini-Green Local Advisory Council, 1999). And Charles Coats, former resident of Robert Taylor, resents the suggestion that public housing families need training in order to live in middle-class neighborhoods: We don't "need help being people" (McRoberts & Pallasch, 1998).

The second strategy of self-representation is a narrative one: We are people with histories. The metaphor of *rootedness* occurs frequently in these documents. Barbara Moore says, "We poor people get uprooted a lot, but we are people with roots too. We want our grandchildren to grow up in our neighborhood. We don't want to be moved to a new place every year" (Jewish Council on Urban Affairs, 1999, p. 2). Similarly, resident leader Ferrell Freeman criticizes the ABLA redevelopment plan because "People with roots in the community will be moved to racially segregated and economically depressed areas of the city" (National Center on Poverty Law, 1999). In an interview with the *NewsHour with Jim Lehrer*, Cabrini-Green LAC president Cora Moore defends her wish to stay put in the place she has called home for 30 years: "We still want to live here because our kids [have] grown up [here], three sets of families, you know, and you feel more comfortable" (quoted in Brackett, 1997). Likewise, Cheryl Russon, another Cabrini-Green resident, asked of the city's plans to demolish the project, "How can they take our roots from us without our input? They're planning to move the poor and destitute and build for rich folks" (Oldweiler, 1998). Attached to places that outsiders see as uninhabitable, the residents claim a history in the projects that they are not willing to erase: "We're proud of where we are from," says Verlee Gant, who has lived at Robert Taylor since 1970; and former resident Patricia Cathery refers to Taylor as "my roots" (Rogal, 1999a).

One of the traits shared by characters in both Lemann (1992) and Kot-lowitz (1991) is their surprisingly fond memories of growing up in Chicago projects. When Ruby Haynes saw the Robert Taylor Homes for the first time in the early 1960s, writes Lemann, she thought they were magnifi-cent: tall, sturdy buildings with elevators and balconies, fresh paint and central heating. When her family moved in, there was excitement and a feeling of festivity. As Ruby's son Larry, 12 years old at the time, later put it: "I thought that was the beautifullest place in the world" (quoted in Lemann, p. 107). So too LaJoe Rivers's memories of the Henry Horner Homes—when opened in the late 1950s it was a dazzling place to her: "The building's brand-new bricks were a deep and luscious red, and they were smooth and solid to the touch. The clean windows reflected the day's movements with a shimmering clarity that gave the building an almost magical quality" (Kotlowitz, pp. 19–20). In an interview with the *Chicago Reporter*, Patricia Reed also remembers moving into the projects long ago: "I'll never forget the day my father called all of us together and asked if we wanted to live in the projects, and we were so excited, we just started saying, 'yes, yes'" (Rogal, 1999a).

Third, public housing residents represent themselves as rhetorical agents, that is, as speakers, writers, arguers, and critics. In the Jewish Council on Urban Affairs' *Community Views* (1999), they write of the need "to speak for ourselves" about issues affecting them: "These voices are often not heard in community planning and decision making." In a let-ter inviting community leaders to a public meeting, Cabrini-Green resi-dents write that the redevelopment of the project is "our" endeavor, based on our vision, our history, our plans, our achievements and struggles (Cabrini-Green Local Advisory Council, 1999). "Only the residents," they claim, "can fully inform developers and planners about the achievements and struggles experienced in creating community at Cabrini and convey how they intend to continue strengthening the neighborhood." Though people had said they were not competent to speak for themselves, "[f]rom our panelists and speakers today we can see that there is hope, that *we are capable of speaking on our own behalf*" (emphasis added).

Rhetorical agency for public housing residents is also expressed in le-gal documents, where they are seen not as poor, black, or socially disor-dered, but as plaintiffs, that is, individuals who sue someone in a court of law. Claiming here is best seen not as a matter of articulating logical propositions, but in the words of Crosswhite (1996), as a medium of self-creation (pp. 54, 65). To claim, says Crosswhite, is to invite others to share a particular way of seeing something (p. 62). It is also to anticipate a response to that invitation. So seen, residents' self-representation as claimants is a crucial assumption of rhetorical power on their part. In the 1998 Cabrini-Green lawsuit, for example, note the kinds of verbs used with resident subjects (argumentative verbs noted):

The LAC [Cabrini-Green Local Advisory Council] *brought* this case *alleging* that the NNRI [the city's Near North Redevelopment Initiative] . . . displaced Cabrini-Green residents and reduced the supply of affordable housing units at Cabrini, thereby resulting in a discriminatory impact upon African Americans, women, and children. . . . [T]he LAC *asserted* that the CHA defendants had violated the Fair Housing Act . . . and Title VI of the Civil Rights Act. . . . Finally, the LAC *asserted* that the CHA defendants had excluded the residents of Cabrini-Green from the planning process that gave rise to the NNRI and consequently violated Sections 18 and 24 of the United States Housing Act. . . . The LAC further *claimed* that the City defendants' NNRI violated the Fair Housing Act. . . . Plaintiff's complaint and amended complaint *sought* declaratory and injunctive relief prohibiting the defendants from implementing the NNRI and CHA's HOPE VI plans. (paragraphs 2–4)

Clearly, the language here is coming from lawyers who are not themselves tenants; but the rhetorical effect, I would argue, is to imbue public housing residents with a discursive power that they lack in other discourses about them.

In the courts, in other words, public housing residents have control over their world, something that is typically denied them in other contexts, as we saw above. This control is often literal: According to the terms of the Cabrini-Green consent decree, signed by the interested parties in 1998, but then blocked by the Habitat Corporation (the appointed receiver in the *Gautreaux* case), the Cabrini-Green LAC would be co-general partner in the redevelopment of the neighborhood with a 51% interest, participating fully in profits, personnel decisions, planning, etc (Section I(C)). In that document, public housing families also have relocation options (they have the right to choose whether they will stay in a rehabilitated building, move to a new unit in the neighborhood, move to a "scattered-site" unit somewhere else in Chicago, or take a Section Eight rent voucher for use anywhere on the private market), job training and employment opportunities, and full participation in all decision-making concerning the project.

Likewise, ABLA tenants filed a class action discrimination lawsuit in

1999 alleging racial discrimination, accusing the CHA of failing to negoti-
ate with them about demolition and development, and demanding that all
displaced tenants be provided with replacement housing of their choice
and receive assistance in finding affordable replacement housing (National Center on Poverty Law, 1999). According to Ferrell Freeman, 40-
year resident of ABLA and president of the Concerned Residents of
ABLA, "We can't allow our homes to be torn down without having a say in
the decision and without the opportunity to live in any new units that are
built" (paragraph 7).

Finally, the Henry Horner plaintiffs, in their 1991 lawsuit against the
city, the CHA, and HUD alleged de facto demolition of their project without being provided replacement housing. Four years later the plaintiffs
won a comprehensive revitalization of the entire Horner development
(*Henry Horner Mothers Guild v. Chicago Housing Authority*, 1995). Residents of the Horner Annex (which sits next to the new United Center on
the Near West Side), for example, were given the right to determine
whether they wanted the annex to be demolished or rehabilitated. Other
residents in the Horner complex were given their choice of a scattered-
site unit, a Section Eight certificate, an apartment in a rehabilitated high-
or mid-rise, or a new replacement unit on site. Further, the consent decree
requires that the CHA consult and attempt to agree with the plaintiffs on
all aspects of the revitalization program, including location and design of
new units, the hiring of developers and managers, and the determination
of management and security policies: "No site for new construction or acquisition shall be selected, no design approved, and no development or
management entity selected, and no management plan . . . or security
plan adopted unless the CHA defendants first agree with the HRC
[Horner Residents Committee]" (pp. 31–32). Unlike the blocked Cabrini-
Green agreement, the Horner decree is legally enforceable and currently
under implementation.

As rhetorical agents, Chicago's public housing residents are, by at least
one criterion, the most sophisticated users of language in the debate, consistently decoding language and bringing out its biases and interests when
others seem to take it at face value. There are numerous examples of this
in the collected documents: Cabrini-Green tenant leader Carole Steele
claimed in one interview that "mixed-income" was just another word for
gentrification; and "redevelopment," a code word for kicking people out
(Kamin, 1997b, p. 65). Similarly, Rene Maxwell, a resident of ABLA, con-

tended, "The president of the United States lives in public housing. No one calls it public housing, but that is what it is" (Jewish Council on Urban Affairs, 1999). Residents are also frequently concerned to debunk "myths" about public housing (e.g., Cabrini-Green Local Advisory Council, 1999). But nowhere do they represent their rhetorical sophistication more ably than in their general wariness about others' speech acts: The late Wardell Yotaghan, cofounder of the Coalition to Protect Public Housing and president of 2450 W. Monroe Resident Management Corporation (Rockwell Gardens), put it this way in an interview: "Public housing residents don't trust anyone. They have been lied to and exploited. We saw what they did at Lakefront properties. They closed them to rehab them and never opened them again" (Jewish Council on Urban Affairs, 1999, p. 1). In the same publication, Barbara Moore, president of a tenant board at Robert Taylor, is quoted as saying, "The government never keeps their word" (p. 1). And Cabrini-Green resident leader Carol Steele says, "I don't trust the government" (p. 1). Others agree: "The government is fooling people." "The government is trying to wiggle their way out of public housing" (p. 2). Two high school students who had entered the *Chicago Tribune's* 1993 design competition for the new Cabrini-Green expressed doubts about whether the city would actually deliver on its pledge to include public housing residents in the mixed-income developments being planned for the area (Kamin, 1997b). Venkatesh (1997) writes that public housing residents "question the sincerity of housing authority officials who equate high-rise demolition with social betterment." And, in an interview with the *Chicago Sun-Times*, one tenant remarks, "everyone just wants us to leave so they can make their money" (Dreazen, 1997).

Conclusion

Clearly, the debate about the future of public housing in Chicago has generated an enormous amount of discourse, thousands of documents discussing in great detail the problems of low-income housing projects, and various proposals for their redesign and revitalization. A prominent function of such discourses is to identify the people who live in the projects, an act that almost always pretends to be neutral, but actually functions to construct individuals in rhetorically charged ways. What we have seen is that there is enormous variation in such constructions: the residents of Cabrini-Green appear one way in some of the discourses and another way in others. Strategies of style and argument operate to emphasize some features and obscure others; they focus, reduce, omit, compare, divide, juxtapose, and link each in a different way and with different effect. And this variation is not random; rather, it can be tied to the conflicting interests at play in the inner city.

But we can go further. Representations do not just conflict with one another; some emerge victorious. Certain constructions of public housing residents, in other words, are picked up, repeated, and disseminated across time and space, developing into bona fide argumentative topoi with genuine persuasive power. Especially prominent in these discourses, I hope to have shown, are representations that work to disempower public housing residents, to leave them symbolically shorn of the ability to individually and collectively determine their own fate. As we have seen, this does not mean that public housing residents are so rhetorically oppressed that they lose all power to criticize others' representations and forge their own. On the contrary, the self-representations of such people show that there are powerful topoi at the disposal of inner-city residents, that they know how to use these topoi, and that they are enormously sensitive to issues of writing and representation. The problem, of course, is that their discourses are so marginal in the overall discussion.

Let me conclude by pointing out one final topos of representation, one that is almost completely absent from the discourses surrounding public housing in Chicago: this is language that identifies the resident as a citizen, where "citizen" is a person who shares in self-government, who possesses not just constitutionally-protected rights, but a broader, more substantial, more explicitly political agency. The word "citizen" does show up once or twice in these discourses, for example, in an interview with former Rockwell Gardens tenant leader Wardell Yotaghan: "Residents want to be accepted like any other citizen of Chicago. Residents of public housing have been isolated from the rest of the community and aren't seen as neighbors . . . we are a part of the City of Chicago" (Jewish Council on Urban Affairs, 1999, p. 2). The word also shows up in the CHA's 1999 *Plan for Transformation*: "Residents should be treated as true citizens of the City of Chicago" (p. 4). But "citizen" here seems to mean consumer of government services. In no document that I reviewed were public housing residents represented as citizens in a political sense, individuals empowered to participate fully in the collective self-determination of their city.

That is an enormous loss for us all. Because if the city is an important topic of writing, a site of argumentative contention, even at times a product of linguistic representation, it is also, of course, a school of public discourse, a place where young people learn what it means to be responsible users of civic language. We can hardly expect the children of Chicago's housing projects to develop into good citizens if they are rarely treated as such.

Notes

1. According to the U.S. Department of Housing and Urban Development (1999b), the median income for a family of four in Chicago in 1999 was $63,800

2. In 1998, the line was at $16,530 for a family of four with two children, or $13,133 for a family of three (U.S. Census Bureau, 2000b).

References

Admission to, and occupancy of, public housing, 24 C.F.R. § 960.204 (1999). Available at http://www4.law.cornell.edu/cfr/24p960.htm#start.

Bennett, L. (1998). Do we really wish to live in a communitarian city?: Communitarian thinking and the redevelopment of Chicago's Cabrini-Green public housing complex. *Journal of Urban Affairs, 20*, 99–116.

Bowly, D., Jr. (1978). *The poorhouse: Subsidized housing in Chicago, 1895–1976.* Carbondale, IL: Southern Illinois University Press.

Brackett, E. (1997, July 3). Rethinking public housing. *The News Hour with Jim Lehrer.* Washington, DC: Public Broadcasting Service.

Breitbart, M. M., & Pader, E. J. (1995). Establishing ground: Representing gender and race in a mixed housing development. *Gender, Place, & Culture: A Journal of Feminist Geography, 2*, 5–24.

Burke, K. (1969). *A grammar of motives.* Berkeley: University of California Press. (Original work published 1945)

Cabrini-Green Local Advisory Council. (1999, July 16). *Vision 2000: The future is now.* Agenda for August 5, 1999, public meeting.

Cabrini-Green Local Advisory Council v. Chicago Housing Authority and City of Chicago, No. 96 C 6949 (N.D. Ill. 1998).

CHA vote belies housing dilemma. (1995, December 25). *Chicago Sun-Times*, p. 31.

Changes to admission and occupancy requirements in the Public Housing and Section 8 Housing Assistance Programs (proposed rule), 64 Fed. Reg. 23460ff (1999, April 30) (to be codified at 24 C.F.R. § 5.603). Available at http://www.access.gpo.gov/su_docs/aces/aces140.html.

Chicago Housing Authority (2000). Web site containing information about Chicago's public housing projects: http://www.thecha.org/.

Chicago Housing Authority (1999, September 30). *Plan for transformation.* Draft for public comment.

City of Chicago Department of Housing. (1998, January 30). *Near North Development Initiative. Request for Proposals for Purchase and Redevelopment of the Halstead North Property.*

Congress for the New Urbanism. (1999, Winter). Rebuilding communities: Hope VI and new urbanism principles for inner city neighborhood design. Report of the Inner City Task Force. *Task force report, 2.* Available at http://www.cnu.org/.

Crosswhite, J. (1996). *The rhetoric of reason: Writing and the attractions of argument.* Madison: University of Wisconsin Press.

Dahl, R. A. (1979). Procedural democracy. In P. Laslett & J. Fishkin (Eds.), *Philosophy, politics, and society, fifth series* (pp. 97–133). New Haven, CT: Yale University Press.

Darden, J. T. (1998). Segregation. In W. van Vliet (Ed.), *The encyclopedia of housing* (pp. 323–325). Thousand Oaks, CA: Sage.

Daskal, J. (1998, June). *In search of shelter: The growing shortage of affordable rental housing.* Washington, DC: Center on Budget and Policy Priorities. Available at http://www.cbpp.org/615hous.htm.

Davis, S. (1996). Metonymy. In T. Enos (Ed.), *Encyclopedia of rhetoric and composition: Communication from ancient times to the present age* (pp. 444–446). New York: Garland.

Dewey, J. (1991). *The public and its problems.* Athens: Ohio University Press. (Original work published 1927)

Dolbeare, C. N. (1999, September). *Out of reach: The gap between housing costs and income of poor people in the United States.* Washington, DC: National Low Income Housing Coalition. Available at http://www.nlihc.org/oor99/index.htm.

Dreazen, Y. (1997, May 28). Study questions Cabrini plan. *Chicago Sun-Times.*

Finkelman, P. (Ed.) (1997). Dred Scott v. Sandford: *A brief history with documents.* Boston: Bedford.

Fisher, R. B. (1985). Origins of federally aided public housing. In J. P. Mitchell (Ed.), *Federal housing policy and programs: past and present* (231–244). New Brunswick, NJ: Center for Urban Policy Research at Rutgers University. (Original work published 1959)

Frug, G. E. (1999). *City making: Building communities without building walls.* Princeton, NJ: Princeton University Press.

Garza, M. M. (1999a, September 20). Old problems plague new low-rises. *Chicago Tribune.*

Garza, M. M. (1999b, October 5). CHA tenant leaders decry major makeover. *Chicago Tribune.*

Garza, M. M., & McRoberts, F. (1999, October 1). Leaner, cleaner CHA envisioned in overhaul. *Chicago Tribune.*

General HUD program requirements, 24 C.F.R. § 5.100 et seq. (1999). Available at http://www4.law.cornell.edu/cfr/24p5.htm#start.

Habermas, J. (1970). Towards a theory of communicative competence. *Inquiry, 13,* 360–375.

Hays, R. A. (1995). *The federal government and urban housing: Ideology and change in public policy* (2nd ed.). Albany: State University of New York Press.

Henry Horner Mothers Guild v. Chicago Housing Authority, No. 91 C 3316 (N.D. Ill. 1995).

Hirsch, A. R. (1983). *Making the second ghetto: Race and housing in Chicago, 1940–1960.* Cambridge: Cambridge University Press.

Holsten Real Estate Development Corporation. (1998a, March 30). *Proposal for Halstead North community.* Chicago.

Holsten Real Estate Development Corporation. (1998b, June 10). *Reply to city's questions.* Chicago, IL.

Jacobs, J. (1961). *The death and life of great American cities.* New York: Vintage.

Jewish Council on Urban Affairs. (1999, October). Public housing: Voices rising above the bulldozers. *Community Views: Voices from Chicago's Neighborhoods*. Chicago. Available at http://www.jcua.org.

Kamin, B. (1995, June 18–23). *Sheltered by design: How architects, officials, and residents can create public housing that works* (Special reprint). *Chicago Tribune*. Individual articles available at http://www.chicagotribune.com/.

Kamin, B. (1997a, February). Can public housing be reinvented? *Architectural Record, 185*, 84–89.

Kamin, B. (1997b, September). Who controls the future of Cabrini-Green? *Architectural Record, 185*, 62–69.

Kamin, B. (1999, November). At first glance, it seems that the master plan for Cabrini-Green is finally taking shape. *Architectural Record, 187*, 83.

Kotlowitz, A. (1991). *There are no children here: The story of two boys growing up in the other America*. New York: Anchor/Doubleday.

Lanham, R. A. (1996). *A hypertext handlist of rhetorical terms* [Computer software]. Berkeley, CA: University of California Press.

Lemann, N. (1992). *The promised land: The great black migration and how it changed America*. New York: Vintage.

Lubell, J., & Sard, B. (1998, August 3). *Proposed housing legislation would divert subsidies from the working poor and weaken welfare reform efforts*. Washington, DC: Center on Budget and Policy Priorities. Available at http://www.cbpp.org/8-3-98hous.htm.

Martin, A., & McRoberts, F. (1998, December 8). Scattered CHA sites? hardly. *Chicago Tribune*.

Massey, D. S. , & Denton, N. A. (1993). *American apartheid: Segregation and the making of the underclass*. Cambridge, MA: Harvard University Press.

Mayer, M. (1997, Summer). The enemies of the good. *The Brookings Review, 15*, 3. Available at http://www.brook.edu/default.htm.

McCormick, J. (1991, August 19). Chicago housecleaning: How the city is winning back crime-ridden projects. *Newsweek, 118*, 58–59.

McCormick, J. (1992, June 22). A housing program that actually works: Chicago's Lake Parc Place, one year later. *Newsweek, 119*, 61–63.

McCormick, J. (1993, March 15). Can houses become homes? A contest to rethink Chicago's troubled projects. *Newsweek, 121*, 71.

McRoberts, F. (1998a, July 30). When two worlds collide at Cabrini. *Chicago Tribune*, p. 1

McRoberts, F. (1998b, October 8). A new world—Down the block. *Chicago Tribune*, p. 1

McRoberts, F. (1998c, October 25). Home is where the problem is. *Chicago Tribune*, p. 1.

McRoberts, F., & Pallasch, A. (1998, December 28). Neighbors wary of new arrivals. *Chicago Tribune*.

Meehan, E. J. (1985). The evolution of public housing policy. In J. P. Mitchell (Ed.), *Federal Housing Policy and Programs: Past and Present* (287–318). New Brunswick, NJ: Center for Urban Policy Research at Rutgers University. (Original work published 1979).

Meyerson, M., & Banfield, E. C. (1955). *Politics, planning, and the public interest: The case of public housing in Chicago*. Glencoe, IL: The Free Press.

Mitchell, J. P. (1985). Historical overview of direct federal housing assistance. In J. P. Mitchell (Ed.), *Federal housing policy and programs: past and present* (187–206). New Brunswick, NJ: Center for Urban Policy Research at Rutgers U.

Mumford, L. (1961). *The city in history: Its origins, its transformations, and its prospects*. New York: Harcourt, Brace, & World.

Myers, L. (1998, December 30). From a world of despair to life of promise. *Chicago Tribune*.

National Center on Poverty Law. (1999, July 29). Chicago Housing Authority and U.S. Department of Housing and Urban Development sued for racial discrimination. Press release. Available August 2, 1999, at *http://www.povertylaw.org/abla.htm*. Complaint in *Concerned Residents of ABLA v. Chicago Housing Authority and United States Department of Housing and Urban Development,* No. 99 C 4959 (N.D. Ill. 1999), available at http://povertylaw.org/.

Nivola, P. (1999). *Laws of the landscape: How policies shape cities in Europe and America.* Washington, DC: Brookings Institution Press.

Oldweiler, C. (1998, March). Cabrini changes come all too slowly. *Chicago Reporter.*

Oldweiler, C., & Rogal, B. J. (2000, March). Public housing: Reading between the lines. *Chicago Reporter.*

On Cabrini, a deal best not made. (1998, August 3). *Chicago Tribune*, p. 12.

Pallasch, A. M. (1998, September 20). Developer building a dream at Cabrini. *Chicago Tribune*.

Perelman, C. (1982). *The realm of rhetoric* (W. Kluback, Trans.). Notre Dame, IN: University of Notre Dame Press.

Perelman, C., & Olbrechts-Tyteca, L. (1969). *The new rhetoric: A treatise on argumentation* (J. Wilkinson & P. Weaver, Trans.). Notre Dame: University of Notre Dame Press. (Original work published 1958)

Peroff, K. et al. (1979). *Gautreaux housing demonstration: An evaluation of its impact on participating households.* Washington, DC: U.S. Department of Housing and Urban Development, Office of Policy Development & Research.

Polikoff, A. (1978). *Housing the poor: The case for heroism.* Cambridge, MA: Ballinger.

Porter, M. E. (1995). The competitive advantage of the inner city. *Harvard Business Review*, 75, 55–71.

Riis, J. A. (1996). *How the other half lives.* D. Leviatin (Ed.). Boston: Bedford. (Original work published 1890).

Roeder, D. (1999, July 26). Developer puts new spin on affordable. *Chicago Sun-Times.*

Rogal, B. J. (1998, July–August). CHA residents moving to segregated areas. *Chicago Reporter.*

Rogal, B. J. (1999a, June). Survey casts doubt on CHA plans. *Chicago Reporter.*

Rogal, B. J. (1999b, November). Private firm keeps tight grip on public housing. *Chicago Reporter.*

Rosenbaum, J. E. (1994, November 9). *Housing mobility strategies for changing the geography of opportunity.* Working paper. Evanston, Ill: Institute for Policy Research, Northwestern University. Available at http://www.nwu.edu/IPR/index.html.

Rumbler, B. (1998, March 15). Integration project leads to a sense of community. *Chicago Sun-Times*.

Sard, B., & Daskal, J. (1998, November). *Housing and welfare reform: Some background information.* Washington, D.C.: Center on Budget and Policy Priorities. Available at http://www.cbpp.org/hous212.htm.

Sard, B., & Lubell, J. (1998, December). *How the statutory changes made by the Quality Housing and Work Responsibility Act of 1998 may affect welfare reform efforts.* Washington, DC: Center on Budget and Policy Priorities. Available at http://www.cbpp.org/12–17–98hous.htm.

Sarkissian, W. (1976). The idea of social mix in town planning: An historical review. *Urban Studies, 13*, 231–246.

Schill, M. H. (1993). Distressed public housing: Where do we go from here? *University of Chicago Law Review, 60*, 497ff.

Schill, M. H. (1997). Chicago's mixed-income new communities strategy: The future face of public housing? In W. Van Vliet (Ed.), *Affordable housing and urban redevelopment in the United States* (pp. 135–157). Thousand Oaks, CA: Sage.

Schorr, A. L. (1986). *Common decency: Domestic policies after Reagan.* New Haven, CT: Yale University Press.

Schwartz, A., & Tajbakhsh, K. (1997). Mixed income housing: Unanswered questions. *Cityscape: A Journal of Policy Development and Research, 3*, 71–92.

Smith, R. (1997). *Civic ideals: Conflicting visions of citizenship in U. S. history.* New Haven, CT: Yale University Press.

Traub, J. (2000, January 16). What no school can do. *New York Times Magazine*, pp. 52ff.

U.S. Census Bureau. (2000a). Age data. Available at http://www.census.gov/population/www/socdemo/age.html#national.

U.S. Census Bureau. (2000b). Poverty. Available at http://www.census.gov/hhes/www/poverty.html.

U.S. Department of Housing and Urban Development. (1996a, May). *Public housing that works: The transformation of America's public housing.* Washington, DC.

U.S. Department of Housing and Urban Development. (1996b, June). *New American neighborhoods: Building homeownership zones to revitalize our nation's communities.* Washington, DC.

U.S. Department of Housing and Urban Development. (1997, April). *Community building in public housing: Ties that bind people and their communities.* Washington, DC.

U.S. Department of Housing and Urban Development. (1998a, March). Characteristics of households in public and assisted housing. *Recent Research Results.* Available at http://www.huduser.org/periodicals/rrr/3_98pub.html.

U.S. Department of Housing and Urban Development. (1998b, April). *Rental housing assistance-The crisis continues: The 1997 report to Congress on worst case housing needs.* Washington, DC.

U.S. Department of Housing and Urban Development. (1998c, December). Summary of the Quality Housing and Work Responsibility Act of 1998. Available at http://www.hud.gov:80/pih/legis/titlev.pdf.

U.S. Department of Housing and Urban Development. (1999a, September). *The widening gap: New findings on housing affordability in America.* Washington, DC. Available at http://www.hud.gov/pressrel/afford/afford.html.

U.S. Department of Housing and Urban Development. (1999b). Revised FY 1999 income limits and section 8 fair market rents. Available at http://www.huduser.org/datasets/il/fmr99rev/index.html.

U.S. Department of Housing and Urban Development. (1999c). HOPE VI fact sheet. Available at http://www.hud.gov/pih/programs/ph/hope6/facts.pdf.

U.S. Department of Housing and Urban Development. (2000, March 23). Cuomo issues policy directive to increase racial and economic integration of public housing (press release). Available at http://www.hud.gov/pressrel/pr00–62.html.

U.S. Housing Act of 1937 (as amended), 42 U.S.C. § 1437 et seq. (1998). Available at http://www4.law.cornell.edu/uscode/42/ch8.html.

Venkatesh, S. A. (1997, September/October). An invisible community: Inside Chicago's public housing. *The American Prospect, 34*, 35–40.

Walker, S. (1997, September 9). US eyes public housing—and begins to remodel. *Christian Science Monitor.*

Will, G. (2000, March 5). Seven blunders short circuit Bradley campaign. *Wisconsin State Journal*, p. 2B.

Wilson, W. J. (1978). *The declining significance of race: Blacks and changing American institutions*. Chicago: University of Chicago Press.

Wilson, W. J. (1987). *The truly disadvantaged: The inner city, the underclass, and public policy*. Chicago: University of Chicago Press.

Wilson, W. J. (1996). *When work disappears: The world of the new urban poor*. New York: Knopf.

Wirth, L. (1938). Urbanism as a way of life. *American Journal of Sociology, 44,* 1–24.

4
Closing Remarks

9

The Future of Writing Ability

Robert Gundlach

I

In his autobiography, biologist Edward O. Wilson (1994) reports that during the 1960s he often made long trips by train. The confinement imposed by this mode of travel served him well as a writer:

> I found an advantage in the restriction. It gave me, in the case of the Miami run [from Boston], eighteen hours in a private roomette, trapped . . . like a Cistercian monk with little to do but read, think, and write. It was on such a journey that I composed a large part of *The Theory of Island Biogeography*. (p. 319)

No doubt many writers continue to find advantage in the restriction of solitude. For them, it is "essential to their craft," as Mencken (1956) once remarked, "to perform its tedious and vexatious operations a capella" (p. 169). But if a need for solitude and concentration remains steady, much else in writers' ways of working has changed dramatically in the few decades since Wilson wrote about the geographical distribution of plants and animals. The most significant difference, of course, is that many writers now write with computers.

It is not difficult to find conjecture about the significance of the rise of the computer as a tool for both reading and writing. Roger Chartier (1995), for example, argues that "the substitution of screen for codex is a far more radical transformation than that brought by Gutenberg's invention of the printing press; it changes methods of organization, structure, consultation, and even the appearance of the written word" (p. 15). Carla Hesse (1996), who like Chartier is a historian of reading, is careful to note that new forms of discourse emerge from social and cultural processes, not directly from technological innovation. Hence the story of "what kind of literary system we will (re)invent" with the new tools becoming available to us is one that "historians are not yet able to tell" (p. 32). Nonetheless, she observes that new modes of writing already in use—real-time email, interactive hypertext, on-line public forum discussions—"make it possible to imagine a world in which writing loses its particular relation to time, in which the space created by the structure of deferral gives way to pure textual simultaneity." If these "performative modes supersede structural ones," Hesse adds, "the history of the book will become nothing more than memory" (pp. 32–33).

Although attempts to project the future of writing from the experience of change in the present are often provocative, it is easy to fall prey to hazards encountered in such speculation. One hazard is the temptation to organize such a vision by imagining a single key transformation as the driving element of many kinds of change. But as Anthony Grafton (1999) observes in "The Humanist as Reader," an essay on the uses of reading in the Renaissance, historians are wise to "eschew grand theses and rapid transitions." They should expect to find instead a tangle of "paradox and contradiction" (p. 183). Grafton notes that "[e]ven in the heartlands of Renaissance classicism, then, medieval and Renaissance conventions, the desire to bring the ancient world up to date, and the desire to reconstruct it as it was, coexisted" (p. 187).

Historical coexistence of another kind is emphasized by Walter D. Mignolo (1994) in his "Afterword" for *Writing without Words: Alternative Literacies in Mesoamerica and the Andes*. "The coexistence of conflictive literacies" in the colonial and post-colonial phases of the history of the New World, Mignolo writes, "brings about the need, first, to theorize co-evolutionary histories of writing and, second, to move toward a pluritopical interpretation of the history of writing in colonial situations when alphabetic literacy coalesced with non-Western writing systems" (p. 293). Writing with nonalphabetic systems, he notes, can be understood as analogous not only to speaking and drawing but also to weaving (p. 296). The introduction of alphabetic writing can be experienced not only as extending the range of speech but also as "taming the voice" (p. 294). Given the complexities of sorting out writing's history, it is daunting indeed to try to imagine its future. Even in moments when the shape of what is to come may seem clear, other conceptual hazards loom; the preoccupations of the present can never be shaken off entirely in our attempts to look ahead.

Geoffrey Nunberg (1996) exaggerates only a little when he remarks, "Nothing betrays the spirit of an age so precisely as the way it represents the future" (p. 103).

II

How, then, shall we think about the future of writing? If it is a mistake to try to construct broad cultural visions of the future, it seems equally unwise simply to ignore changes now clearly in progress. Since the abiding question in my own work is how people learn to use written language to say what they want or need to say, my approach to questions about the future of writing begins by recasting them as questions about the future of writing ability. From this perspective, it becomes possible to frame either informal observation or formal inquiry that concentrates on the present, which then tracks, so to speak, trajectories of experience from the present into the future. By paying attention to an individual's development of writing ability, it becomes possible to learn not only about the individual, but also about the nature of the ability itself, at least as one person in a particular set of circumstances exhibits it. It also becomes possible to think about the interaction between teaching and learning, and about writing ability as it relates to general language ability.

The "future" to be observed as it unfolds in such cases is both specifically biographical and broadly cultural. Generalizations about the development of writing ability come, when they come at all, in the form of questions about learning to write in particular circumstances—circumstances that are local, variable, and in our time, unquestionably changing. An individual's development of writing ability, viewed in such a framework, is understood as a function of interacting histories: technological, certainly, but also cultural, social, educational, biographical, and especially linguistic. Particularly illuminating are the glimpses of the nature of writing ability provided by the evidence of learning-in-progress found in the written language of beginners.

To make these ideas more concrete, let me discuss an example of learning-in-progress. Some years ago I gave a talk on the development of writing ability to a group of alumni at the university where I teach. A week or so later, I received a note, with several enclosures, from a person who had been in the audience. "After attending your recent lecture," my correspondent wrote, "I collected these 'samples' from my Sunday School

class. I thought they were great examples of what you had discussed."
Among the samples was an ordinary paper napkin with a message written
in blue ink: "Be! cwyiT! Now!"

I received no further details. I don't know the precise age of the writer,
though I imagine that the writer was a child 6 or 7 years old. I don't know
why the sentence was written, nor how the document came into the hands
of the author's Sunday School teacher. Nonetheless, this modest piece of
writing strikes me as engaging, not least because of its mysteries, both
dramatic and linguistic. Was the text composed as a message to a specific
reader, or was it created as a record of someone else's utterance? Who said
what to whom? What sort of speech act was this? As for orthography, the
spelling of "cwyiT" for "quiet" suggests its own logic, but why the lower
case initial "c," especially alongside the initial "B" in "Be" and the initial
"N" in "Now"? Why the capital "T" in the final position of "cwyiT"?

And what about the three exclamation marks? M. B. Parkes (1993), in
*Pause and Effect: An Introduction to the History of Punctuation in the
West*, notes, "The fundamental principle for interpreting punctuation is
that the value and function of each symbol must be assessed in relation to
other symbols in the same immediate context, rather than in relation to a
supposed absolute value and function for that symbol when considered in
isolation" (p. 2). Parkes himself cites the possible ambiguity of exclamation marks, suggesting that in some instances they are meant to serve as
notation for an imagined "increase in decibels." In other contexts (for example, "Stop!!" he whispered), they imply expressive intensity of a different kind. In such instances, Parkes adds, "punctuation can encourage
readers to import to the process of interpretation elements of their own
wider behavioural experience" (p. 2). In everyday life, that is, the interpretation of punctuation often turns on inferences based on knowledge of
how the world works.

We can add that in the case of "Be! cwyiT! Now!" an experienced
reader's habits of interpreting punctuation may actually obscure a plausible interpretation. Such a reader, knowing from long experience that exclamation marks represent expressive intensity of some kind, may not easily recognize the possibility that at least the first two exclamation marks in
this inexperienced writer's message may be meant simply to provide
graphic markers reinforcing the boundaries between words.

In my talk to the aforementioned group, I offered informal analyses of
several examples of young children's writing, along with comments about

examples of writing by high school students, university undergraduates, graduate students, an engineer, a novelist, and two or three poets. One point I emphasized was that writers at every level make crucial use of their reading experience as a source of information about how writing works and what writers can do. Cultivating this way of reading—reading from the perspective of a writer, asking what can be learned from what one reads—is no less important for a high school junior, a second year law student, or an engineer than for a novelist or a poet. Young children are often especially adept at drawing on their reading experience in their early experiments with writing, though it requires some practice for adult readers to learn to detect evidence of linguistic and rhetorical learning-in-progress in children's improvisations.

With respect to the models for writing available to developing writers, there is no absolute boundary between written and spoken "texts." Most developing writers recognize that, for all the differences between the conventions of written and spoken language, the act of writing can be approached as a way of speaking, a way of saying something to someone. Some developing writers also intuitively appreciate the reciprocal insight that reading can be approached as a way of being spoken to, a way of listening. The trick in detecting evidence of learning-in-progress in young children's writing is to see that children take on and often transform the resources of both the spoken and written language they have encountered—that is, they draw very broadly upon their reading experience when they try to write themselves.

So it is with "Be! cwyiT! Now!" which suggests both an appropriation of a dramatic bit of everyday speech, and simultaneously a sorting out, still in progress, of various loosely coordinated principles of spelling, punctuation, and capitalization. There is much evidence of learning-in-progress to be found here, and several interesting glimpses of the nature of writing ability.

III

Reflecting on this example, we can easily imagine a future for writing ability that involves increasingly complex interactions between writers and writing tools. The chief tool, the computer, will almost certainly provide more of what might be called mechanized collaboration. Computer programs already help not only with transcribing words but also with making linguistic judgments. Suppose the young writer who puzzled out the spelling of "cwyiT" were to consult the spell-check program included with Microsoft Word 98 for Macintosh. The writer's own rendition, "cwyiT," would be marked as "not in the dictionary," and two possible alternatives would be suggested: *quit* and *quiet*. It is not difficult to imagine an enhanced spell-check program that would allow the writer to hear a spoken version of each choice. Indeed, some on-line dictionaries now provide pronunciations for every word the writer chooses to look up. Icons clarifying the options could easily be included as well—for "quiet," perhaps an index finger raised to lips. Written, spoken, and iconic representation might thus converge in service of helping the writer determine the appropriate convention.

The availability of collaboration from the machine does not, of course, preclude help from other people or from models of written language encountered elsewhere. Nor does this kind of mechanized help "violate the lone principle that present teachers of composition have salvaged from the twenty-five hundred years of the discipline of rhetoric," as Porter G. Perrin (1933, quoted in Connors, 1997) identifies this principle in his classic condemnation of workbook instruction, "The Remedial Racket": "[T]hat one learns to speak and write by speaking and writing" (1997, p. 149). The interactive support offered by such software is contingent on, and prompted by, the writer's particular linguistic choices. In this respect, the machine's collaboration operates in Vygotsky's zone of proximal development, pinpointing and offering specific cultural information designed to allow the writer to succeed with help where the writer might not succeed alone.

In time, interactive software might well provide reliable mechanized collaboration in making judgments not only about spelling but also about diction, sentence structure, and the use of discourse markers associated with specific genres. Already available are speech-to-text dictation programs that allow writers to compose by speaking, and translation programs that enable writers to convert their own written texts from one language to another. Also in the works is software that combines functions in increasingly powerful ways, such as Raymond Kurzweil's program designed to integrate speech recognition, language translation, and speech synthesis. Computer programs that help people write and manipulate text in these ways are in some ways analogous to calculators—knowledge required for the necessary operations is stored not in the mind of the user but in the programming of the machine. The potential reconfigurations of familiar human abilities and the implications for human learning are far-reaching indeed.

An exploration of the future of writing ability, then, should certainly consider the increasing role of mechanized collaboration of the sort noted above. However, an approach limited to this focus would also miss much. Most immediately apparent is that such an approach would fail to take into account a writer's development of the various kinds of social and rhetorical knowledge on which both writers and readers depend. Less apparent, perhaps, is the degree to which a focus on the capacities of new writing tools might also obscure key questions about the shifting character of learning to write in relation to the broader process of language development.

John J. Gumperz (1997) offers a perspective on emerging changes in the development of the social and rhetorical knowledge upon which linguistic communication relies in his essay, "On the Interactional Bases of Speech Community Membership." "If there is anything that sociolinguistic research of all kinds has in common," Gumperz notes, "it is the premise that studies of language in society must be grounded in the everyday discursive practices of human populations." The starting point of sociolinguistic inquiry, then, is the notion of the speech or discourse community, defined in the broadest sense as "interacting individuals" (p. 188). Yet the concept of a speech or discourse community has itself become problematic, as Gumperz acknowledges: "[B]ecause of the ever increasing pace of change during the last decade and the large scale population migrations, sociologists as well as anthropologists have all but given up attempts at finding empirical ways of defining the bounds of community" (p. 188).

Gumperz asserts that it nonetheless remains possible to define social groups or networks as the key unit of analysis in sociolinguistic inquiry by recognizing that the ability of group members to make common inferences in communicative interactions gives the group its shape. Such inferences "rely both on linguistic presuppositions and on knowledge of the world, much of which is culturally specific" (p. 188). The relevant knowledge is "rhetorically grounded and rhetorically controlled," Gumperz suggests, since the ability to make inferences from what is said—and what is omitted—"is a precondition for entering into the kind of social relationship that being a member of a group involves, and, by implication, profiting from the advantages that participation entails" (p. 200).

To clarify this link between the ability to infer and rhetorical knowledge, Gumperz quotes Edward Sapir: "Generally speaking, the smaller the circle and the more complex the understandings already arrived at within it, the more economical can the act of communication afford to become" (Sapir, 1953, quoted in Gumperz, 1997, p. 201). Sapir's observation in turn allows Gumperz to offer a sociolinguist's formulation of the rhetorician's concept of ethos: "It is because of the relationship of knowledge to actual participation in human groups that knowledge of rhetorical strategies can become a badge of membership" (p. 201). More broadly, Gumperz emphasizes that the rhetoric of everyday life turns primarily on the expectation that interlocutors share particular strategies of inference and interpretation—strategies appropriate to the groups with whom the interlocutors identify and the situations in which they interact. Seen from this point of view, Gumperz writes,

lexical and grammatical knowledge as well as potentially applicable general norms and values provide only a rough template to be fleshed out by additional interpretive mechanisms that operate in a cultural environment which shapes and constrains the ways in which utterances are interpreted. (p. 189)

Hence a speaker or writer simultaneously signals and situates meanings, using not only nouns and verbs, but also ellipsis and silence. An attuned listener or reader recognizes the cues that matter.

These ideas will be familiar to contemporary scholars of rhetoric and composition, who have also articulated an ambivalence about the notion of "community" as an organizing concept for understanding the situated character of written discourse (e.g., J. Harris, 1997). Martin Nystrand (1990) has argued persuasively that a perspective emphasizing social interaction, built on the insights of Rommetveit and Bakhtin, solves many of the theoretical problems created by the metaphor of bounded discourse communities. In some respects, Gumperz makes a similar argument, though he emphasizes less the process by which interlocutors construct meaning together, and gives more attention to the individual language user's reliance on "interpretive mechanisms" learned through such interactions: "My main point is that subconsciously internalized communicative conventions acquired through interaction are a key factor . . . [for] understand[ing] how community membership enters into communication" (Gumperz, 1997, p. 202).

It is important to note that the beginnings of such learning do not await the onset of learning to write. Even in the initial phases of developing writing ability, a person learning to write draws upon social and rhetorical abilities learned earlier. The insights that support what might be understood in traditional terms as a writer's 'sense of audience' may thus actually have their origins in communicative experience prior even to speech. The social and rhetorical abilities used in writing may thus be formed through the making and remaking of basic insights about the link between intended meaning and conventional gesture, as well as about perceived gesture and interpreted meaning. Catherine Snow (1999) observes, "[T]he most salient need that early conventional communicative means can fulfill for young children is the need to participate in social interaction—waving bye-bye, playing peek-a-boo, exchanging markers of attention while looking at pictures in books, and marking the transfer of objects or the occurrence of an unexpected event" (p. 265).

Snow emphasizes the significance of children's "precocious social capacities," which are expressed in even the youngest child's selective alertness to the human face and human voice, and the ability to establish, sustain, and redirect joint attention with a caregiver (p. 273). In his essay, "From Joint Attention to the Meeting of Minds," Jerome Bruner (1995) offers a synopsis of the long-term developmental path: "[J]oint visual attention in infancy and early childhood, more ideational attention once language becomes established, shared presuppositional attention as we become acculturated into specialized interpretive communities" (p. 12). A promising approach to studying the development of these social and rhetorical abilities in older children and adolescents is suggested by Nystrand, who has outlined a framework for research on the development of particular kinds of writing ability in the context of what he characterizes as the ecology of discourse (Nystrand & Graff, 2000).

To consider the future of writing ability, then, is to consider how people learning to write will interact not only with new tools available for writing, but also with changing contexts: changing spheres of knowledge, changing roles for readers and writers, changing relations of power and authority. Adopting Nystrand's phrase, the future of writing ability will be shaped mainly by shifts in the ecology of discourse in which developing writers find themselves. These shifts might be brought about by the use of new technology, by new social and cultural arrangements, or, most likely, by a combination of both technological change and social change.

Thus, we must remain alert to the interactions between new tools for

writing and changes in patterns of discourse in order to be able to recognize, and perhaps even to anticipate changes in what it means to write and
in how people develop writing ability. Olson and Homer (1998), however,
add a sobering caveat. In their generally admiring review of Katherine
Nelson's book, *Language in Cognitive Development: Emergence of the
Mediated Mind*, they assert that neither Nelson nor anyone else has yet
provided an adequate explanation of precisely "how culture shapes mind"
(p. 254). A fully illuminating account, they suggest, would have to accommodate two well-supported and apparently irreconcilable ideas: "One is
that the child has to make up his or her own knowledge—the premise of
constructivism. The second is that the knowledge constructed by the child
is just that proffered by the culture" (p. 254). In their view, the familiar notion of internalization—an explanation invoked by Gumperz ("subconsciously internalized communicative conventions acquired through interaction")—is simply a placeholder, a theoretical shortcut to be abandoned
in favor of a fuller account.

IV

One step in addressing this problem is to bring to the foreground the
question of how individual language users develop, as Gumperz phrases
it, a "rough template" of "lexical and grammatical knowledge as well as potentially applicable general norms and values" that complements, and perhaps interacts with the language user's inferential and interpretive strategies. In fact, there is spirited debate on this question , and issues that have
arisen through this debate suggest implications not only for deeper understanding of the basic dynamics of language learning, but also for new
perspectives on the development of writing ability.

"The fundamental scientific problem raised by language," Steven
Pinker (1999) observes, "is to explain its vast expressive power." Pinker
elaborates by posing a question: "What is the trick behind our ability to fill
each other's heads with so many kinds of thoughts?" (p. 11). Pinker's answer is that our ability to use language depends on the interaction of two
principles. When we speak or listen, and presumably when we read or
write, we rely on two basic mental tricks, not one: "[M]emory, for the arbitrary sign that underlies words, and symbolic computation, for the infi-
nite use of finite media underlying grammar" (p. 13). He explains:

We have a lexicon of words for both common and idiosyncratic entities like ducks and dogs and men, which depends on the psychological mechanism called memory. And we have a set of grammatical rules for novel combinations of entities, for dogs biting men and men biting dogs, which depends on mental mechanisms of symbol combination. (p. 11)

Many cognitive scientists regard this dual-level generative concept of language ability as the standard view. No doubt in part as a consequence of becoming the standard view, this concept has also become the target of increasingly powerful and often useful criticism. Connectionists who reject the idea that language use depends on a language user's mental representation of abstract, universal, and specifically linguistic rules or principles advance one line of criticism. Joseph Allen and Mark Seidenberg (1999) cast their challenge in a sharply drawn contrast:

Whereas the standard approach is committed to the uniqueness of linguistic representations vis-à-vis other cognitive domains, and to the existence of representations whose fundamental character is shaped by the repertoire of innate ideas, the alternative view sees cognitive representations as one component of a system that includes both the organism and its environment. (p. 119)

In the connectionist view, our ability to use language depends not on symbolic, guiding representations—general, abstract structures that Pinker characterizes as something like recipes or blueprints—but on cognitive networks of information derived from our encounters with language. The human mind sorts out our experience with language on the basis of statistical regularities and probabilities. As the title of Seidenberg's (1997) recent essay for *Science* states, acquiring and using language are matters of "learning and applying probabilistic constraints." Such learning and application involve processes not unique to language; they are processes that are broadly cognitive, coming into play in many domains of knowledge and activity. In Seidenberg's (2000) view, languages are thus best understood as "quasiregular: They are systematic and productive, but admit exceptions that deviate from central tendencies in different ways and degrees" (n.p.).

In an essay recently published in *Cognition*, Michael Tomasello (2000) also challenges the Chomskian generative position held by Pinker and others, though he develops his critique with a different line of reasoning, proposing "an alternative, usage-based theory of child language acquisition" (p. 209). Every theory of language acquisition, Tomasello notes, "must posit local learning—so that children can learn the particular structures of the particular languages into which they are born"; in his view, there is no need to stipulate a "universal grammar with which the child's local learning must link up" (p. 246). A more convincing theory of language acquisition can be fashioned from an appreciation of even the youngest child's "cognitively sophisticated learning and abstraction processes involved in intention reading, cultural learning, analogy making, and structure combining" (p. 247). These processes are intertwined with the child's "biological preparation for acquiring language, which consists not of a narrow set of abstract grammatical principles but rather a broader set of neural predispositions or capacities involving basic processes of cognition, social interaction, symbolization, and vocal-auditory processing" (p. 247). In the account of children's language development he proposes, Tomasello emphasizes that there is "continuity of process—the basic cognitive and learning mechanisms are the same at all developmental periods—but there is discontinuity of structure" (p. 246).

There is more to the current debates about the theoretical premises of language acquisition than is suggested in these brief comments (see, for example, Marcus, 2001). It is also fair to guess, not just about the standard model, but about all of the current proposed accounts, that each model is, at best, "only metaphorically related to the brain processes involved in producing and comprehending language" (Allen & Seidenberg, 1999, p. 119). Even so, from just these brief observations, we see many things that are relevant to our consideration of the development of writing ability. In one form or another, the current debates will produce a more refined and illuminating account of language learning than is suggested by the shorthand term, "internalization." It is reasonable to suppose that a durable model will encompass at least these two processes: (a) the learner gives selective attention to the phenomena of experience (including language); and (b) the learner then in some way extends, generalizes, or abstracts from observed experience, and is thus equipped to transpose the analogous, generalized, or abstracted principle to a new situation. Furthermore, it seems likely that such a process recurs, with the learner's attention in new situations directed and perhaps constrained by understandings the learner has constructed from previous experience. Though learning to speak and learning to write are certainly not parallel processes, the learner's basic cognitive strategies may extend to both, especially in instances where children encounter a great deal of written language as well as spoken language early in their lives (see Teale and Sulzby, 1986). Hence, 'goed' for *went*, 'did went' for *did go*, and 'cwyiT' for *quiet*—or, more generally, evidence of learning-in-progress.

V

One way to observe the unfolding future of writing ability, then, is to pay attention to the development of writing ability, beginning with its earliest phases. In this essay, learning to write is conceived as a dimension of the broader process of language development. Knowledge of writing is understood as linguistic knowledge; writing ability is understood as linguistic ability. In Peter T. Daniels' (1996) careful formulation, writing can be defined as "a system of more or less permanent marks used to represent an utterance in such a way that it can be recovered more or less exactly without the intervention of the utterer" (p. 3). As Florian Coulmas (1989) puts it, a writing system provides for "the materialization of language" (p. 272).

But writing is not a simple extension of speaking, of course. Indeed, the relations between spoken and written language and the interactions of the two modes of discourse vary not only according to culture, language, script and orthography, but also according to discourse community and even specific discourse situation. The complexity and variability in the relations between writing and speaking suggest a number of issues relevant to both formal inquiry and informal observation. For example, as we have already seen, a person learning to write learns to incorporate aspects of speaking into writing. Even at the basic level of learning to spell, however, a close look discloses both complexity and variability. As Bryant, Nunes, and Adinis (1999) suggest in "Different Morphemes, Same Spelling Problems: Cross-Linguistic Studies," if the cognitive processes involved in learning to spell certain kinds of morphemes are similar for beginners learning to write in different alphabetic written languages, "the actual instances of this link—the particular morphemes, the sounds and the spelling patterns—vary tremendously from script to script" (p. 113).

At the same time, the person learning to write may also incorporate aspects of writing into speaking, perhaps without noticing it. In a report of a study of changes in children's word segmentation and word writing from preschool through second grade in Hebrew and Spanish (languages selected for the study in part because their written forms use not only different spelling systems, but also different scripts), Liliana Tolchinsky and Ana Teberosky (1998) note that in the case of both languages, "[d]evelopmentally, [a child's] intuitive perceptual segmentation may influence writing decisions but later on orthographic knowledge shapes phonology-segmentation preferences" (p. 18). Tolchinsky and Teberosky add:

The interplay of these dimensions changes with development but it is enduring and begins very early, to the extent that in urban environments where exposure to writing is intense and constant, it may be hard to posit phonological performance untouched by knowledge of writing. (p. 18)

The picture of learning to write as a dimension of language development suggested by these observations is one of exchange between spoken and written language development. That learning to speak and learning to write might interact in a linguistically significant way is an idea that many linguists have resisted (see Aronoff, 1994). Even so, the idea merits further exploration, at least because it is made more plausible by the recent theoretical challenges to the generative theory of language acquisition. If key learning mechanisms used in initial language acquisition do not rely chiefly on innate linguistic principles, it would seem to follow that an individual's overall linguistic knowledge is shaped and reshaped through the mind's continuing interaction with linguistic experience, including, in some cultural contexts, experience with written language.

The picture becomes still more complex when we consider that for some children writing emerges not only from speech, but also from drawing, gesture, and various kind of play, including play with social roles, cultural themes, conceptual objects, and language itself (McLane & McNamee, 1990). In differing ways and with varying consequences the emergence of writing may operate, both developmentally and historically, as an instance of the recruitment to language of nonlinguistic forms and nonlinguistic tools. If, as Roy Harris (1986) has argued, the cultural origins of writing involved the appropriation of the conventions of spoken discourse to already formed sets of graphic relations in proto-writing systems (conventionalized systems for recording information that combined elements of drawing and tallying), it can also be argued that the process of appropriation went both ways, with language acquiring new technologies of recording and transmission, along with discourse forms devised to be seen as well as heard. Perhaps it is in this sense that Florian Coulmas (1989) is right that the "invention of writing is the answer to the limitations of speech" (p. 272). Perhaps it is also in this sense that John Durham Peters (1999) is right that with the invention of phonograph machines and motion pictures in the nineteenth century, "[p]honography and film attack[ed] the monopoly on the storage of intelligence once held by writing" (p. 163).

With continuing advances in communication technology, we may find in the years ahead that a person learning to write learns not only to differentiate written language from other forms of notation, but also learns to reintegrate writing with speech, drawing, and other systems of symbolic representation. Indeed, we may observe something like this even now, with the emergence of "multi-media" texts. The familiar scholarly tradition for exploring such matters is cultural history. Distinguished and often provocative work of this kind has been offered over the past several decades by Elizabeth Eisenstein, Ruth Finnegan, Jack Goody, Marshall McLuhan, Henri Jean Martin, Walter Ong, Raymond Williams, and many others. Studies in the cultural history of writing and literacy are valuable not only as history, but also in that they offer perspectives regarding present issues. "Revisiting old shocks can be highly illuminating," as John Durham Peters (1999) observes in his recent book, *Speaking into the Air: A History of the Idea of Communication*: "The urgent questions about communications today—the telescoping of space-time (e.g., the Internet) and the replication of human experience and identity (e.g., virtual reality)— were explored in analogous forms in the eras of the telegraph and photograph, the phonograph and telephone, the cinema and radio" (p. 143). Yet, as Jason Epstein (2000), a long-time literary publisher, argues, familiar shocks will be felt and perennial questions will be asked in entirely new contexts: "The invention of moveable type created opportunities for writers that could barely be imagined in Gutenberg's day. The opportunities that await writers in the near future are immeasurably greater" (p. 59).

To understand this movement into the future, it will be useful to balance analyses of large-scale cultural trends with the close observation of the development of writing ability, even in its beginning phases, and especially as it is suggested by linguistic evidence of learning-in-progress. From a close view of writing ability as it takes shape in the experience of individual writers, we stand to learn much about what it means to write even as the character of writing itself shifts with the use of new technology and the emergence of new forms of social interaction. With this approach, we get the added benefit of a fresh perspective on the issues, problems, and possibilities of writing instruction. We see, for example, that a fundamental premise of writing instruction, acknowledged or not, is that learning to write involves more than being taught. If we recognize the sense in which learning to a write can be understood as a dimension of language development, we will recognize as well that writing instruction always seeks to contribute to a process of individual learning that begins before instruction starts and continues after instruction is completed. We can see, too, that writing instruction has its own ambitions. Whatever its local aims and limitations, and however it is grounded in the cultural traditions and social structures that both support and constrain it, the teaching of writing can be understood as an effort to contribute to the future of writing ability.

Note

Thanks to Martin Nystrand and Susan Gundlach for helpful comments on earlier versions of this essay.

References

Allen, J. & Seidenberg, M. (1999). The emergence of grammaticality in connectionist networks. In B. MacWhiney (Ed.), *The emergence of language* (pp. 115–155). Mahwah, NJ: Lawrence Erlbaum Associates.

Aronoff, M. (1994). Book notice. *Language, 70*, 619.

Bruner, J. (1995). From joint attention to the meeting of minds: An introduction. In C. Moore and P. J. Dunham (Eds.), *Joint attention: Its origins and role in development.* Hillsdale, NJ: Lawrence Erlbaum Associates.

Bryant, P., Nunes, T., & Aidinis, A. (1999). Different morphemes, same spelling problems: cross-linguistic studies. In M. Harris & G. Hatano (Eds.), *Learning to read and write: A cross-linguistic perspective* (pp. 112–133). Cambridge: Cambridge University Press.

Chartier, R. (1995). *Forms and meanings: Texts, performances, and audiences from codex to computer.* Philadelphia: University of Pennsylvania Press.

Coulmas, F. (1989). *The writing systems of the world.* Oxford: Blackwell.

Connors, R. J. (1997). *Composition-rhetoric: Backgrounds, theory, and pedagogy.* Pittsburgh: University of Pittsburgh Press.

Epstein, J. (2000, April 27). The rattle of pebbles. *New York review of books*, pp. 55–59.

Daniels, P. T. (1996). The study of writing systems. In P. T. Daniels & W. Bright (Eds.), *The world's writing systems* (pp 3–17). New York: Oxford University Press, 1996.

Grafton, A. (1999). The humanist as reader. In G. Cavallo & R. Chartier (Eds.), *A history of reading in the west.* Cambridge, MA: Polity Press.

Gumperz, J. (1997). On the interactional bases of speech. In G. Guy, C. Feagin, D. Schiffrin, & J. Baugh (Eds.), *Towards a social science of language: Papers in honor of William Labov* (Volume 2: *Social interaction and discourse structures*) (pp. 183–203). Amsterdam: John Benjamins Publishing Company.

Harris, J. (1997). *A teaching subject: Composition since 1966.* Upper Saddle River, NJ: Prenctice Hall.

Harris, R. (1986). *The origin of writing.* London: Duckworth.

Hess, C. (1996). Books in time. In G. Nunberg (Ed.), *The future of the book* (pp. 21–36). Berkeley: University of California Press.

Marcus, G. F. (2001). *The algebraic mind.* Cambridge, MA: MIT Press.

McLane, J. B. & McNamee, G. D. (1990). *Early literacy.* Cambridge, MA: Harvard University Press.

Mencken, H. L. (1956). The author at work. In A. Cooke (Ed.), *The vintage Mencken* (pp. 167–170). New York: Vintage Books.

Mignolo, W. D. (1994). Aferword: Writing and recorded knowledge in colonial and post-colonial situations. In E. H. Boone & W. D. Mignolo (Eds.), *Writing without words: alternative literacies in Mesoamerica and the Andes* (pp. 292–313). Durham, NC: Duke University Press.

Nunberg, G. (1996). Farewell to the information age. In G. Nunberg (Ed.), *The future of the book* (pp. 103–138). Berkeley: University of California Press.

Nystrand, M. (1990). Sharing words: the effects of readers on developing writers. *Written communication, 7,* 3–24.

Nystrand, M., and Graff, N. (2000). Report in argument's clothing: An ecological perspective on writing instruction. *Elementary school journal.*

Olson, D. R. & Homer, B. D. (1998). How children create knowledge. *Cognitive development, 13,* 249–255.

Peters, J. D. (1999). *Speaking into the air: A history of the idea of communication.* Chicago: University of Chicago Press.

Pinker, S. (1999, October 29) Regular habits: How we learn language by mixing memory and rules. [Edited extract of the Colin Cherry Memorial Lecture on Communication, Imperial College, London]. *Times Literary Supplement,* pp. 11–13.

Perrin, P. G. (1933). The remedial racket. *English Journal, 22,* 382–388.

Sapir, E. (1951). Communication. In D. G. Mandelbaum (Ed.), *Selected writings of Edward Sapir* (pp. 104–109). Berkeley: University of California Press.

Seidenberg, M. (1997). Language acquisition and use—learning and applying probabilistic constraints. *Science, 275,* 1599–1603.

Seidenberg, M. (2000). The quasiregular nature of language. Abstract for a lecture in the language and cognition program lecture series, March 6, 2000. Northwestern University, Evanston, IL.

Snow, C. E. (1999). Social perspectives on the emergence of language. In B. MacWhiney (Ed.), *The emergence of language* (pp. 257–276). Mahwah, NJ: Lawrence Erlbaum Associates.

Teale, W. H. & Sulzby, E. (Eds.) (1986). *Emergent literacy.* Norwood, NJ: Ablex.

Tomasello, M. (2000). Do young children have adult syntactic competence? *Cognition, 27,* 209–253.

Tolchinsky, L. & Teberosky A. (1998). The development of word segmentation and writing in two scripts. *Cognitive development, 13,* 1–24.

Wilson, E. O. (1994). *Naturalist.* Washington, DC: Island Press.

Index

Contributors

Martin Nystrand is professor of English at the University of Wisconsin–Madison. He is author of *The Structure of Written Communication: Studies in Reciprocity between Writers and Readers* (1986) and *Opening Dialogue: Understanding the Dynamics of Language and Learning in the English Classroom* (1997) and editor of *Language as a Way of Knowing* (1977) and *What Writers Know: The Language, Process, and Structure of Written Discourse* (1982). His research on the intellectual history of composition studies included in this volume was funded by the Spencer Foundation.

John Duffy is assistant professor of English at the University of Notre Dame, where he directs the Writing Center. He recently received a fellowship from the National Endowment for the Humanities to continue his work on the historical development of Hmong literacy.

Ralph Cintron is associate professor of English at the University of Illinois at Chicago. He has been a Rockefeller Foundation Fellow, and his book *Angels' Town: Chero Ways, Gang Life, and Rhetorics of the Everyday* (1997) was the runner-up winner of the Victor Turner Prize for Ethnographic Writing. He is currently doing interdisciplinary fieldwork in the Puerto Rican neighborhoods of Chicago and conducting fieldwork in Kosovo under the auspices of the International Center for the Study of Human Responses to Social Catastrophe.

Carolyn R. Miller is professor of English at North Carolina State University. Her primary interests are in rhetorical theory and criticism and the rhetoric of science and technology. She has published essays in *Argumentation, College English, Journal of Business and Technical Communication, Quarterly Journal of Speech, Rhetorica*, and the *Rhetoric Society Quarterly*, as well as in numerous essay collections. She currently serves on the editorial boards of *College Composition and Communication, Philosophy and Rhetoric, Rhetoric Society Quarterly*, and *Written Communication* and was 1996–98 president of the Rhetoric Society of America.

John Ackerman is associate professor of English at Kent State University, where he teaches in the Rhetoric and Composition Program. His research focuses on social theory, disciplinarity, and educational reform. He is the author of "The Promise of Writing to Learn"(*Written Communication,* 1993) and coauthor, with Berkenkotter and Huckin of "Social Context and Socially Constructed Texts" in *Texts and the Professions: Historical and Contemporary Studies of Writing in Academic and Other Professional Communities* (1990) and reprinted in *Landmark Essays on Writing Across the Curriculum* (1994).

Anne Haas Dyson, professor of education at Michigan State University, studies the social lives and literacy learning of schoolchildren. Among her publications are *The Brothers and Sisters Learn to Write: Popular Literacies in Childhood and School Cultures* (2003), *Writing Superheroes: Contemporary Childhood, Popular Culture, and Classroom Literacy* (1997), and *Social Worlds of Children Learning to Write in an Urban Primary School* (1993), which was awarded NCTE's David Russell Award for Distinguished Research.

Catherine Prendergast is assistant professor in the Department of English at the University of Illinois at Urbana–Champaign. She received the 1999 Richard L. Braddock award for her article, "Race: The Absent Presence in Composition Studies." Her book, *Literacy and Racial Justice: The Politics of Learning after Brown v. Board of Education* is forthcoming from Southern Illinois University Press.

David Fleming is assistant professor of English at the University of Wisconsin–Madison, where he teaches undergraduate courses in writing and graduate courses in rhetorical theory. He has written a book manuscript partly about the Cabrini-Green redevelopment, titled *City of Rhetoric: Revitalizing the Public Sphere in Metropolitan America.*

Robert Gundlach is director of the Writing Program and professor in the Department of Linguistics at Northwestern University, where his interests include children's language development and the uses of writing in childhood and adolescence. He has served on the editorial boards of *Written Communication* and *Discourse Processes,* and has been a consultant or adviser to the National Institute of Education, the National Assessment of Educational Progress, the Center for the Study of Writing, the Center for English Learning and Achievement, and the Illinois State Board of Education.

David J. Depew, Deidre N. McCloskey, John S. Nelson, and John D. Peters
General Editors

Lying Down Together: Law, Metaphor, and Theology
Milner S. Ball

Shaping Written Knowledge: The Genre and Activity of the
Experimental Article in Science
Charles Bazerman

Textual Dynamics of the Professions: Historical and Contemporary
Studies of Writing in Professional Communities
Edited by Charles Bazerman and James Paradis

The Meanings of the Gene: Public Debates about Human Heredity
Celeste Michelle Condit

Politics and Ambiguity
William E. Connolly

The Rhetoric of Reason: Writing and the Attractions of Argument
James Crosswhite

Democracy and Punishment: Disciplinary Origins of the United States
Thomas L. Dumm

Philosophy, Rhetoric, and the End of Knowledge: The Coming of
Science and Technology Studies
Steve W. Fuller

Machiavelli and the History of Prudence
Eugene Garver

Language and Historical Representation: Getting the Story Crooked
Hans Kellner

Body Talk: Rhetoric, Technology, Reproduction
Edited by Mary M. Lay, Laura J. Gurak, Clare Gravon, and Cynthia Myntti

Therapeutic Discourse and Socratic Dialogue: A Cultural Critique
Tullio Maranhão

The Rhetoric of Economics
Donald N. McCloskey

The Rhetoric of Economics, Second Edition
Deirdre N. McCloskey

Tropes of Politics: Science, Theory, Rhetoric, Action
John S. Nelson

The Rhetoric of the Human Sciences: Language and Argument in Scholarship and Public Affairs
Edited by John S. Nelson, Allan Megill, and Donald N. McCloskey

Towards a Rhetoric of Everyday Life: New Directions in Research on Writing, Text, and Discourse
Edited by Martin Nystrand and John Duffy

What's Left? The Ecole Normale Supérieure and the Right
Diane Rubenstein

Understanding Scientific Prose
Edited by Jack Selzer

The Politics of Representation: Writing Practices in Biography, Photography, and Policy Analysis
Michael J. Shapiro

The Legacy of Kenneth Burke
Edited by Herbert W. Simons and Trevor Melia